LARRY BURKETT AND CHUCK BENTLEY

GOD

is

Faithful

Biblical Wisdom for Money and Life

DAILY DEVOTIONAL

CROWN
Do Well

ISBN: 978-156427-269-0

Portions originally published under the title *Great Is Thy Faithfulness*
by Larry Burkett (Barbour Publishing, Inc., 1998).

Printed in the U.S.A.

November 2013 Edition

DEDICATED TO

every faithful steward
who loves our Faithful God.

G O D

i s

is presented

To: _____

By: _____

Date: _____

*"God, who has called you into fellowship with his Son
Jesus Christ our Lord, is faithful."*
I CORINTHIANS 1:9

INTRODUCTION

It is a privilege to update and release the original devotional titled, *Great is Thy Faithfulness,* written by Larry Burkett. Many of you who read this book will do so because of your great appreciation for the impact of Larry's teaching on your life. I, too, fall into that category.

My life verse for many years has been 1 Corinthians 1:9: *"God, who has called you into fellowship with his Son Jesus Christ our Lord, is faithful."* The truth of God's faithfulness jumps from the pages of Scripture and history alike. He is the constant in a world of variables. And He was the constant in the life of my beloved friend, Larry Burkett.

In these pages, we share our heart on issues and insights that will encourage you in your walk to become or continue as a good and faithful steward. The devotional also establishes a plan for you to read through the Scriptures throughout the course of the year. Larry and I shared a mutual love for God's Word. I do hope you will be encouraged to read through the entire Bible as you use this devotional.

My prayer is that this devotional will be used by the Holy Spirit to lead you to know Christ more, to love Him more, and to serve Him more than the year before.

To our faithful God be the glory.

Chuck Bentley

"You shall love the Lord your God with all your heart,
and with all your soul, and with all your mind. . . . You
shall love your neighbor as yourself"
(Matthew 22:40, 37, 39).

NEW YEAR'S COMMITMENT

As the new year opens, I'd like to challenge you to make one commitment (you'll notice I didn't say resolution). I believe the most important issue in this New Year is to set priorities for your life. It is imperative that you stay focused on the things that are really important.

We find out what is important by reading God's Word. In Matthew, when someone asked Jesus, "Which is the great commandment in the Law?" Jesus answered with what is in our Scripture passage for today. Read that again.

What does that have to do with setting priorities? Those are the priorities: love God and love people. If you do, everything else will fall into place.

Decide today what your priorities will be for the coming year, write them down, and ask for God's help in setting those priorities in your everyday life this year.

Larry Burkett

Daily Scripture Reading:
Genesis 1-3

"Not one of us lives for himself, and not one dies for himself; for if we live, we live for the Lord; therefore whether we live or die, we are the Lord's"
(Romans 14:7-8).

WE ARE THE LORD'S

I grew up in a non-Christian atmosphere. I never saw Christianity manifested in my parents, so I didn't know anything about Christianity; nor did I have any interest in it.

My wife Judy was saved through door-to-door evangelism by Campus Crusade for Christ. In all honesty, at that time I thought, "That's okay. If it helps her, it keeps her off my back and let's me do what I want to do."

A lot of people shared Christ with me after that; I was pulled into Christian circles because of Judy. It didn't matter. I only wanted to have success, which to me meant buying the houses and cars I wanted.

Happiness doesn't come from material things. So, I started attending a Bible study with Judy, but I went looking for error, not for truth. I argued every point that was made, until the teacher finally asked to meet with me privately. He asked me to do two things: "Read the Bible, ask God if it is the truth, and if it is accept it; if not, put it down because it isn't for you. And two, don't come back to my Bible study. You are a disruptive influence."

Well, I picked up the Bible and read it with a different attitude and I accepted the Lord at age 32. My life changed from that moment. I became a different person, which is what the Lord asks of all of us.

What a joy it is to serve our God!

Father, am I the person You want me to be?

Larry Burkett

Daily Scripture Reading:
Genesis 4:1-6:8

*"He who loves money will not be satisfied with money,
nor he who loves abundance with its income"*
(Ecclesiastes 5:10).

AT WHAT PRICE?

I often think of people, like Howard Hughes, who made tremendous successes of their lives financially and materially. These people did what they thought was best, but when they got to the end of life they asked, "What is life all about?" "What good is money now that I'm going to die?"

If I hadn't received Christ, that's exactly where I would be. There is no question. I would never have been happy and would have died thinking, "What is this all worth? What a worthless effort this has been!"

But, in Christ, life is totally different. I made a promise to God that, to the best of my ability, to this day I have not violated. I said, "God, if You will make it clear, I'll do whatever You say. You'll have to deal with my ignorance, because I am really ignorant about You, God, but I will never be rebellious or disobedient again. So, if You'll make it clear, I'll do it."

God's Word is really clear about what He wants us to do. We just aren't very obedient about following it. And, I'm not just talking about money (although that's what I teach about). That's true in the area of loving other people and putting the right priorities in our lives. It's putting God first.

It doesn't cost anything to say "I believe in God; I put God first." But, if you live it, it will cost something.

Have you put God first in your life? Is there some area of your life that you are holding back? Ask God to show you what that is and then surrender it to Him.

Larry Burkett

Daily Scripture Reading:
Genesis 6:9-9:29

"All of you, clothe yourselves with humility toward one another, because, 'God opposes the proud but gives grace to the humble' "
(1 Peter 5:5 NIV).

HUMILITY

Humility is the priceless cornerstone of financial wisdom. It will change the way you think about money, the way you make money, and the way you spend money.

Eliminating pride is important because God is not neutral about our pride, He "opposes" those who are proud. Notice that He doesn't just withdraw from them or look the other way. He actively opposes or resists people who think too highly of themselves. In other words, He stands against them.

The day you realize this fact, you will truly want to repent of your pride and grow in humility. You won't mind having less notoriety in the world while others seek increasing levels of popularity and approval, because you can have far greater rewards in heaven.

Pride puts you in an adversarial position with God. And, even though your efforts to impress others may gain you some temporary notoriety, they will bring God's opposition and cost you blessings not only in this world but also in the world to come.

Chuck Bentley

Daily Scripture Reading:
Genesis 10-11

*"Trust in the Lord forever, for in God the Lord,
we have an everlasting Rock"*
(Isaiah 26:4).

TRUSTING TOTALLY

If I could wake up tomorrow, having gained one ability I don't have, I would want it to be the ability to absolutely trust God in everything I do—to have no doubts and no fears.

I believe there have been people in the past who had that ability and I admire them greatly. (The apostle Paul is one great example.)

From a human perspective, I could be perfectly content if I had really turned everything over to God and was trusting in Him completely.

My personality is such that I think too much sometimes. Then I remember the passage from God's Word in which Jesus asked, "Why do you worry so much? No matter how much you worry, you can't add even a moment to your life. Each day has enough trouble of its own; therefore, trust in Me" (paraphrased from Matthew 6:19-34).

How would you measure the amount of trust you have in God? Is it total, complete, unconditional, or is it limited by your circumstances?

God's Word says, *"Trust in the Lord with all your heart, and do not lean on your own understanding. In all your ways acknowledge Him, and He will make your paths straight"* (Proverbs 3:5-6).

Larry Burkett

Daily Scripture Reading:
Genesis 12-14

"Everyone who is proud in heart is an abomination to the Lord"
(Proverbs 16:5).

DEALING WITH PRIDE

In order to cure a disease, we must first be able to recognize its symptoms.

Once we are trapped by our pride, we are of no service to God. Without a change and a commitment to accountability, we will not even be aware of our attitude of pride.

God will give us plenty of opportunity to recognize and correct the attitude of pride. The difficulty most times is admitting we have a problem.

It is vital for us to stay open to criticism, particularly from those who are spiritually discerning. Those most consistent in discerning our faults are usually our spouses. God has placed them in our lives as a balance, and they will help to offset our extremes if we will listen.

When we find that we only want to associate with the "right" people and look down at others because they're less educated, less intelligent, or less successful, then we are no longer useful to God and His work.

We must actually demonstrate that no one person is more or less important than another.

Who do you think is most important in God's sight?

The apostle Paul wrote, *"With humility of mind let each of you regard one another as more important than himself"* (Philippians 2:3).

How do you break out of the pride trap? Vow to serve God and God's people, and then make yourself accountable to others.

Is pride a problem in your life?

Larry Burkett

Daily Scripture Reading:
Genesis 15-17

"The deceitfulness of riches, and the desires for other things enter in and choke the word, and it becomes unfruitful"
(Mark 4:19).

JUST A LITTLE EXTRA

Dr. Brown had been the pastor of one of the larger churches in the city for only three months but had brought some fine messages that were an encouragement to many church members.

One afternoon, Dr. Brown went through the checkout line of one of the local grocery stores. He did not recognize the cashier as a member of his church and the cashier didn't identify himself.

After leaving the store, Dr. Brown realized that he had received $20 more in change than he should have. But being in a hurry, he got in his car and went on his way. Almost immediately the $20 began to haunt him. The next day he returned the money to the cashier and explained what had happened. The cashier simply took the money and said, "Yes, I know. Thank you."

After the service the following Sunday morning, the pastor was greeting the people as they left the church. One of the hands he shook was that same grocery cashier, who said, "Pastor, I know now that you believe what you preach."

The deceitfulness of riches did not destroy the fruitfulness of Dr. Brown's testimony to the cashier who belonged to his church.

How sad it is when we allow ourselves to be caught in Satan's snares—even small ones. Just a little extra change we don't return can destroy our testimony.

Have you ever taken something that didn't belong to you? Kept extra change? Taken office supplies home? How did you feel about it? Have you allowed it to "choke the word"?

Larry Burkett

Daily Scripture Reading:
Genesis 18-19

"Being found in appearance as a man, He humbled Himself by becoming obedient to the point of death, even death on a cross"
(Philippians 2:8).

CONVERSION

At the heart of the Gospel is Christ's atonement and resurrection. Jesus came to earth for one purpose: to die for our sins.

When we were created, God gave us the ability to make choices. One of those choices is whether or not to become a Christian.

I've been a Christian since age 32, but I have several members of my family who are unsaved. I don't have a great many unsaved friends anymore. Those that have been around me for a long period of time either accepted the Lord or moved on.

It's a fine balance that we walk sometimes, between sharing Christ and being obnoxious. Others must see consistency in our lives as we live for the Lord. That is what will attract them.

When I'm with the unsaved members of my family I don't hesitate to talk about the Lord—just as I would around my Christian family members. We are called to give an account for our faith. I'm believing God for the salvation of those who are unsaved.

If you have a close friend or family member who is not a believer, you are responsible to share the message: *"By grace you have been saved through faith; and that not of yourselves, it is the gift of God"* (Ephesians 2:8). So, you should share your gift.

The Bible asks, How will they hear unless someone tells them? Think of those you know who are unsaved and make it a practice to pray regularly for their salvation.

Larry Burkett

Daily Scripture Reading:
Genesis 20-22

"Whoever loves money never has money enough; whoever loves wealth is never satisfied with his income. This too is meaningless"
(Ecclesiastes 5:10 NIV).

WHAT'S IN A BRAND NAME?

When it comes to shopping, are you trapped in a cycle of buying products with the most prestigious brand names? Have luxuries become necessities?

Satan never wants you to be happy with equality. Instead, he wants you to engage in a process of comparison that constantly drives you to buy those "top-of-the-line" brands, those that make you appear slightly better than those with lesser brands. Doing so may help you feel better about yourself, but it can put you on a treadmill that demands higher and higher levels of spending.

For many people, only the "deluxe" package will do. This means that if they have a choice of low, middle, or high, they'll always choose high, whether they're considering a house, a car, a handbag, a wristwatch, or even a pair of eyeglasses.

Having a roof over your head, getting from one place to another, and keeping track of time can be had for a lot less money than what many people feel compelled to spend. And when it comes to eyeglasses, the most important thing is not the fashionable brand but whether your vision is corrected!

Don't buy into the lie that only the "best" will do. Satisfaction isn't found in a name. Freeing yourself from the cycle of comparison can save you a lot of money and take a tremendous burden from your shoulders.

Chuck Bentley

Daily Scripture Reading:
Genesis 23-24

"Whatever you do, work at it with all your heart, as working for the Lord, not for men. . . . It is the Lord Christ you are serving"
(Colossians 3:23-24 NIV).

A REFLECTION OF VALUES

It is enlightening to reflect on what the Bible has to say about business. Many Christians say they have a Christian business, but what does that mean? In order to understand business from a biblical perspective, it is necessary to first define what is meant by "Christian business."

Obviously, the actual business entity is neither Christian nor non-Christian. A Christian business, therefore, is one that is controlled by a Christian. The more control this Christian has, the more the business can reflect his or her spiritual values.

It is interesting how many Christians would like for God to make them successes so they can be witnesses for the Lord and how few really are once God does.

Clearly, Christians in business can be used by the Lord but only if the correct priorities have been preestablished.

One key to being useful to the Lord is to make decisions on the basis of God's Word and not on circumstances, feelings, or what is acceptable to society. To do this without compromise requires unwavering obedience.

If you know people who either own or manage a business, pray that God will help them not to compromise their beliefs.

Larry Burkett

Daily Scripture Reading:
Genesis 25-26

"You are the light of the world. A city on a hill cannot be hidden. Neither do people light a lamp and put it under a bowl. Instead they put it on its stand, and it gives light to everyone in the house. In the same way, let your light shine before men, that they may see your good deeds and praise your Father in heaven"
(Matthew 5:14-16 NIV).

INTEGRITY IN THE MIDST OF FEAR

In times of great financial stress, you may be more tempted to compromise. But as a believer, it's critical that you not allow financial fears to discredit your witness for Christ.

Always act with transparency, honesty, and complete integrity. Treat others fairly, and avoid even the appearance of dishonesty.

Difficult times may cause you to be plagued with fears and want to hold on tightly to money, but remember the wisdom of God's Word: "Give everyone what you owe him: If you owe taxes, pay taxes; if revenue, then revenue; if respect, then respect; if honor, then honor" (Romans 13:7 NIV).

Remain generous to God and to His Kingdom, remembering that He, as Owner of all things, is more than capable of meeting your needs.

Continue to shine your light in every circumstance by honoring the Lord in all you do, so that others will be drawn to Him. It is in these times of testing that you will have the opportunity for your light to shine brightly for the glory of God.

Chuck Bentley

Daily Scripture Reading:
Genesis 36-37

*"Consider it all joy, my brethren, when you encounter various trials,
knowing that the testing of your faith produces endurance"*
(James 1:2-3).

RESPONDING TO THE TESTING PROCESS

In His great wisdom, God has ordained that the perfecting of our faith and walk with Him should come by way of testing. God allows problems and circumstances to occur that will break our stubbornness, keep us dependent upon Him, and make us profitable for His service.

So often our first reaction to the pressures that accompany the testing process is to question God or try to escape, but should we?

Of course, there are times in all our lives when we feel defeated and would like to get away from it all. If that happens to 40- to 50-year-olds, we usually blame it on mid-life crisis. In reality, such crises come at every stage of life.

The great preacher, Charles Spurgeon, said, "Many men owe the grandeur of their lives to their tremendous difficulties."

Until we come to the point of total dependence on God, in good times or bad, we are not really useful in His plan.

God, what is Your plan for me this day? I know You will be with me, no matter what happens.

Larry Burkett

Daily Scripture Reading:
Genesis 38-40

"Therefore I ask you not to lose heart at my tribulations on your behalf, for they are your glory"
(Ephesians 3:13).

BROKENNESS

Brokenness, whether it is financial, physical, or emotional, has at its center the purpose of teaching us to trust in God. Paul knew that his tribulations were the result of his persistent battle against Satan. They were neither pleasant nor enjoyable to Paul, but he knew they were necessary in order to build his character.

Remember, our loving Father's goal throughout our lives is to conform us to the image of His Son. But to that end, our ego and pride, which naturally oppose God and His purposes, must be broken.

"The Lord is near to the brokenhearted, and saves those who are crushed in spirit" (Psalm 34:18).

Is there anything in your life that might result in brokenness? Pray about it today. Do you see brokenness in someone else's life? Pray for that person now.

Larry Burkett

Daily Scripture Reading:
Genesis 41-42

*"Therefore I shall make the heavens tremble,
and the earth will be shaken from its place at the fury
of the Lord of hosts in the day of His burning anger"*
(Isaiah 13:13).

CHANGING OPINIONS

After I received Christ I accepted many things I heard from others without questioning them. Then, as I matured in the Lord, I began to study for myself and developed my own conclusions.

Probably the most predominant in my mind is the position that I held on the Rapture. It was the opinion of many of the people I met that Christians would be raptured before the Tribulation. After studying the Scriptures for myself, I concluded that Christians may not be raptured before the Great Tribulation.

When people ask my position, I say, "I'm praying that I won't have to go through it and planning as if I will."

I do believe God will rapture Christians before He pours out His wrath upon Earth, but it's hard to imagine that God would equip this great army and then remove us from the earth just before the great battle occurs.

I don't look forward to going through the tribulation battle, but I surely would hate to miss it. I believe we're going to see miracles such as have not been seen since the Lord Jesus Christ and His apostles departed.

Instead of worrying about the Tribulation, we should be concerned with being prepared for eternity. The future is in God's hands.

"We have obtained our introduction by faith into this grace. . . and we exult in hope of the glory of God" (Romans 5:2).

Larry Burkett

Daily Scripture Reading:
Genesis 43-45

*"Such is the will of God that by doing right
you may silence the ignorance of foolish men"*
(1 Peter 2:15).

POLITICAL CONVICTIONS

When I first became a Christian, it was my conviction that politics was a corrupting influence and that Christianity and politics didn't mix.

However, as I look back over history, especially reading the early history of America, it's clear that Christianity and politics were intricately entwined—they were one and the same—and the religious convictions of our Founding Fathers are clear in everything they wrote: the Declaration of Independence, the Constitution, and the Bill of Rights.

So, now I'm more convinced that Christians must be involved in politics. I believe we have the responsibility to make our positions well known. We have the right to vote for the candidates of our choice and to speak out against the candidates who don't stand for the value systems we hold dear.

If we don't get involved in politics, we will end up with exactly what we have today: a secular society. My spirit is grieved when I think of what we are leaving the generation of Americans who will follow us. Without the Christian foundation that was established in this country, we can easily become an evil society.

With a Christian foundation, we are God's unique creation and subject to God's unique blessings. So I would implore you to get involved. Pray about it and spend your money supporting candidates that best reflect your value system.

Larry Burkett

Daily Scripture Reading:
Genesis 46-47

*"The prudent see danger and take refuge,
but the simple keep going and suffer for it"*
(Proverbs 27:12 NIV).

INVESTING VS. GAMBLING

If you or someone you know has lost money in the stock market, you may be wondering if lotteries would be a better investment. After all, don't both of these "investments" involve risk? I have been asked this question on numerous occasions by well meaning Christians.

The truth is, risk is present when you invest in the stock market as well as when you gamble. But consider this: During the twentieth century, the average stock market return was about 5 percent. And, any rate of return is better than zero, which is what essentially all but a few lottery players will receive.

In one multi-state lottery, the odds of winning the grand prize were almost 200 million to one, which means that the lottery ticket you buy doesn't significantly reduce your risk. In fact, one example compared the probability of winning represented by one lottery ticket to picking the correct 12 inches of a line stretched the 240,000-mile distance between the earth and the moon!

For most people, the return on investment represented by a lottery ticket is nothing more than the paper on which it's printed.

Christians should never take the money God has entrusted to them and waste it on gambling. God is more than able to meet our needs, and when we begin putting more trust in chance than in Him, it's time to reevaluate our priorities.

Chuck Bentley

Daily Scripture Reading:
Genesis 48-50

"By wisdom a house is built, and through understanding it is established; through knowledge its rooms are filled with rare and beautiful treasures"
(Proverbs 24:3-4 NIV).

GOD OR CHANCE?

In Proverbs 24:3-4, God taught us to rely on what He gives us in order to build our houses. This means we rely on the truth he puts in our minds to develop wisdom, understanding, and knowledge.

Lotteries are promoted as a simple way to get what we need. Tickets are purchased based on chance, to obtain a large sum of money that will be gained quickly and easily.

Using that philosophy, Proverbs 24:3-4 would read something like this: "By the lottery my house has been built, and through great luck it has been established. Through random chance its rooms have been filled with rare and beautiful treasures."

When we rely on the lottery instead of on what God has given us, we put our faith in luck and random chance. And, we ignore what God taught us to use instead.

However, if we'll rely upon God's wisdom, understanding, and knowledge and seek godly counsel, we'll improve our opportunity for financial success through investing, work, and business.

Don't put your faith in luck. God is in control. In fact, the Bible teaches that He is sovereign even in the outcome of casting lots! *"The lot is cast into the lap, but its every decision is from the LORD"* (Proverbs 16:33 NIV).

The difference between investing and gambling is where you put your faith and confidence. God wants us to use the minds He gave us and trust Him for our provision, not random chance.

Chuck Bentley

Daily Scripture Reading:
Job 1-3

January 22

"Let this mind be in you, which was also in Christ Jesus"
(Philippians 2:5).

THE MIND OF CHRIST

What does it mean to have the mind of Christ? Even though Jesus was God, He humbled Himself, became a servant, and obeyed even to death.

It's important to see that Scripture instructs us to have the mind of Christ and the humble attitude of a servant. God's grace is given to those who exhibit humility through their attitudes, words, and actions.

The Lord Jesus experienced humility in rank, because He left the heavens and came to Earth as a man. He remained humble throughout the disbelief, accusations, and physical pain associated with His trial and crucifixion.

Most of us have been humbled in specific circumstances; however, being humble is an act of our own will and occurs when we voluntarily serve others. Usually we prefer to be served and may even feel deserving, but this is when we don't have the mind of Christ.

Just as Jesus humbled Himself to do the will of the Father, we are to humble ourselves in obedience to God's will.

Having the mind of Christ is not a mystical experience; it is the humble act of an obedient servant.

Think of times when you definitely have not had the mind of Christ. You might want to list them. Then ask for forgiveness for those times.

Larry Burkett

Daily Scripture Reading:
Job 4-7

"[If] my people who are called by My name humble themselves and pray, and seek My face and turn from their wicked ways, then I will hear from heaven, will forgive their sin, and will heal their land"
(2 Chronicles 7:14).

HUMILITY

Even though Christ is the most exalted being in the eternal kingdom of God, He assumed the lowliest, most humbling position possible during His lifetime.

God wants us to question the condition of our hearts. Do we really consider ourselves higher than someone else, simply because we may have special talents that give us the ability to earn more money or have more advantages? Did you "earn" your looks or your size or your intelligence?

Having humility means we can accept our unique differences without feeling superior to any other individual. It is more than just an attitude, though. It is living a life of servanthood.

Larry Burkett

Daily Scripture Reading:
Job 23-28

*"Forgetting what is behind and straining toward
what is ahead, I press on toward the goal to win the prize
for which God has called me heavenward in Christ Jesus"*
(Philippians 3:13-14 NIV).

SYMPTOMS OF FINANCIAL BONDAGE

Like Paul, it's critical that you keep an eternal perspective while you're in this life. When your focus shifts to the things of this world, you run the risk of financial bondage as you seek to accumulate everything you feel is necessary to make you comfortable.

The more you accumulate, the busier you become, and before you know it, you're too entangled in worldly things to completely fulfill God's purpose for your life.

Following is a list of common symptoms associated with financial bondage.

1. You think so much about money and the future that you have no peace with God and can't focus on things outside of day-to-day existence.

2. You can't give as generously as you want to give.

3. You're not at peace living on what God has provided and often yearn for things you don't have.

4. You're not working as if the Lord was your employer. Perhaps you're underperforming, or maybe you're on the opposite end of the spectrum and you're a workaholic.

5. You constantly argue with other family members over money.

6. You can't or don't pay off consumer debt obligations in full each month.

7. You're considering a consolidation loan.

8. You're receiving notices of past due bills and charging items because you can't pay cash.

9. You're spending money as a form of emotional therapy.

If some or all of these symptoms describe you, take action to bring your finances into line with God's financial principles. The path to financial freedom may not be easy. After all, you didn't get into debt overnight, and chances are you won't come out of it overnight. But the result is worth the effort as you become better able to have an eternal impact in a temporary world.

Chuck Bentley

Daily Scripture Reading:
Job 29-31

"Do not conform any longer to the pattern of this world, but be transformed by the renewing of your mind. Then you will be able to test and approve what God's will is—his good, pleasing and perfect will" (Romans 12:2 NIV).

OVERCOMING FINANCIAL BONDAGE

Yesterday's devotion focused on the symptoms of financial bondage. If you saw one or more symptoms that applied to you, it's important to bring your finances into line with biblical financial principles.

You may believe that financial bondage is common to everyone, but I assure you, there are people following God's financial principles who are living a joyous, victorious life of financial freedom. You can, too.

Although I have seen some exceptions, you're likely to be in financial bondage because of what you believe about money more than any other root cause.

The solution is found in today's verse, Romans 12:2. God tells us we've been conformed, or molded, into the pattern of the world. You may profess to be a child of God and a follower of Christ, and yet your financial habits have been subtly conformed to what everybody else is doing.

That's why it's important to be transformed by the renewing of your mind, because it's what you *believe* that changes your *behavior.* Applying spiritual truth leads to very practical results!

If you change what you believe about money from what society has taught you to what God wants to teach you, and you then apply that truth to your financial decisions, your behavior will change. It will remain consistent as you stay in God's Word and are fed and nurtured by the Holy Spirit.

"As for God, his way is perfect; the word of the LORD is flawless. He is a shield for all who take refuge in him" (Psalm 18:30 NIV).

Chuck Bentley

Daily Scripture Reading:
Job 32-34

"Whatever you do, do your work heartily, as for the Lord rather than for men; knowing that from the Lord you will receive the reward of inheritance. It is the Lord Christ whom you serve"
(Colossians 3:23-24).

THE WORK ETHIC

In addition to supplying our physical needs, work plays a very important role in our spiritual lives. It provides the opportunity to put into practice spiritual principles that would otherwise be mere academics.

A Christian can study every passage in the Bible dealing with serving others and read every biography of those who were noted servants, such as George Mueller, and still not really understand the principle of surrendering rights.

The way we do our work provides the best exterior reflection of our commitment to serve the Lord in a real, physical way. It doesn't matter whether that work is in the home, on an assembly line, or in a corporate office.

Our true Christian beliefs will be reflected in our work situation, as we interface with others, more than in any other environment outside the immediate family relationships.

In his second inaugural address, Abraham Lincoln said, "With malice toward none; with charity for all; with firmness in the right, as God gives us to see the right, let us strive on to finish the work we are in."

Do you do all your work heartily and "as unto the Lord"? If not, what changes could you make?

Larry Burkett

Daily Scripture Reading:
Job 35-37

"You will be blessed, since they do not have the means to repay you; for you will be repaid at the resurrection of the righteous"
(Luke 14:14).

TIME OUT

Most Christians would never refuse to do God's will; it's just that the timing is not right.

When God calls us, He wants obedience first and excuses last. We have allowed the urgent things of this society in which we live to overshadow the important things.

That fact is neither new nor unique to our generation. In fact, Christ witnessed it in His walk and predicted it for us. He gave a parable of God's calling to follow Him. People were invited to a dinner, but most were far too busy to attend right then. They wanted to be a part of what was happening but had a great many responsibilities. The result was that others were chosen in their places.

We all, to a greater or lesser degree, suffer from being too busy to serve God. Some are so busy doing things for God they fail to do the things of God.

Does this description fit you? Ask God to help you set your priorities in the right order.

Larry Burkett

Daily Scripture Reading:
Exodus 12-13

> *"Do not be deceived, God is not mocked;*
> *for whatever a man sows, this he will also reap"*
> (Galatians 6:7).

SOWING AND REAPING

Most Christians are familiar with the principle of sowing and reaping as it applies to giving—though few really believe it.

That same principle applies to sharing time in the Lord's work. Just as God can multiply the fruits of our labor, He can also multiply the use of our time. Any good administrator knows that ten minutes spent in productive planning is more valuable than two hours spent in confusion and frustration.

Therefore, one of the first things a busy, frustrated, overworked Christian needs to do is to dedicate the best part of the day, week, month, and year to the Lord.

To do so will mean reordering priorities at work and at home to allow for time alone with God.

No other goals are going to be meaningful until the first and most important one is settled: your relationship with God.

Larry Burkett

Daily Scripture Reading:
Exodus 14-15

"You are the salt of the earth"
(Matthew 5:13).

YOU ARE SALT

Salt has two major purposes: to season and to preserve.

Seasonings make things taste better and they become more palatable. When other people look at us, as Christians, they should see love, kindness, joy, and peace—pleasant things that make life more palatable.

Preservatives keep things from spoiling. When I was a boy, we raised hogs, and after butchering them we would smoke them and then cure them in salt. Since we didn't have much refrigeration then, the salt would preserve the meat.

We must preserve the truth by telling others about the Lord and by providing a light for those who are looking for the truth.

When things in our society start to "go bad," we must preserve life by making the Gospel message known. It will preserve life for all eternity.

I challenge you to be salt in your home, your church, and your community.

Larry Burkett

Daily Scripture Reading:
Exodus 16-18

"Whoever serves, let him do so as by the strength which God supplies; so that in all things God may be glorified through Jesus Christ, to whom belongs the glory and dominion forever and ever"
(1 Peter 4:11).

THE CALL OF GOD

Some have been called by God to go into full-time Christian service, but they weighed the call against the cost and rationalized that they could serve God best where they were.

Others clutter their lives with so much materialism that they never have time to listen to God. The desire for more "things" overwhelms them and the call to Christian service is shelved until "a better time."

We can all give thanks to those committed saints, from the apostles forward, who did not feel that fame and success in the eyes of the world were as important as God's blessings.

Without fear of contradiction, I can say that one day each of us will grade 100 percent of our success or failure on the basis of our service to Jesus Christ and nothing else.

I trust that each of us will hear Him say, "Well done, My good and faithful servant."

Larry Burkett

Daily Scripture Reading:
Exodus 19-21

"Whoever in the name of a disciple gives to one of these little ones even a cup of cold water to drink, truly I say to you he shall not lose his reward"
(Matthew 10:42).

GET INVOLVED

Be certain when you give that you are not using a gift of money to avoid a larger responsibility.

It may be that God desires your physical involvement as well. In other words, don't just give your money; give of yourself.

I know a Christian who helps to care for the poor in a major city. By caring, he not only gives money but also gives of himself by establishing thrift shops for the poor in the downtown ghetto areas.

Those shops supply clothing, furniture, food, and other necessities to the poor at prices they can afford. Although his time is limited, like everyone else's, he does it out of obedience to God and love for others.

He says that, often, when he contacts other Christians to help, the vast majority would rather give a little money to God's work than to get personally involved.

In today's Scripture verse, Jesus was saying that we must be involved in giving—including our time—if we don't want to lose our rewards.

Larry Burkett

Daily Scripture Reading:
Exodus 22-24

*"I will instruct you and teach you in the way which you should go;
I will counsel you with My eye upon you"*
(Psalm 32:8).

A LESS STRESSFUL APPROACH TO FINANCES

Are you experiencing new levels of insecurity? Have the things you placed your confidence in disappointed you? God tells us in Psalm 32:8 that He is prepared to instruct us and teach us the way that we should go.

This world will try to convince you that your purposes, goals, significance, self-worth, ambition, and life energy should be wrapped up in material things. For many, the world's message is simple: make as much as you can, as quickly as you can, to retire as soon as you can, to enjoy a life of leisure as long as you can.

In addition, this world will tell you that if you have enough money, you can live free of fear and anxiety. In other words, place your faith and security in your net worth, your assets, and your ability to generate income.

But true financial peace comes from accepting God's lordship over all things, including our money; managing the resources He entrusts to us according to His financial principles; and being a generous giver.

When you adopt this pattern of thinking, you're no longer pressured from within to meet the world's demands. Instead, you begin to define success by whether or not you're faithful with what you have, regardless of the amount.

God does not measure success by worldly achievements and accumulation. He knows that if you are faithful with little, He can trust you with much.

Chuck Bentley

Daily Scripture Reading:
Exodus 25-27

*"Seek first His kingdom and His righteousness;
and all these things shall be added to you"*
(Matthew 6:33).

SEEK HIS KINGDOM

The admonition to seek first the kingdom of God is given by the Lord as a contrast to worrying about material possessions. I believe there never has been a generation of Christians so caught up in worry about possessions as we are.

We have a greater abundance available on a day-by-day basis than any previous generation. Most of us have machines that reduce the daily household labor required, our children are well-clothed and well-educated, and life expectancy is more than God's promise of three score and ten.

We have insurance plans, retirement plans, unemployment plans, and disability plans. Yet, we are so caught up in making more money and buying bigger and better things that we have lost most of our thrust to reach the unsaved world.

As I read through God's Word, it keeps asking the same fundamental question: "Are we seeking first the kingdom of God?"

If we are going to spend an eternity in God's presence and only seventy or so years on earth, we should be more concerned about what we will receive than what we are getting now.

Larry Burkett

Daily Scripture Reading:
Exodus 28-29

"Where your treasure is, there will your heart be also"
(Matthew 6:21).

WHAT DO YOU STAND FOR?

The question often is asked, "What do Christians stand for?" The answer the world would give is, "Not much other than what we do."

The sad part about it is that most people really want to know a personal God, but because of their desires they make gods out of material possessions and worship them instead. Time, energy, and money all are spent on the wrong things.

We have the only hope to offer a generation that is without hope, and yet we're spending the majority of our time pursuing vain things.

Our energies are so depleted in accumulating bigger homes, businesses, cars, computers, and retirement plans that we don't have much time to see that our priorities are out of order.

We can stand for accumulating things, or we can stand for building the kingdom of God.

Larry Burkett

Daily Scripture Reading:
Exodus 30-31

*"You will be enriched in everything for all liberality,
which through us is producing thanksgiving to God"*
(2 Corinthians 9:11).

A SPIRITUAL GIFT

There's only one reason God supplies a surplus of wealth to a Christian: so that he or she will have enough to provide for the needs of others. True wealth comes with the gift of giving. God promises His blessings to all who freely give and promises His curse on those who hoard, steal, covet, or idolize.

The apostle Paul defines the reason for having wealth as meeting the needs of the saints. In today's Scripture verse, the gift of giving is defined as the foundation for a life of selfless devotion to others.

Being a wealthy Christian establishes a greater responsibility than being a poor Christian. Being rich or being poor is a matter of providence in God's will, and He will give us only what we are capable of handling.

But the duties and responsibilities of wealth are very heavy because of the temptations. You can step outside of God's plan simply by attitude.

Becoming content without God in our abundance is a much more subtle sin than stealing. We just slip outside of God's will and never realize it until calamity hits.

The Christian's responsibility is awesome and sobering. God, in His eternal plan, has decided to use us to supply His work. One day we must all stand before God and give an account of what we have done with His resources.

God allows an accumulation of wealth so His people can exercise the spiritual gift of giving.

Larry Burkett

Daily Scripture Reading:
Exodus 32-34

"He has given freely to the poor; his righteousness
endures forever; his horn will be exalted in honor"
(Psalm 112:9).

SHARING OUT OF OBEDIENCE

Many of the decisions we make in our Christian lives don't make sense to the world. Therefore, we make them because of a commitment to God's Word—in other words, out of obedience. We must predetermine that if God defines a course of action in Scripture, we will follow it.

Attitudes play an important part in sharing with others. Have you ever given to someone resentfully? I have and almost immediately realized I had given up more than money.

Anyone who gives willingly receives a blessing that comes only with true love. God will honor your attitude more than the amount.

Remember, when you give to meet the needs of others, you give to God. He doesn't need the money; He's allowing us to share in His work.

When God places the needs of others on your heart and you supply those needs, that's obedience. But I'd like to emphasize that sharing from obedience differs from giving the tithe.

The tithe is given in recognition of God's ownership; obedience is sharing with those in need, out of a conviction that they should not be deprived.

I read somewhere that when you give of your possessions you give little, but the real gift is giving of yourself.

Pray for direction in your giving.

Larry Burkett

Daily Scripture Reading:
Exodus 35-36

"He said, 'Truly I say to you, this poor widow put in more than all of them;
. . . she out of her poverty put in all that she had to live on'"
(Luke 21:1-4).

SACRIFICIAL GIVING

Sacrificial giving with a right attitude is possible only for Christians submitted to God. In the United States, giving sacrificially is almost unknown. Worldly attitudes have clouded our thinking and dulled our sensitivity to others.

God will not allow His work to tarry for lack of funds. He will redistribute the necessary funds to Christians who have the correct attitudes—primarily those who are seeking His will and are willing to sacrifice their luxuries for the needs of others.

The use of our money is a very objective measure of our commitment to Jesus Christ and to His work. Christians who bypass God's work because they refuse to experience even a slight discomfort have missed the mark.

Sacrificial giving is possible for those who have a little as well as those who have much. All Christians can give sacrificially.

Begin to sacrifice a small portion from your wants or desires for the needs of others. Ask God to lay their needs on your heart and then put your commitment to sacrificial giving into action.

Larry Burkett

Daily Scripture Reading:
Exodus 37-38

"Poverty and shame will come to him who neglects discipline,
but he who regards reproof will be honored"
(Proverbs 13:18).

SELF-DISCIPLINE

In the natural order of things, God designed us to be disciplined people. The lack of self-discipline usually leads to all kinds of problems: debt, obesity, bad health—to name a few.

Self-discipline can't be limited to one's "self" or even to standards of society. If the majority of people are self-indulgent, instead of self-disciplined, does that make the lack of discipline acceptable? God's Word says it does not.

True self-discipline is not self-oriented at all; it is God-oriented. *"Cease listening, my son, to discipline, and you will stray from words of knowledge"* (Proverbs 19:27).

Only by knowing and applying God's self-discipline can a Christian be free and, therefore, receptive to God's direction.

Larry Burkett

Daily Scripture Reading:
Exodus 39-40

"Blessed is the man who finds wisdom, the man who gains understanding, for she is more profitable than silver and yields better returns than gold" (Proverbs 3:13-14 NIV).

RAISING CREDIT SMART KIDS

What would parents like to see their children accomplish? If you surveyed thousands of people, you'd probably get a broad range of answers, ranging from professional ice skater to company president.

If you reversed the question and asked parents what they hope their children never do, many of them would probably list their own financial mistakes. Chances are that many of those mistakes would involve credit.

If you want to build a good financial foundation for your children, it's important to start when they're young. One of the most important lessons they can learn is saving. If kids never learn to be patient and save, credit may become a way of life for them in later years.

Teach your kids to save some of the money they receive from their allowances or the paid work they do around your house. Then, allow them to spend a certain amount of their savings during a shopping trip.

Before going shopping with your kids, make purchasing decisions in advance. Tell them they can buy a treat, if that is in the budget, and set a price limit. But also emphasize that you won't be buying any other items.

If they want something that costs more, teach them to be patient, save, and buy that item on a later shopping trip. As your children grow older, encourage them to set larger savings goals.

By teaching your children to plan ahead for the future and save enough to fulfill their plans, they will learn God's ways are better and debt is not necessary.

Chuck Bentley

Daily Scripture Reading:
Leviticus 1:1-5:13

"The Lord is the defense of my life; whom shall I dread?
The Lord is my light and my salvation; whom shall I fear?"
(Psalm 27:1).

WHAT IF?

Our anxieties and worries usually are not related to the lack of things but, rather, to the loss of things. One of Satan's favorite tools is the question, "What if?"

Dedicated Christians get trapped in fear: the "what if" of extended illness, retirement, disability, unemployment, economic collapse. God wants us to consider these things and even plan for them, within reason; but, a Christian must consciously reject the attitude of fear.

Fear is the antithesis of trust; therefore, if we live in fear of the future, we suffer from the problem of not putting our trust in God. That doesn't mean that we shouldn't plan for the future, but if we live in fear it means that we have taken on a responsibility that belongs to God.

If other people see us living lives of fear, we lose our witness. Don't get trapped in fear. Father, help me to remember that You are my light and my salvation—my deliverance.

Larry Burkett

Daily Scripture Reading:
Leviticus 5:14-7:38

*"I am the Lord your God who upholds your right hand,
who says to you, 'Do not fear, I will help you'"*
(Isaiah 41:13).

FEAR OF THE FUTURE

Christians cannot truly serve God and live in fear of the future. Many of the decisions God's people make on a day-by-day basis are motivated by fear of the future, not by trust in God.

For instance, many people stay with jobs they dislike because they fear change. This is particularly true with those who are 40 and older. Society has convinced us to a large degree that those over 40 are past their prime. What nonsense this is! It runs totally contrary to God's intention.

Fear of the future causes Christian families to scrimp and sacrifice for the elusive day known as retirement.

Often the total focus of the earlier years is toward the eventual day when "we can relax and enjoy ourselves." Unfortunately, the same fear that necessitated the hoarding for the retirement years forces further sacrifices—"just in case."

I don't mean to imply that planning is not God's will; obviously, it is. But when a Christian looks inside and finds primary attitudes of fear and worry, bondage has occurred. Ask God to deliver you from that bondage.

Larry Burkett

Daily Scripture Reading:
Leviticus 8-10

*"In the fear of the Lord there is strong confidence,
and his children will have refuge"*
(Proverbs 14:26).

FAITH CONQUERS FEAR

The opposite of fear is faith. Therefore, when dealing with fear, one must first understand faith. In Hebrews it is described as "things we hope for and things that we do not presently have." So, if we have no needs, we have no need of faith.

Martin Luther said, "Faith is a living, daring confidence in God's grace."

It is God's plan that we have some needs in order that we may develop faith in Him, and it is vital that we view these future needs as opportunities to exercise and develop our faith.

We are told in God's Word that He is a rewarder of those who diligently serve Him. We must decide if we believe that or if those are just words.

F.B. Meyer said, "God incarnate is the end of fear; and the heart that realizes He is in the midst will be quiet in the middle of alarm."

No Christian can truly serve God and live in fear. It's a choice.

Larry Burkett

Daily Scripture Reading:
Leviticus 11-12

*"Do not be anxious for tomorrow; for tomorrow will care for itself.
Each day has enough trouble of its own"*
(Matthew 6:34).

WOULD YOU ROB GOD?

Many families literally rob God and their families because of this underlying fear. They start a savings or insurance plan, initially with an eye toward family provision, but then more and more contingencies must be provided for.

Finally, there are so many contingencies that no amount of protection is adequate, and fear pervades all decisions about money. Some are willing to give a tithe from regular income, but any invasion of their surplus is viewed with resentment and alarm.

The net results of this lifestyle are bitterness, conflict within the family, and growing separation from God.

My heartfelt concern for this spiritual illness is that it is increasing among dedicated believers and is being rationalized as good planning for the future. That is an absolute lie. Any action that is not done from faith is done from sin.

The mania we have in the United States about buffering ourselves from any possible future event is straight from the deceiver. When our "sand castle" of affluence comes tumbling down—and it shall—our faith had better be founded in the person of Jesus Christ and not in material security.

God's Word says it better than I can: *"Everyone who hears these words of Mine, and does not act upon them, will be like a foolish man, who built his house upon the sand. And the rain descended, and the floods came, and the winds blew, and burst against the house; and it fell, and great was its fall"* (Matthew 7:25-26).

Larry Burkett

Daily Scripture Reading:
Leviticus 13-14

*"Be sincere and blameless until the day of Christ;
having been filled with the fruit of righteousness which
comes through Jesus Christ, to the glory and praise of God"*
(Philippians 1:10).

THE NEED FOR QUALITY

We live in a society in which average is exceptional and slothful is normal. The trend today is to seek the path of least resistance, and when the going gets difficult to give up.

In school, when the total grades are averaged, it's called "grading on the curve." As Christians we have allowed our standards to be graded by the curve of the world.

To avoid the trap of "curve grading," each of us must establish some minimum, godly goals. It means that we cannot be content to just "get by."

God's Word requires believers to make quality products and make them available at a fair price. Quality really means putting the best possible effort into whatever we are doing—whether it be a product or a service—because, by doing so, it reflects our value system.

There's nothing more honoring to God than quality service or a quality product from a professing Christian. And there's probably nothing more dishonoring to God than poor service or a poor quality product from a professing Christian.

Larry Burkett

Daily Scripture Reading:
Leviticus 15-17

*"The Lord is the defense of my life. . . Though a host
encamp against me, my heart will not fear; though war arise
against me, in spite of this I shall be confident"*
(Psalm 27:1, 3).

GEORGE WASHINGTON

In 1776 King George was not about to concede a very successful and prosperous part of his empire. England had the greatest military force on earth and its Navy truly ruled the seas.

When George Washington and the others committed themselves to open rebellion, they all knew the ultimate decision would either be freedom or the gallows. In the winter of 1777 the Continental Army was all but defeated. Washington warned that the prospect of defeat was all but certain, except for the intervention of the Almighty.

The ragtag army of 8,000 was trapped in Yorktown, with its back to the river and its front to 21,000 crack British troops. Although the circumstances were desperate, two things drove them as they retreated to their last stand along the river: their burning desire for freedom and their hope for better lives for their children.

Washington rallied his men with the cry: "If God be for us, who then can stand against us?" He was convinced that God would not bring them so far to let them fail.

In the midst of a heavy fog, Washington's troops made their escape to the other shore, and the American dream was born—the dream that our founders gave us.

Washington was right: With God's providence we all can "reach the other shore" if we place ourselves in His hands.

Larry Burkett

Daily Scripture Reading:
Leviticus 18-20

*"Do you see a man skilled in his work? He will stand before kings;
he will not stand before obscure men"*
(Proverbs 22:29).

EXCELLENCE IN A MEDIOCRE WORLD

There's an old saying: "If you want someone to do a good job, find a busy person."
The precept is that a person who is not busy probably doesn't want to be.

Obviously that's not always true, but in the long run I have found a great deal of
truth in it.

Many (or even most) people do no more than is necessary to meet the minimum
standards set for them. They will continually belittle others who work to capacity and will
demand more and more "protection" for their positions.

Solomon described these people well: *"Poor is he who works with a negligent hand, but
the hand of the diligent makes rich"* (Proverbs 10:4).

Larry Burkett

Daily Scripture Reading:
Leviticus 21-23

*"In the house of the wise are stores of choice food and oil,
but a foolish man devours all he has"*
(Proverbs 21:20 NIV).

ESCAPE VACATIONS

You'll often hear costly vacations referred to as "escapes," but running away is never a good remedy for financial problems.

When people experience financial crises, they commonly react by getting away from it all. The logic is simple: Escape to an exotic place that will be remembered as a happy experience, even if you have to go deeper into debt to get there.

But burying your head in the sand won't erase your financial problems. If you choose the "escape" option, the long-term result is that your financial problems are only going to become worse.

Indebtedness can destroy your relationship with your spouse. After all, you can't have a good relationship when all you ever talk about are problems!

If you're suffering from a financial crisis, stop overspending immediately and get on a budget. Adopt a frugal lifestyle and pay down your debt. This is a far better "escape" than a debt funded trip.

This won't prevent you from taking a vacation. It simply means that the vacation you take can be paid for in cash, not with more debt.

Chuck Bentley

Daily Scripture Reading:
Leviticus 24-25

"For all these things the Gentiles eagerly seek; for your heavenly Father knows that you need all these things"
(Matthew 6:32).

THE CHRISTIAN VIEW OF SUCCESS

As Christians we have to be careful not to fall into Satan's traps. We must have our guard up so thoroughly that we recognize the dangers.

If you spend too much time building security, the family grows up without proper guidance. When material priorities are substituted for spiritual priorities, children are spoiled by things and, thus, have an indifferent attitude.

Unfortunately, Christians do fall into traps. Why? Because the lies are so convincing we believe they have to be true. From one perspective, big homes, new cars, and private schools seem great. However, what had to be surrendered in the pursuit of them may have been greater: family relationships.

Remarkably, God's Word says that things are not the problem; in fact, God promises us that we will be blessed.

However, if we have the same desires as unbelievers do, our priorities probably are misplaced.

Father, show me a true picture of my own priorities.

Larry Burkett

Daily Scripture Reading:
Leviticus 26-27

*"If I give all my possessions to feed the poor, and if I deliver my body
to be burned, but do not have love, it profits me nothing"*
(1 Corinthians 13:3).

THE POVERTY SYNDROME

Since the world puts so much store in material success, many Christians have naturally concluded that the opposite extreme is God's way and Christians should be poor. Or, if they aren't poor, at least they ought to look that way.

Satan is very tricky. Those he can't trap into his plan he tries to drive through and out the other side. So he naturally perverts one of God's blessings so that God's people will be careful to avoid it.

Poverty is a reality in Scripture, but it certainly is not a promise. God said there always would be poor in the land, but He never said they would be His people. The norm taught in God's Word is either "enough" or an "abundance" for those who believe and follow.

Many Christians believe that giving up something makes them spiritual. Although they may not believe they earned their salvation, they now believe that by self-sacrifice they must earn God's acceptance.

Surely the apostle Paul laid this deception to rest once and for all in his letter to the Corinthians (see today's Scripture verse above).

God is not looking for martyrs; He's looking for believers (literally, doers). We are to be doers of the Word and not hearers only.

Larry Burkett

Daily Scripture Reading:
Numbers 1-2

"Do not defraud your neighbor or rob him"
(Leviticus 19:13 NIV).

HONESTY

I have traveled to many beautiful places in the world that are totally devastated by corruption. Like cancer of the body, dishonesty spreads death and destruction, and its miserable effects are difficult to contain.

Some Christians have conducted surveys of the population living in countries plagued by bribery and extortion. The surveys revealed that the majority of individuals totally agree that corruption is a major problem in their country. However, when asked if they see any problem with lying to have their own needs met, the same people believe that lying under conditions in which they benefit is acceptable.

This type of thinking must make God's heart ache.

God placed you and I in this world to reveal Himself through us. In order for this to happen, we must take a stand to live by His standards of absolute honesty.

There may be times when our honesty results in personal loss or persecution. But our biggest potential losses involve much more than money.

If we are not honest with something as trivial as money, we will not be entrusted with something far greater. *"So if you have not been trustworthy in handling worldly wealth, who will trust you with true riches?"* (Luke 16:11 NIV).

We should pray for a personal revival of absolute honesty in our own hearts and then in our respective nations.

Chuck Bentley

Daily Scripture Reading:
Numbers 3-4

*"So then it does not depend on the man who wills
or the man who runs, but on God who has mercy"*
(Romans 9:16).

GOD'S VIEW OF SUCCESS

A look into God's Word quickly reveals that material blessings were given because God loved His people, not because they deserved the blessings. They were withdrawn from those who used them foolishly and were transferred to more faithful stewards.

To be a success from a biblical perspective, some prerequisites must be met.

Surrender: To be a successful servant of the Lord and to be entrusted with material and spiritual rewards, we must first demonstrate an acceptance of God's leadership.

Obedience: To be truly blessed by God, we must demonstrate a willingness to use our material resources for God. The more we "let go and let God," the more God is able to glorify Himself through us.

Persistency: To be successful we must be persistent in the face of problems. We cannot give up easily. If all the doors were supposed to be open and waiting, there would not be so many Scriptures directing us to "knock."

Nothing and no one can shake a true believer from doing God's will once it is understood. The evidence of this can be observed in the lives of every servant who ever was used by God. God's Word is full of examples.

Larry Burkett

Daily Scripture Reading:
Numbers 5

*"The sorrow that is according to the will of God
produces a repentance without regret"*
(2 Corinthians 7:10).

REFLECTION

As I look back over the years, I have a few regrets; one, that I was not saved at an younger age so I would have had longer to serve the Lord. Also I regret that I didn't know more while my children were at home so I could have spent more time teaching them God's ways.

Obviously I can't do anything about the past, so I'm trying to pass along what I know to my grandchildren.

Other than those, I have no conscious regrets. For the last 25 years, God has allowed me to do exactly what He called me to do; and, I've never done anything in my life that I have enjoyed more. Of course, there were some parts I didn't enjoy, but that's true with anything, isn't it?

It is unfortunate that so few people can look back over their lives with few regrets.

It's a good idea to examine this past year, to see if there's anything you regret. You can correct it right now. It's never too late. Make up your mind that next year will be different.

We will all face judgment one day and should be prepared. You can't do anything about the past, but you don't have to continually live in it either.

"We shall all stand before the judgment seat of God" (Romans 14:10).

Larry Burkett

Daily Scripture Reading:
Numbers 6

"He who is kind to the poor lends to the LORD,
and he will reward him for what he has done"
(Proverbs 19:17 NIV).

HELPING THE LEAST

Many of God's people are surrounded by so much wealth that they tend to compare themselves to the wealth they see, not the poverty they do not see.

In America, one of the world's most prosperous nations, even people considered to be in "poverty" have access to resources and services that much of the world cannot imagine.

Throughout the world there are 2.6 billion people classified as "Poor" who live on $2 per day. And, there are 1.2 billion "Ultra-Poor" who live on $1 per day.

Together, these two groups account for almost 4 billion among a world population of about 7 billion.

Although these people are among the least in the world, they are precious in God's sight. *"I tell you the truth, whatever you did for one of the least of these brothers of mine, you did for me"* (Matthew 25:40 NIV).

Helping these people does not require a major investment. For them, a little goes a long way. Support organizations that render aid but also teach stewardship principles and introduce the Gospel. This will meet their needs—not only now but for all of eternity.

Chuck Bentley

Daily Scripture Reading:
Numbers 7

*"For the despairing man there should be kindness from his friend;
lest he forsake the fear of the Almighty"*
(Job 6:14).

CHRISTIAN CONCERN

Perhaps the number one cause of discouragement for those with problems is the lack of support on the part of other Christians.

Often children are cruel to those who are different, and in this matter I often wonder if some Christians have reverted to childhood.

What most troubled people don't need is for someone else to point out their problems or to counsel them about the sins in their lives that are causing the problems.

The majority of people who are discouraged already recognize they have erred (if they have) and have more than adequately condemned themselves. What they need is love and support.

The lack of loyalty to Christians undergoing problems is not new. All through the apostle Paul's letters there is evidence that his problems caused others to doubt his calling and to avoid him. Looking back further in time, the record of Job's friends stands as a testimony to disloyalty.

Outwardly, treat your troubled friends with patience, kindness, and love. And lift them up in intercessory prayers.

Larry Burkett

Daily Scripture Reading:
Numbers 8-10

"Who is the one that overcomes the world,
but he who believes that Jesus is the Son of God?"
(1 John 5:5).

BE AN OVERCOMER

I have counseled many people who are discouraged about their problems—many to the point of suicide. Satan knows where we're vulnerable, and in America it's usually in our self-esteem concerning material things.

In a land of plenty like ours, even those who are poor are better off than the majority of the world. So why do we see despair and discouragement? Because we have adjusted our expectations and made them relative to everyone else around us. It's the same symptom that causes despair in a multimillionaire whose assets have shrunk to a few hundred thousand dollars.

Discouragement abounds today because of unemployment or underemployment. When everyone is poor, it seems that most people can adjust to that. But when someone has lost a job and others still have theirs, it's hard to handle. High debt loads and creditor pressures simply add to the feelings of inadequacy and failure.

Discouragement, depression, and self-pity are the result of problems and adversity for some. For others, problems are a challenge and help bring about faith, trust, and victory.

As Christians we are admonished to be overcomers.

Think about something in your life that you need to overcome and ask the Lord to help you.

Larry Burkett

Daily Scripture Reading:
Numbers 11-13

"Consider it all joy, my brethren, when you encounter various trials"
(James 1:2).

EXPECTATIONS

Most of us suffer from unrealistic expectations of what God promised. In Christians it is sometimes worse, because we fear that others will think of us as being less spiritual.

We actually have come full circle from the Christians of the first and second century who believed that problems were the evidence of spiritual depth.

Actually neither extreme is scripturally correct, but the case for Christians undergoing trials is more scriptural.

The trials James is addressing in today's Scripture verse are a consequence of serving God without compromise. However, most of our current problems are the result of violating biblical principles.

If we follow the teachings of God's Word, we will have realistic expectations of what He has promised. There's a promise in His Word for every circumstance or happening in our lives. All you have to do is to learn those verses and apply them to your life.

Larry Burkett

Daily Scripture Reading:
Numbers 14-15

*"The overseer must be above reproach as God's steward,
not self-willed, not quick-tempered. . .not fond of
sordid gain. . .hospitable, loving what is good, sensible, just,
devout, self-controlled, holding fast the faithful word"*
(Titus 1:7-9).

UNREASONABLE EXPECTATIONS

Unreasonable expectations often create discouragement, particularly in the lives of our church leaders. The pastor obviously should be a Christian of very high character, but where in that description does it imply that he is to be perfect?

Unfortunately, according to the "Book of Christian Opinions," pastors don't have the right to have problems. So those who have trouble communicating with their wives or who are trying to live on much less than what others live on often get discouraged.

One of Satan's favorite weapons is discouragement. He knows that if he can get you to doubt God there's a chance you will give up.

It would shock many Christians to find out that their pastors even doubt God from time to time and that their problems get so overwhelming that they suffer depression.

Some collapse into despair and self-pity, but others grow stronger. Those who grow stronger can be categorized, as James said, as doers of the Word and not hearers only who delude themselves (see James 1:23).

Examples of doers are Abraham, Nehemiah, Daniel, and Paul. It's pretty clear they weren't perfect, but they were obedient. In their times of difficulty they did not panic or get depressed; they turned to the Lord. They were a good example for all of us.

Lord, are my expectations unreasonable?

Larry Burkett

Daily Scripture Reading:
Numbers 16-18

*"Like apples of gold in settings of silver
is a word spoken in right circumstances"*
(Proverbs 25:11).

EXPECTATIONS ABOUT CHILDREN

Even the most humble Christians are quick to brag about achievements by their children, particularly if it's something in the Lord's work.

It's as if we want to validate our commitments through our children. If we are elevated spiritually by the achievements of our children, then we also are demoralized by their failures.

It's probably time for us to realize that God doesn't have grandchildren or stepchildren—only children. Everyone decides individually to follow or not to follow the Lord. This doesn't mean that we shouldn't lead our children, correct them, or encourage them, but we must recognize their right to choose, just as we did.

It would be great if all children were as smart as most parents and could learn without any personal difficulties, just as we did—right?

Share failures you've had with your children and allow them to observe that Christians haven't totally arrived—we're still on the way. I experienced such an event when one of my sons came home from college to ask me for help in clearing up his checking account.

He had eight checks overdrawn and $70 in overdraft charges. Needless to say, I was discouraged. The only thing worse for me, as a Christian financial counselor, would be for my own account to be overdrawn (which happened one summer when I forgot to make a deposit).

God used my son's problem to help me realize that just because I teach financial discipline doesn't mean my children understand it. I was able to share why financial principles are in God's Word.

First, set an example; then, lead and encourage your children.

Larry Burkett

Daily Scripture Reading:
Numbers 19-21

*" 'For I know the plans I have for you,' declares the LORD, 'plans to prosper
you and not to harm you, plans to give you hope and a future'"*
(Jeremiah 29:11 NIV).

THE PURPOSE OF MONEY

God gave you money in order to help you fulfill His purpose for your life. That's why
it's important for you to manage your money according to His financial principles.

Being financially free makes you able to respond to God's leading. He does not give
us money simply to spend as we desire.

If you handle money according to your own purposes, then money will become the
driving force of your life.

Ask yourself: "What am I spending my life energy to accomplish? What did God
really call me to do? And, how does money fit into that calling?"

Christ is the most valuable gift that you possess. So, while you're on this earth, use
money to advance His kingdom and not to build your own.

*"The kingdom of heaven is like treasure hidden in a field. When a man found it, he hid it
again, and then in his joy went and sold all he had and bought that field. Again, the kingdom
of heaven is like a merchant looking for fine pearls. When he found one of great value, he went
away and sold everything he had and bought it"* (Matthew 13:44-46 NIV).

Chuck Bentley

Daily Scripture Reading:
Numbers 22-24

> *"But in all these things we overwhelmingly
> conquer through Him who loved us"*
> (Romans 8:37).

HOW TO DEFEAT DISCOURAGEMENT

There is a cliché that summarizes this subject: "Keep on keeping on." You must decide what you believe and trust God, regardless of the outside circumstances.

Also, your response to any situation should be determined in advance. If anyone, Christian or otherwise, waits until a problem occurs to decide how he or she will handle it, that person will be controlled by the events—not God's Word.

If all we are looking for is what we can have in this world, then we're only slightly better off than the lost.

Be ready at all times to "overwhelmingly conquer" whatever comes into your life. You can do it with God's help.

God wants to bless us with peace in this life and eternal rewards in the next.

Larry Burkett

Daily Scripture Reading:
Numbers 25-26

"A worthless person, a wicked man, is the one who walks with a false mouth, who winks with his eyes, who signals with his feet, who points with his fingers"
(Proverbs 6:12-13).

HOW DECEIT DESTROYS

Deceit is an external, visible expression of inner spiritual flaws. The most devastating loss associated with deceit is the dulling of our spiritual awareness.

Guilt associated with a known deception will cause us to withdraw from God's presence. Once withdrawn, subsequent deceptions (lies) become easier, and we feel less conviction.

Often the pretense of spirituality remains (church, conferences, Bible studies), but the sensitivity and fellowship are gone. Literally, we no longer feel worthy and believe that we have failed God. If we allow this to continue, the result can easily be a life of defeat and frustration.

Fortunately, God knew we wouldn't be perfect and made allowances for our weaknesses by a principle called confession. Confession is often more difficult than honesty would have been originally, but it is absolutely necessary to restore fellowship with God.

Since confession is so painful, total honesty will look more attractive the next time.

Larry Burkett

Daily Scripture Reading:
Numbers 27-29

"He who conceals his transgressions will not prosper,
but he who confesses and forsakes them will find compassion"
(Proverbs 28:13).

TEMPTATION TO DECEIVE

No one is immune to the temptation to deceive, particularly when money is concerned. Some people establish their responses prior to the situation and are able to resist, not on the basis of their own strength but on God's.

When I was an unsaved businessman, the temptation to deceive was a constantly nagging problem. Quite often it was not a desire to lie but, rather, to just simply omit a few pertinent facts about a product to a potential buyer. After all, I would tell myself, what they don't know won't hurt them.

Sometimes that old cliché is right and sometimes it's wrong, but invariably I found the one it did hurt was me. I felt guilt and a loss of honor each time. As a Christian, I naturally assumed such weaknesses would never tempt me again, especially as I became more familiar with God's Word.

The one way to fail is to deceive yourself into believing you're too strong to fail. Many times in our lives there are situations in which an undetected compromise to God's way could be made; in fact, many times it is.

Fortunately, when Jesus went to the cross He opened the way of repentance. All we have to do to restore fellowship with God is to repent and ask for forgiveness.

Forgiveness follows genuine repentance.

Larry Burkett

Daily Scripture Reading:
Numbers 30-31

"Put away from you a deceitful mouth, and put devious lips far from you"
(Proverbs 4:24).

HYPOCRISY

There is nothing more devastating to a believer's life than to look spiritual but live in defeat. The immediate consequence is the loss of esteem in the eyes of loved ones, close friends, and business associates.

Children are rarely attracted to a weak, watered down version of Christianity that says one thing and does another. If they see mom and dad put on their "church" faces only on Sunday, they will believe that's what being a Christian is all about.

When we live lifestyles that are contrary to God's way, the step from hypocrisy to a critical spirit is a short one. It is the desire to cut others down to our level that brings about the critical or judgmental attitudes. Every small flaw in others will be amplified and expounded on in an effort to justify the flaws in our own attitudes.

Instead of accomplishing the desired result of hiding the deceptive spirit, usually the opposite occurs, and others who normally would not notice are even more aware.

I'm sure you've heard it before, but you may be the only "Gospel" that someone near you will "read." It may be a loved one, a friend, or a business associate. If unbelievers see hypocrisy in your life, they'll have no desire to be Christians.

Is someone "reading" your life? What do they see?

Larry Burkett

Daily Scripture Reading:
Numbers 32-33

"Have this attitude [mind] in yourselves which was also in Christ Jesus"
(Philippians 2:5)

THE MIND OF CHRIST

In order to have the mind of Christ, I believe we must separate ourselves from the wicked influences of the world.

This means that you literally turn off the television when something comes on that you shouldn't be watching. You don't go to movies that exert wrong influence over your mind. You don't read books that are contrary to the teachings of God's Word.

We must learn to discipline ourselves to live Godly lives in this world. We are told that we are to be in the world—not of the world.

I believe too many Christians have become a part of the world, and that's why they don't have the mind of Christ.

The world puts emphasis on self above all else, but when we inflate our own self-worth, we don't have the attitude of Christ. The verse following today's verse says about Christ: *"Although He existed in the form of God, did not regard equality with God a thing to be grasped. . . . And being found in appearance as a man, He humbled Himself by becoming obedient to the point of death"* (Philippians 2:6-8).

Larry Burkett

Daily Scripture Reading:
Numbers 34-36

"Four things on earth are small, yet they are extremely wise: Ants are creatures of little strength, yet they store up their food in the summer"
(Proverbs 30:24-25 NIV).

SHORT-TERM PLANNING

One of the noblest characteristics of ants is the way they plan for the future by storing food in good times for use when times are bad. It's an example that we can use to improve our lives, as well.

Do you often face cash "shortages" that require you to use credit cards? Short-term planning can help you avoid this dilemma. It takes a little time, but it can save you a lot of headaches.

Take utility bills, for example. By averaging them over one year, you can store money from low-use months to offset the cost of high-use months. Check with your utility company to see if it has a plan that allows you to pay an average, constant amount each month of the year. That way, you'll always know what your monthly bills will be, and huge bills won't overwhelm you in peak usage months.

Clothing, medical, and dental costs are also good candidates for short-range planning. These costs usually occur on an irregular basis, and when you don't have the right amount of reserves, you'll find yourself turning, once again, to credit. So, set aside an average monthly amount for these needs based on how much you spent the year before and how much you expect to spend in the coming year.

You can plan your vacations in the same way by establishing a vacation budget and dividing that amount by 12 to determine what must be set aside on a monthly basis.

In addition, you need to include appliances in the short-range planning process. When a dishwasher or clothes dryer suddenly quits working, it can be shocking to go to an appliance department or store and see how much prices have increased since the last time that you purchased such items.

And, of course, there's your automobile. Set aside something each month for parts replacement and maintenance, because failed parts can cost you hundreds of dollars to repair.

Chuck Bentley

Daily Scripture Reading:
Deuteronomy 1-2

"Without consultation, plans are frustrated,
but with many counselors they succeed"
(Proverbs 15:22).

BE ACCOUNTABLE

We need to be accountable to others, so that when we stray off the path they will correct us. Unfortunately, many Christians are accountable to no one because they don't have to be. This is particularly true of those who are materially successful; they isolate themselves behind a wall of ego and pride.

The best accountability comes from the home between husband and wife. With rare exception, one spouse is acutely aware of the other's strengths and weaknesses. If a couple has an open and honest relationship, one will detect the other's deceptions quickly.

Correcting must be done gently and in love, or the result may be bitterness. Always remember that the purpose is to restore a loved one to the right relationship with God, not to accuse.

Children can participate wholeheartedly in the detection and correction process. (Mine never failed to detect when I exceeded the posted speed limit.)

In addition to family, every Christian should become accountable to one or more other Christians who care enough to admonish and correct. Sometimes it's painful for both parties, but it is absolutely necessary for spiritual growth.

God's Word says it better than I can. *"With gentleness correcting those who are in opposition, if perhaps God may grant them repentance leading to the knowledge of the truth, and they may come to their senses and escape from the snare of the devil, having been held captive by him to do his will"* (2 Timothy 2:25-26).

Larry Burkett

Daily Scripture Reading:
Deuteronomy 3-4

*"Everyone who is proud in heart is an abomination to
the Lord; assuredly, he will not be unpunished"*
(Proverbs 16:5).

RECOGNIZING PRIDE

Pride is what caused Satan's eternal ruin and it is also what led Saul astray. When we take things into our own hands, it becomes easier to disobey God.

Once we are trapped by pride, we are not of service to God. Without a change and a commitment to accountability, we will not be aware of our attitude of pride.

Dr. Samuel Johnson wrote, "Pride is a vice, which pride itself inclines every man to find in others, and to overlook in himself."

God will give plenty of opportunities to recognize and correct this attitude. The difficulty most times is admitting that the problem exists.

Pride is deceptive because it's so normal today. We are told to achieve and to be the best we can be so we can be effective witnesses. Then, somewhere along the way, the goal of achieving takes a higher priority than witnessing—the result of pride.

It's good to remember what we read in God's Word: *"Everyone who exalts himself shall be humbled, but he who humbles himself shall be exalted"* (Luke 18:14).

Larry Burkett

Daily Scripture Reading:
Deuteronomy 5-7

*"Do you see a man skilled in his work? He will stand
before kings; He will not stand before obscure men"*
(Proverbs 22:29).

HARD WORK: REWARD ENOUGH?

Work plays a very important role in our lives as believers. It provides the opportunity to put into practice spiritual principles that otherwise would be mere academics.

We can read every passage in the Bible dealing with noted servants and still not really understand the principle of surrendering rights. On the job, however, the opportunity to yield our rights presents itself every day.

The way we do our work day by day provides the best exterior reflection of our commitment to serve the Lord in a real, physical way. It doesn't matter whether that work is in the home, on an assembly line, or in a corporate office. Our true Christian beliefs will be reflected more clearly there than in any other environment outside of the immediate family relationships.

Somehow we've been duped into believing that work is a secular activity and, therefore, we shouldn't expect to feel spiritual about our jobs. This attitude destroys our greatest area of outreach and witness. Few Christians, if any, who view their work as a "chore" have much of a witness on or off the job.

What is your attitude toward your job? Do your coworkers and your employer know that you are a Christian by your attitudes and work habits?

Larry Burkett

Daily Scripture Reading:
Deuteronomy 8-10

"Before destruction the heart of man is haughty,
but humility goes before honor"
(Proverbs 18:12).

ESCAPING THE PRIDE TRAP

I think Robert Burton said it best when he wrote, "They are proud in humility, proud in that they are not proud." Does that sound like anyone you know?

How do you break out of the pride trap? First, vow to serve God and then make yourself accountable to others.

Too often Christian leaders are not accountable to anyone. Consequently, they have little or no feedback from those who can recognize the symptoms associated with pride.

First and foremost, a husband and wife must be accountable to each other. Major decisions should be discussed together and opinions and insights exchanged. If a wife has the liberty to be honest, she usually will detect (and expose) his pride (and vice versa).

Second, Christian businesspeople should be accountable to peers or people they respect who are strong enough to be totally honest. Those I know who practice accountability find they must meet regularly and learn each other's basic flaws. They both must be studying God's Word and be seeking to truly serve God or it won't work.

One rule I use for those I have helped to get started: the criticism must be honest and based on God's Word.

Also, the person pointing out the problem must suggest a way to change the attitude and must testify how the change helped in his or her own life.

Sophocles wrote, "Pride, when puffed up, vainly, with many things unseasonable, unfitting, mounts the wall, only to hurry to that fatal fall."

Larry Burkett

Daily Scripture Reading:
Deuteronomy 11-13

"Where your treasure is, there will your heart be also"
(Matthew 6:21).

THE DANGER OF AFFLUENCE

It is not necessary to live poorly to serve the Lord. The only people who think poverty is spiritual are those who haven't tried it.

But, just as certainly, it is clear from God's Word that affluence presents the greatest threat to our walk with the Lord.

Poverty is not God's norm; but, neither is lavishness.

It is a rare individual who can actually handle much wealth and keep his or her priorities straight.

While we are laying awake wondering whether to buy a big screen television, over half the world's children are going to bed hungry and cold.

Everything starts with a first step and that is to get involved with the needs of others. This will help us focus more clearly on what our actual needs are.

Perhaps you think you don't have much, but compared to someone else you are very affluent.

Lord, please show me someone that I can help—someone who really needs what I can give.

Larry Burkett

Daily Scripture Reading:
Deuteronomy 14-17

"Without faith it is impossible to please Him, for he who comes to God must believe that He is, and that He is a rewarder of those who seek Him"
(Hebrews 11:6).

FAILING GRACEFULLY

There are many Christians who are "graceful failures." They don't demand anything of God and, in fact, expect nothing. Usually, they get what they expect: nothing. Many people accept failure as God's will when it isn't.

The Scripture says God wants to bless us and wants us to ask of Him. We must believe that God wants to bless us.

And, until God individually convicts someone that His plan is otherwise, we are not to accept failure. If you believe you should accept failure, you should read Christ's parables in Luke 11:5-13 and Luke 18:1-8. One of God's principles is persistence in the face of discouragement.

Satan wants you to fail. He will plant a dark thought in your mind and then "fertilize" it daily. But you don't have to listen to him. God's Word says plainly to resist Satan and his tricks. The Bible is full of encouragement.

Do you trust God, or do you just say you trust God?

Larry Burkett

Daily Scripture Reading:
Deuteronomy 18-21

"Then Moses said to the Israelites, 'See, the LORD has chosen Bezalel son of Uri, the son of Hur, of the tribe of Judah, and he has filled him with the Spirit of God, with skill, ability and knowledge in all kinds of crafts'"
(Exodus 35:30-31 NIV).

MAXIMIZING YOUR SKILLS

Mention stewardship, and money will probably be the first thing that comes to most people's minds. But we should be good stewards of everything entrusted to us, including God-given skills as well as money.

If a skill enables you to do something easily, you may take it for granted. Suppose you're a "natural" at something and can perform, up to a point, with little effort. Because going beyond this point would require more effort, you may be tempted to remain where you are.

But as we look throughout history, we can see the benefits of skills that were developed into excellence. As a result, we have beautiful art and music, medical advancements, technological wonders, and an abundance of conveniences that enhance our lives today. All of these resulted from people who made good use of their skills.

Yet, even in our high-tech world, there is still plenty of room for innovation.

Regarding your children, make it a point not to limit your view of their skills. If you have children who can't sing or play sports well, don't be quick to conclude that they aren't skilled.

Your children are "wired" for certain tasks. You can do them a great service by helping them recognize this and encourage the development of their talents. As a result, they could experience fulfillment in life and work that many people miss. God may use their skills to improve the lives of many others in the process.

Chuck Bentley

Daily Scripture Reading:
Deuteronomy 22-25

*"When Cephas came to Antioch, I opposed him
to his face, because he stood condemned"*
(Galatians 2:11).

IS IT GOD'S WILL?

Have you ever witnessed to a Christian who was obviously doing something rather dumb but rationalized it by saying, "God told me to do it"?

You found that hard to argue with, because by challenging it you felt like you were doubting God. But later the whole thing fell apart, and you found yourself wishing you had had the courage to speak up.

Why don't we speak up when we see another Christian who is obviously wrong? Because most of us are timid about applying biblical truth to a real-life situation.

The soundest and most mature believers can and do make mistakes about God's will. Usually, when confronted by either a loving but firm challenge from another Christian (or the resulting problems), they will change direction.

In today's Scripture verse we find that the apostle Paul knew the truth—Peter's actions didn't conform to the truth—so Paul confronted the leader of the Christian church.

Of course, some Christians simply refuse to believe they could be wrong and cloak themselves in spirituality by saying "I know God wants me to do this." Those are the ones who confirm the cliché: "Often wrong, but never in doubt."

Lord, show me Your will for me in everything I do today, and as I read in Your Word, *"Give me understanding, that I may know Thy testimonies"* (Psalm 119:125).

Larry Burkett

Daily Scripture Reading:
Deuteronomy 26-28

*"Be devoted to one another in brotherly love; . . . contributing
to the needs of the saints, practicing hospitality"*
(Romans 12:10, 13).

DEVOTED ASSISTANCE

One Sunday after church, Paige, a single mother, was leaving the sanctuary, dragging her two-year-old beside her. Paige was exhausted. She'd been working 11-hour days and had worked all day Saturday. Her toddler needed her but she had nothing left to give. She needed rest and time to regroup, so during the service she had silently asked for God's help.

One of the ladies in the church noticed her as she walked by and said, "Paige, would you let me take Rachel for the afternoon? You look like you could use a break."

It was the best thing anyone could have done for this young mother. It was an answer to prayer.

As the body of Christ, or as individuals, we can be the answer to a single parent's prayer. God will be honored by our service and we will be blessed.

Do you have someone in your church (or your neighborhood) who needs your help for an afternoon now and then? Sometimes we think the only way to help others is to give money, but time is a valuable commodity in situations like this one.

Ask God to show you someone you can be a blessing to by giving of your time and resources. Single parents are in a daily tug-of-war and they need to know that there's hope.

Larry Burkett

Daily Scripture Reading:
Deuteronomy 29:1-31:29

"The faith which you have, have as your own conviction before God. Happy is he who does not condemn himself in what he approves"
(Romans 14:22).

CONFIRMED BY SUCCESS

Material success does not necessarily constitute God's endorsement of our actions. This applies to businesses and ministries alike. Every action must meet two criteria for a Christian.

First, it must be in accordance with God's written Word. Some decisions are objective enough to be eliminated on the basis of direct contradiction to the Bible.

The second criterion that must be met is personal conviction. The Christian life is not just a set of rules that can be obeyed to the letter and thus satisfy our commitment. We are held to an even higher standard that requires constant input from the Holy Spirit to keep us going in the right direction.

It means we are accountable if we defile our consciences by doing something we feel is wrong. This feeling must be based on a firm conviction from God.

How do you know? You will lack the feeling of inner peace that comes from being in God's will.

"From Thy precepts I get understanding; therefore I hate every false way" (Psalm 119:104).

Larry Burkett

Daily Scripture Reading:
Deuteronomy 31:30-34:12

*"Therefore, my dear brothers, stand firm. Let nothing move you.
Always give yourselves fully to the work of the Lord, because
you know that your labor in the Lord is not in vain"*
(1 Corinthians 15:58 NIV).

THE VALUE OF GOD'S APPROVAL

The world is constantly trying to conform us to its image. But Romans 12:2 says, *"Do not conform any longer to the pattern of this world, but be transformed by the renewing of your mind. Then you will be able to test and approve what God's will is—his good, pleasing and perfect will"* (NIV).

Conforming to God's pattern may not make us popular or rich. But we don't serve God because of what He can do for us; we serve Him because He is God. Job was so sure of this fact that he told his friends, *"Though he slay me, yet will I hope in him"* (Job 13:15 NIV).

Shadrach, Meshach, and Abednego were so sure of this fact that they refused to bow before a golden idol erected by the Babylonian king, Nebuchadnezzar, even at the risk of being thrown into a *"blazing furnace"* (Daniel 3:15 NIV).

They boldly told the king, *"If we are thrown into the blazing furnace, the God we serve is able to save us from it, and he will rescue us from your hand, O king. But even if he does not, we want you to know, O king, that we will not serve your gods or worship the image of gold you have set up"* (Daniel 3:17-18 NIV).

All of us must come to the point where we value and seek God's approval more than the world's fame or riches.

Chuck Bentley

Daily Scripture Reading:
Joshua 1-4

*"Whoever does not carry his own cross and
come after Me cannot be My disciple"*
(Luke 14:27).

COMMITTING TO LORDSHIP

There are many dedicated Christians who are willing to accept God's direction at any moment and surrender their jobs, homes, and comforts to accomplish their assigned tasks. However, they do not represent a majority within the Christian community.

We have an Americanized standard for Christian service that requires very little of us. It yields a sizable body of believers who never mature.

It seems in God's discipleship plan that some adversity and self-denial are necessary ingredients for spiritual maturity. One has to wonder what Bible some Christians read that promises them perfect health, unlimited success, and permanent residence at the location of their choice. Certainly it's not the one that gave us the Scripture verse for today.

A commitment to the Lordship of Christ means that we must be willing to go where and when God determines we can best be utilized. There's a hymn that goes something like this: "I'll go where You want me to go, Dear Lord; I'll do what You want me to do."

The apostle Paul describes us as soldiers in God's army, and we are admonished not to get so caught up in the everyday affairs of this life that we take ourselves out of the battle.

Remember that in Psalm 91 we read, *"He will give His angels charge concerning you, to guard you in all your ways."*

Larry Burkett

Daily Scripture Reading:
Joshua 5-8

"Seek first His kingdom, and these things shall be added to you"
(Luke 12:31).

GOD, FAMILY, WORK

Most Christians know that in God's priority system He must come first, family second, and work and recreation third.

However, it is possible to confuse this priority system and step out of God's will. Putting God first means the active, daily process of knowing and being known by God.

It starts with a thorough understanding of God's handbook for life, the Bible. It requires a heartfelt desire to please God and a willingness to accept God's authority over us.

Many times in the pursuit of this first priority, conflicts will arise in the lower priorities. For instance, what happens when a husband is called by God to serve Him and it requires relocating, which causes family conflicts? Usually, it's a conflict because of family ties to a particular area.

It seems that those who are willing to be used by God through the years are faced with the same conflicts, but determining the first priority—seeking God first—will last for eternity. All other priorities cease at death.

Can you say with the psalmist, *"I will give thanks to Thee, O Lord my God, with all my heart, and will glorify Thy name forever"* (Psalm 86:12)?

Larry Burkett

Daily Scripture Reading:
Joshua 9-11

*"You became imitators of us and of the Lord; in spite of severe suffering,
you welcomed the message with the joy given by the Holy Spirit. And so you
became a model to all the believers in Macedonia and Achaia"*
(1 Thessalonians 1:6-7 NIV).

STRUGGLING WELL

Because of sin's impact on the world, you will face difficulties, pain, and challenges. The way you handle these struggles is a testimony to non-Christians that there is something different about you.

The end product of struggling well will not be the complete elimination of hardships in your life. Quite the contrary, hardships will come, but your mindset will play a major role in your success.

One key to success is to know God's purpose for your life. This is important, because you will be willing to struggle more, harder, and longer for a purpose that will make a difference.

You also need to contextualize your struggle according to your purpose. Paul went through unbelievable struggles, but he viewed his problems within the context of his purpose and found the strength to keep going.

Finally, you need to understand that God uses all things for good and never wastes anything. He may be using your suffering to make an eternal difference in the life of someone else.

No matter what we face, we have the assurance that in the end, God's Kingdom will be victorious. Jesus said, *"In this world you will have trouble. But take heart! I have overcome the world"* (John 16:33 NIV).

Chuck Bentley

Daily Scripture Reading:
Joshua 12-14

"No servant can serve two masters; for either he will hate the one, and love the other, or else he will hold to one, and despise the other"
(Luke 16:13).

CHRIST'S REQUIRED COMMITMENT

A review of Christ's commitment on earth demonstrates pretty clearly that He was seeking those who would commit everything to the service of God's kingdom.

Even as he walked and taught, because of the miracles He was performing, many people were attracted to Him. When others asked Him if they could join His disciples, He directed them to lay aside their own desires and follow Him unreservedly.

With few exceptions, they turned back to whatever they had been doing before; the price was simply too high for them.

The lesson for Christians today should be overwhelmingly clear: All of those who were too busy for Christ will spend an eternity regretting it. So, all that truly matters is what we can do for the kingdom of God.

The things we accumulate are not important. They are tools for us to use in accomplishing God's work. Some will need great resources and some only a little. God owns it all anyway.

Christ said we must make a choice about our commitment, and there are only two choices. These are given in today's Scripture verse.

Whom do you choose?

Larry Burkett

Daily Scripture Reading:
Joshua 15-17

*"The Lord gives wisdom, and from his mouth come
knowledge and understanding. . . .for he guards the course
of the just and protects the way of his faithful ones"*
(Proverbs 2:6, 8 NIV).

CHOICES IN A CHRISTIAN BUSINESS

Being a Christian businessperson is not easy. Many choices that are highly acceptable in most business groups are expressly forbidden to anyone seeking to serve the Lord.

I was talking with the owner of a sizable importing company who boasted that he regularly paid customs officials to "expedite" his goods. When I asked if he thought it was wrong, his reply was "Only if I get caught."

He professed to being a Christian but said he didn't usually tell anyone because some of the things he had to do in business wouldn't look good if people knew he was a Christian.

When I challenged him on his dual ethics, he said that God must approve because He was blessing the business. His sole basis for this analysis was the abundant profit he was making. Such an analysis could just as easily apply to the Mafia.

The purpose of any Christian, in business or otherwise, is to glorify God—not just to make a profit.

"By this is My Father glorified, that you bear much fruit, and so prove to be My disciples" (John 15:8).

Larry Burkett

Daily Scripture Reading:
Joshua 18-19

*"Be strong in the grace that is in Christ Jesus. And the things
you have heard me say in the presence of many witnesses entrust
to reliable men who will also be qualified to teach others"*
(2 Timothy 2:1-2 NIV).

PRIORITIES IN BUSINESS

As in any other area of Christian service, it is important to establish priorities. We can quickly become so involved with the "urgent" things of this world that we neglect the important things.

Early in a business career, the urgent thing is to make payroll. Later it becomes urgent to make a greater profit or build a bigger company.

There will always be a reason to neglect the important areas, most of which will seem pretty trivial one second after death. Therefore, it is always important to strive for balance in business.

This is as true in a spiritual sense as it is in a material sense. For example, sales are important to any business, but if a manufacturing company applies 100 percent of its labor force to sales, the imbalance will be readily apparent.

One of the priorities of a business should be to lead others to a saving knowledge of Jesus. But if all other functions are ignored in pursuit of evangelism, the work will be short-lived.

Therefore, the priorities of a business boil down to this: "What are my goals and can my goals be balanced to achieve the overall objectives of serving God while meeting material needs?"

Compared to eternity, the profile of a business is rather trivial and a lifetime of work rather insignificant. If used wisely, though, a business can be used to change the lives of countless lost people.

Larry Burkett

Daily Scripture Reading:
Joshua 20-22

"A good name is more desirable than great riches; to be esteemed is better than silver or gold. Rich and poor have this in common: The Lord is the Maker of them all"
(Proverbs 22:1-2 NIV).

KEEPING A VOW

It is clear in God's Word that a vow (promise) of any kind is not to be taken lightly. Once someone has given his or her word, it becomes a binding contract to be fulfilled. Thus before agreeing to any terms, it is assumed that an individual has carefully considered the consequences.

For the current generation, this concept is rarely taught and seldom applied. Often a vow is deemed something made under one set of circumstances that may be broken under another—whether it be a financial agreement or a marriage. The original conditions may change and one begins to think he or she should have negotiated a better "deal."

The reason that most Christians aren't able to claim God's promises is because they are not willing to meet His prerequisites. We read in 1 John 3:21-22 that God will answer our prayers when we do the things that are pleasing in His sight and keep His commandments.

Few scriptural principles are clearer than that of keeping our vows—literally keeping our word—both to God and to others.

"Make vows to the Lord your God and fulfill them" (Psalm 76:11).

Larry Burkett

Daily Scripture Reading:
Joshua 23-Judges 1

"Everything is permissible—but not everything is beneficial.
Everything is permissible—but not everything is constructive.
Nobody should seek his own good, but the good of others"
(1 Corinthians 10:23-24 NIV).

RIGHTS OR RESPONSIBILITIES

I believe that we are so conscious of our rights today that our "rights" will ultimately cost us our freedom.

To be responsible means to be accountable for our actions. Christ said His followers must be willing to surrender their rights and become His stand-ins.

We can be truly thankful that God's contract with us is binding and firm. Otherwise, He might really give us what we deserve.

We read in Matthew 20 about various workers who were hired during the day at an agreed sum. At the end of the day, those who had worked all day got paid the same wage as those who had worked only one hour, and they were grumbling at the landowner because they thought it wasn't fair. The issue wasn't whether the wage was sufficient—it was that someone else got a better deal, and that wasn't "right."

It is inconceivable to think that our Lord would have made an agreement with someone and then changed His mind and tried to negotiate a better deal.

We must decide to fulfill our responsibilities—regardless of "rights."

Say with the psalmist, *"The Lord is my portion; I have promised to keep Thy words"* (Psalm 119:57).

Larry Burkett

Daily Scripture Reading:
Judges 2-5

"I can do everything through him who gives me strength"
(Philippians 4:13 NIV).

TOO POOR TO MAKE A DIFFERENCE?

If you compare yourself to others, you may begin to believe that you'll never be rich enough to make a significant difference for God's Kingdom.

But God's purpose for your life can be fulfilled even if you're poor. In fact, giving sacrificially in the midst of poverty can be more rewarding than giving what you can easily spare from an abundance.

One example is the first-century Macedonian churches. They responded enthusiastically to Paul's collection for needy Christians in Jerusalem. He wrote, *"Out of the most severe trial, their overflowing joy and their extreme poverty welled up in rich generosity. For I testify that they gave as much as they were able, and even beyond their ability. Entirely on their own, they urgently pleaded with us for the privilege of sharing in this service to the saints"* (2 Corinthians 8:2-4 NIV).

Paul himself had nothing from the world's perspective, but he had everything from God's perspective. He had been put on the earth to glorify the Lord, and that could not be taken from him. When he was weak, Christ's power rested on him.

Therefore, he wrote, *"That is why, for Christ's sake, I delight in weaknesses, in insults, in hardships, in persecutions, in difficulties. For when I am weak, then I am strong"* (2 Corinthians 12:10 NIV).

The same God who empowered Paul for service will empower us, as well. He remains as capable as ever of carrying out His purposes through us, rich or poor.

Chuck Bentley

Daily Scripture Reading:
Judges 6-8

*"You did not choose me, but I chose you and appointed you
to go and bear fruit—fruit that will last in my name"*
(John 15:16 NIV).

WHOM WILL YOU CHOOSE?

In our society, most people are looking for guidance and unwavering commitment to principles.

Unfortunately, when these can't be found, many people believe the humanists' argument that "values are established by society." The end result of this lie can be seen in the use of drugs to escape reality, sexual immorality, a high rate of divorce and, ultimately, in the collapse of society itself.

Why do people turn to enslavement through a form of government like communism? It is because it offers an uncompromising set of principles that seem to represent stability. In reality, only Christ assures both stability and love.

It is the responsibility of every believer to adhere uncompromisingly to the set of values presented in God's Word. These values encompass every area of life.

We must decide either to follow Christ or to follow Satan; there is no middle road.

Jesus told the disciples, *"You did not choose Me, but I chose you, and appointed you, that you should go and bear fruit, and that your fruit should remain"* (John 15:16).

Larry Burkett

Daily Scripture Reading:
Judges 9

"Since they did not think it worthwhile to retain the knowledge of God, he gave them over to a depraved mind, to do what ought not to be done"
(Romans 1:28 NIV).

THE COST OF COMPROMISE

There's a cost to be paid for every compromise, especially to God's Word. That price is the loss of peace from God.

Compromise at any level results in further compromise—until finally the conscience is seared and right and wrong are no longer distinguishable.

Sometimes an inner conviction about sin decreases and the sins begin to increase. Why? Because fellowship with God was broken at the earliest stage, and from that point selfishness and self-control took over.

Have you allowed yourself to compromise in any area of your life?

Our greatest advantage is that God will restore anyone who will acknowledge sin and return to His way.

"Bless the Lord, O my soul, and forget not all His benefits; Who pardons all your iniquities. . . Who redeems your life from the pit; Who crowns you with lovingkindness and compassion" (Psalm 103:2-4).

Larry Burkett

Daily Scripture Reading:
Judges 10-12

*"Christ in you, the hope of glory. We proclaim him,
admonishing and teaching everyone with all wisdom,
so that we may present everyone perfect in Christ"*
(Colossians 1:27-28 NIV).

GETTING OUT THE MESSAGE

Nothing interferes more with our ability to serve God than our need to earn a living. An observer from 100 years ago would be awestruck by the improvement in our living standards and by the amount of leisure time our technology has provided.

Few Americans regularly work more than a 50-hour week; most work 44 hours or less. In addition, we now live an average of 18 years longer than we did 100 years ago.

When all these factors are weighed together with the fact that in America alone we have perhaps 30 million Christians, it would seem clear that we ought to be getting out the message of Jesus Christ much better than we are.

The simple truth is that most Americans are too busy to serve God. We have grown complacent and comfortable in God's blessings and have forgotten the first commandment.

In the meantime, immorality and cults have grown to alarming proportions, because their advocates are more zealous in their support.

Since God asks for obedience rather than demanding it, we must be sure not to ignore the very reasons for our existence: to glorify God and get out the message.

"Obey My voice, and I will be your God, and you will be My people; and you will walk in all the way which I command you, that it may be well with you" (Jeremiah 7:23).

Larry Burkett

Daily Scripture Reading:
Judges 13-16

*"No one who puts his hand to the plow and looks back
is fit for service in the kingdom of God"*
(Luke 9:62).

CONSIDER THE COST

Service to Jesus Christ is demanding. It may actually be that we will have to work as hard for God's kingdom as we do for earthly riches.

Few salespeople consider it a great imposition on their time to tell about their product line. Being a success at anything requires dedication, training, and perseverance.

A good sales manager knows that not everyone can be good at sales, and many don't even want to be. Christ knew that not everyone would serve God, and some might not even want to.

Some would even like to have a foot in both worlds. They are willing to be called Christians, provided they can pick the times and places to serve.

These poor souls are actually worse off in this life than they were before. They are content to know about God but are fruitless fakers who must generate false blessings. They are poorly nourished spiritually and quickly waste away until there is real doubt in their minds about their salvation. These are the ones who fall prey to every wind of doctrine because they are too "busy" to grow firm roots.

What a loss that we will allow temporary comforts and laziness to rob us of true riches both now and for all eternity.

"I shall not die, but live, and tell of the works of the Lord" (Psalm 118:17).

Larry Burkett

Daily Scripture Reading:
Judges 17-19

"What kind of people ought you to be? You ought to live holy and godly lives as you look forward to the day of God and speed its coming"
(2 Peter 3:11 NIV).

EXCUSE ME PLEASE

Without exception, God has a unique and meaningful plan for every believer, and it does not depend on age, income, or ability.

It is also clear that God calls each of us to fill in our gap. The story of Esther, in the Old Testament, shows us that every believer must decide either to be used by God or to be bypassed and another chosen instead.

Most Christians would never refuse to do God's will; it's just that the timing might not be right. When God calls us, He wants obedience first and worldly wisdom last.

We have allowed the "urgent" things of society to overshadow the "important" things. This fact is neither new nor unique to our generation.

In fact, Christ experienced it during His life and predicted it for us. He told a parable in Luke 14:16-24 of God calling men to follow Him. They were invited to a dinner, but most were far too busy to attend right then. They wanted to be part of what was happening but had to spend their time fulfilling a great many responsibilities.

If we are wise, we will realize that it is God's timetable we want to live by—not our own. This is the only way we will receive the best He has for us.

"My prayer is to Thee, O Lord, at an acceptable time; O God, in the greatness of Thy lovingkindness, answer me with Thy saving truth" (Psalm 69:13).

Larry Burkett

Daily Scripture Reading:
Judges 20-21

"You, my brothers, were called to be free. But do not use your freedom to indulge the sinful nature; rather, serve one another in love"
(Galatians 5:13 NIV).

SERVE ONE ANOTHER

One of the defining marks of the early church was the concern its members had for one another. Acts 4:32 says, *"All the believers were one in heart and mind. No one claimed that any of his possessions was his own, but they shared everything they had"* (NIV).

God's plan for us is to serve one another, but in too many cases, believers seek their own interests, pitting themselves against others even within the church. This leads to division as fellow members choose one or another person's side.

In Galatians 5:13, Paul warned believers not to use their freedom to indulge the sinful nature, because it is this type of indulgence that leads to conflict.

When one or more members allow their personal desires to take precedence over the Kingdom purposes of the church, the unity of the Body is destroyed. As James 4:1 says, *"What causes fights and quarrels among you. Don't they come from your desires that battle within you?"* (NIV).

Those who seek their own desires have fallen out of step with Christ, who noted that He *"did not come to be served, but to serve, and to give his life as a ransom for many"* (Matthew 20:28 NIV).

He set the ultimate example of service. We must follow, because fulfilling our own selfish desires can never justify the eternal consequences of a damaged church witness.

Chuck Bentley

Daily Scripture Reading:
Ruth

*"In vain you rise early and stay up late, toiling for food to
eat—for he grants sleep to those he loves"*
(Psalm 127:2 NIV).

THE WORLD'S YARDSTICK

There is nothing wrong with being successful, even when measured by worldly standards, unless you end up being a failure by godly standards.

The rate of divorce and bankruptcy among Christians is an undeniable indicator that Christians have been duped into using the world's yardstick when setting their priorities.

Each Christian must ask, "Am I certain my priorities are in line with God's?" If not, then a change is in order—no matter what the cost in dollars and cents.

It is remarkable that usually those at the highest end of the material scale are the biggest violators of priorities (executives, doctors, attorneys). But equally guilty are many in full-time Christian service, with pastors leading the group.

We can all give thanks to those committed saints, from the apostles on down, who did not feel that fame and success in the eyes of the world were as important as God's blessings.

One day each of us will be measured on the basis of Christ's evaluation and none other.

Father, I pray that some day I will hear you say, "Well done, my good and faithful servant."

Larry Burkett

Daily Scripture Reading:
1 Samuel 1-3

"I consider everything a loss compared to the surpassing greatness of knowing Christ Jesus my Lord, for whose sake I have lost all things. I consider them rubbish, that I may gain Christ and be found in him"
(Philippians 3:8 NIV).

GOD FIRST

One of the most overwhelming characteristics of those who discern God's will for their lives is that they continually seek to put God first.

Most Christians experience doubts and anxieties when faced with major decisions. However, most major decisions are actually a series of minor decisions that converge into a changed direction.

Consistently putting God first eliminates most decisions before they become crises.

God has already endowed each of us Christians with unique abilities, desires, and gifts to accomplish His will.

As you seek to serve God, the Holy Spirit will make known God's perfect plan for your life. What He wants for you will be different from what He wants for your other family members or friends.

Putting God first and living for Him every day—consistently—is difficult. However, if you exercise self-will, He will do the rest.

"If then you have been raised up with Christ, keep seeking the things above, where Christ is, seated at the right hand of God" (Colossians 3:1).

Larry Burkett

Daily Scripture Reading:
1 Samuel 4-7

"When Judas, who had betrayed Him, saw that He had been condemned, he felt remorse and returned the thirty pieces of silver. . . . And he went away and hanged himself"
(Matthew 27:3).

WHAT'S IT WORTH?

When we celebrate the resurrection of our Lord, we should turn our thoughts to the one who betrayed Him.

How much is your faith worth? I'm convinced that Judas, who sold out the Lord, didn't realize what the outcome would be. Judas was the one Christ had assigned the responsibility of managing all the finances for the disciples. It wasn't that Judas didn't hear the Lord's message—I believe that he even loved Him—he obviously loved money more than he loved Jesus.

When he was approached by the Jews and offered money to betray Jesus, the first thing he should have done was to refuse them and tell the disciples, but he listened to them—much like Eve listened to the serpent in the Garden of Eden. He heard a tempting proposition and was trapped by his own weaknesses.

Judas sold out the Lord for what might have been as little as maybe five weeks of wages—not much when you consider what happened. I really don't know if Judas thought they would kill Jesus or what he would have done if he had known.

What is your faith worth today? Would you sell out the Savior for money? Do you ever sell out your faith to save a little on your income tax? Would you sell it out for the time or things you steal from your employer?

Don't be too critical of Judas until you examine your own life in the light of God's Word. Ask the Lord to help you with a bit of self-examination.

Larry Burkett

Daily Scripture Reading:
1 Samuel 8-10

*"What good will it be for a man if he gains
the whole world, yet forfeits his soul?"*
(Matthew 16:26 NIV).

VOCATIONAL PURPOSE

So often, at the end of a lifetime, a successful person states, "If only I had known 40 years ago what I know now, I would not have wasted my life pursuing wealth."

As Christians, we have the advantage of knowing the certain future. We have the advantage of being able to see life from God's perspective. We will spend eternity reaping the rewards of faithful service to God. Thus, we have the responsibility to orient our lives accordingly.

Vocational planning for us and for our children is based primarily on how we can serve Him best.

It is vital to seek discernment about God's plan and accept nothing less than the vocation that will complement and extend our ministries.

"Let him labor, performing with his own hands what is good, in order that he may have something to share with him who has need" (Ephesians 4:28).

Larry Burkett

Daily Scripture Reading:
1 Samuel 11-13

"Commit to the Lord whatever you do, and your plans will succeed"
(Proverbs 16:3 NIV).

FAMILY GOALS

Goals should be set individually, but they also must become a part of your partnership with your spouse. If your spouse is not a Christian, you have an excellent goal to establish in your personal prayer life.

Don't give up praying for your unsaved spouse (or any other unbeliever). One Christian lady I know prayed for her husband 22 years before he accepted the Lord. It finally took the shock of three years in prison before he responded.

A minimum family goal, which would be a good start, should be to read a few verses of Scripture and pray together regularly.

As Christian parents, we should teach our children God's principles. With very young children, study and prayer are relatively easy habits to develop in the family. Start with a good children's Bible guide and pray for each other.

With older children, start where you can. Read a brief devotional at the breakfast or dinner table, and set aside a few minutes to pray together. You get to know about God by studying His Word, but you get to know God through prayer.

Set a goal with your family to pray regularly and consistently. Even though it may sound trite, it is true: The family that prays together stays together.

You can get your start from God's Word. *"Father, hallowed be Thy name. Thy kingdom come. Give us each day our daily bread. And forgive us our sins, for we ourselves also forgive everyone who is indebted to us. And lead us not into temptation"* (Luke 11:2-4).

Larry Burkett

Daily Scripture Reading:
1 Samuel 14-15

*"Better a dry crust with peace and quiet
than a house full of feasting, with strife"*
(Proverbs 17:1 NIV).

DEALING WITH EXTRAVAGANCE

You've heard the adage, "Enough is enough." But that's easy to forget when spending is involved.

People who look successful on the outside may be pushing the limit of their income or exceeding it through excessive borrowing. Others may have enough money to overspend and get away with it, but extravagance is not a necessity, regardless of how much money you make.

Have you determined when enough is enough, or is your stress level growing because you can't seem to bring your spending under control?

You can change your course by structuring your life goals according to God's purposes; acknowledging His lordship over all things, including your money; and establishing a plan to bring your spending into line with His financial principles.

Unfortunately, you can go from elementary school through college and never learn basic budgeting skills like balancing a checkbook, buying a house, or setting financial goals.

In some people's minds, budgeting is a lot like dieting: both are last-resort measures that people rely on when it's time to tighten the belt a notch or two.

Make yourself an exception. Develop a comprehensive plan for your finances, set monthly limits for all your spending categories, keep track of how much money is coming in and how much is going out, and stick to your plan!

It may hurt a little to pass on buying things you really don't need, but peace of mind is worth its weight in gold and highly preferable to the stress that comes with excessive debt.

Chuck Bentley

Daily Scripture Reading:
1 Samuel 16-17

"Render to all what is due them: tax to whom tax is due;
custom to whom custom; fear to whom fear; honor to whom honor"
(Romans 13:6-7).

PAY YOUR TAXES

Most Christians would consider themselves honest, and yet many violate the tax laws regularly. One of the most common examples is stay-at-moms who are operating a small business, such as a babysitting service or home product sales, but they are not declaring the income for tax purposes.

There is no question that our current tax laws punish married couples and, particularly, stay-at-home moms. For working mothers to have to pay upward of 40 percent of their earnings in taxes is unconscionable.

Moms who babysit at home have to cope with screaming kids to earn precious little income. Then they have to forfeit up to 40 percent of it to some bureaucrat in Washington, who promptly flushes it down the drain called "entitlements."

Yes, it is a problem. But cheating is not the solution. We must get involved personally and do our best to change the system (not to mention the politicians).

God's Word makes it clear that we are to pay taxes. Read today's Scripture verse again.

"Search me, O God, and know my heart; try me and know my anxious thoughts; and see if there be any hurtful way in me, and lead me in the everlasting way" (Psalm 139:23-24).

Larry Burkett

Daily Scripture Reading:
1 Samuel 18-19; Psalm 59

"Let the one who is taught the word
share all good things with him who teaches"
(Galatians 6:6).

MINISTRY SUPPORT

There must be a balance in a Christian's attitude toward ministry support. Too often a Christian will read a spectacular biography of how God used a particular individual and he or she will use that as an absolute rule against everyone else.

Personal testimonies are exciting and rewarding and can be of great value in providing alternatives. However, they are not to be used as yardsticks for giving, unless they are confirmed in God's Word.

Many Christians have read the story of George Mueller's life and how he trusted God for everything without asking. They conclude that no Christian should ever let a material need be known. This is noble and admirable—but not scriptural.

Paul admonished the Corinthians because they felt he didn't have the right to ask them for support. And in Exodus 25:1-3 the Lord told Moses to tell the people of Israel to raise a contribution for the tabernacle.

However, just because asking is acceptable, it doesn't mean that it's God's plan for everyone or that every letter sent to supporters should ask for more money.

Balance is the key principle. Nowhere in the Bible is there any indication that God's people went begging. It's evident that many more needs were met by praying than by asking.

It's also clear that once God's people are made aware of their responsibilities to give and support God's work, the need to ask goes down dramatically.

Jesus said, *"The laborer is worthy of his wages"* (Luke 10:7).

Larry Burkett

Daily Scripture Reading:
1 Samuel 20-21; Psalms 34, 56

*"You are acting faithfully in whatever you accomplish
for the brethren. . . they bear witness to your love before
the church; . . . send them on their way in a manner worthy of God"*
(3 John 1:5-6).

WHICH GROUP TO SUPPORT

God doesn't intend for every Christian to give to every need. Attempting to do so will quickly result in frustration and perhaps poverty. Therefore, we must be able to sort out those we are to help.

This doesn't mean that the cause or the organization isn't worthy—only that the need is meant for someone else to satisfy. There are some simple biblical principles to follow when you are considering giving to any cause.

Limit your giving to groups who are operating in the name of the Lord. Other organizations are serving the needs of the poor, sick, and elderly but make no pretense of doing it in the name of the Lord. It is abundantly clear throughout the Bible that gifts dedicated to God were to be distributed in His name.

Just because a group has an emotional presentation for a seemingly worthy cause doesn't mean it automatically qualifies for support. Determine that the funds actually will be used for the purpose for which they were given. Be a good steward.

Organizations that have met needs in your life should be high on your support list.

Organizations that manage their funds wisely should be considered first. If you have a desire to support a particular type of ministry, locate the most efficient and productive one.

The most important principle of all: Allow God to direct your giving. Ask for His guidance and lean on His wisdom.

Larry Burkett

Daily Scripture Reading: 1 Samuel 22-23; 1 Chronicles 12:8-18;
Psalms 52, 54, 63, 142

"The Lord will deliver me. . .and will bring me safely
to His heavenly kingdom; to Him be the glory forever and ever"
(2 Timothy 4:18).

KEYS TO THE KINGDOM

Over the last few years, I have read and reread Paul's letter to the Romans. It is obvious to me that Paul describes a man (himself) who found the keys to God's invisible kingdom. He's a man who accepts God as the absolute authority in his life and is willing to surrender everything, if necessary, to serve Him, even to the point of death.

Several years ago I met a Chinese Christian who was saved as a member of the "Red Brigade" in communist China. He was imprisoned, tortured, starved, and beaten in an effort to get him to renounce his faith. When he refused, his family was executed to teach others a lesson.

He said the thing that sustained him was an ever-deepening relationship with Christ and an unyielding commitment to serving God. When most of our commitments are weighed against his, it's easy to see why the keys to the kingdom elude us.

Perhaps God hasn't called us to the physical sacrifices that many Christian martyrs have suffered. But, the admonition that Christ gives to all of us is absolutely clear. We must do what Jesus told the disciples: *"If anyone wishes to come after Me, let him deny himself, and take up his cross, and follow Me"* (Mark 8:34).

Is this something you are willing to do?

Larry Burkett

Daily Scripture Reading:
1 Samuel 24-25; Psalm 57

"I gave you an example that you also should do as I did to you"
(John 13:15).

WHERE AM I?

It's always good to have some standard of measure to compare where we are with where God wants us to be.

The evidence in God's Word is clear and simple. All we have to do is eliminate our ego and pride and consistently put the needs of others before our own; then we'll be on the right track. Difficult? No, impossible. But in Romans the apostle Paul gives us God's solution: let go and trust God.

Christ is the most exalted being in the eternal kingdom of God. Even though this is true, He assumed the lowliest, most humbling position possible during His life. Perhaps to us this will mean giving up pride and ego and giving of ourselves to others, as Christ did when He washed the disciples' feet.

It is a contrast in human logic that by giving up something we can receive even more. But Christ taught this principle frequently; it's called sowing and reaping. It's our choice to take what we want now or store it and receive it in God's eternal kingdom.

God's Word tells us that an evidence of our commitment to His way will be shown in our concern for others.

As we start each day we have a choice: follow God or follow the world. If we totally follow God it may be costly. We may be buffeted by Satan as never before, but on the sole authority of God's Word we can clearly know that our priorities are in order.

"Pursue righteousness, faith, love and peace, with those who call on the Lord from a pure heart" (2 Timothy 2:22).

Larry Burkett

Daily Scripture Reading:
1 Samuel 26-29; 1 Chronicles 12:1-7, 19-22

*"For although they knew God, they neither glorified him
as God nor gave thanks to him, but their thinking
became futile and their foolish hearts were darkened"*
(Romans 1:21 NIV).

ACKNOWLEDGING GOD'S BLESSINGS

It's impossible for a nation to be in fellowship with God when its people have forgotten Him in their hearts, given credit for their prosperity to anything but Him, and as a result have a possessive attitude about money.

God designed a system of economics in which He would provide all things. He wants us to remember that everything belongs to Him and that we are stewards of what He has entrusted to us. He wants us to keep our hearts and minds on Him.

If we begin to believe that we are the owners of money and possessions, we embezzle what is rightly God's. We become selfish and think we deserve to be wealthy. This leads to hoarding, covetousness, stealing, and an uncaring attitude toward others.

And, when we begin to regard God's blessings as more important that God Himself, we lose our sensitivity to Him. Shortly before God brought his final judgment on Jerusalem, He told the King of Judah, *"I spoke to you in your prosperity; but you said, 'I will not listen!' This has been your practice from your youth, that you have not obeyed My voice"* (Jeremiah 22:21).

God deals severely with bad attitudes because they lead to behaviors and actions that disrupt the entire economic system. People end up being lovers of the blessings instead of lovers of the One from whom all blessings flow.

"You may say to yourself, 'My power and the strength of my hands have produced this wealth for me.' But remember the LORD your God, for it is he who gives you the ability to produce wealth, and so confirms his covenant, which he swore to your forefathers, as it is today" (Deuteronomy 8:17-18 NIV).

Chuck Bentley

Daily Scripture Reading: 1 Samuel 30-31;
2 Samuel 1; 1 Chronicles 10

"Bring the whole tithe into the storehouse, so that there may be food in My house, and test Me now in this. . .if I will not open for you the windows of heaven, and pour out for you a blessing until it overflows"
(Malachi 3:10).

PURPOSE OF THE TITHE

The purpose of the tithe has been established as a physical, earthly demonstration of our commitment to God. God understood our greedy, selfish nature and provided a readily identifiable sign of our sincerity.

By the act of surrendering some of our physical resources, we are testifying to our origin, just as a farmer does when he surrenders some of his crop back to the earth from which it came.

The tithe is not a law now; nor was it a law in the Old Testament. Although it appears in Leviticus 27, there is no punishment associated with a failure to tithe. There is a consequence (the loss of blessings), but do not misinterpret this. It is not a punishment from God.

Thus, God said that the tithe is an expression of commitment—or the lack of it—by which we can determine our relationship to Him.

What are your thoughts about tithing—why you do (or don't). Do you think it is a reflection of your commitment to God?

Larry Burkett

Daily Scripture Reading:
2 Samuel 2-4

*"All the tithe of the land, of the seed of the land
or of the fruit of the tree, is the Lord's; it is holy to the Lord"*
(Leviticus 27:30).

HOW MUCH IS A TITHE?

This is a difficult question to answer quantitatively. The word tithe in Hebrew literally means "tenth." In Hebrews 7 the tithe is used to describe Abraham's relationship to Christ by drawing a parallel between the tithe and the acknowledgment of authority.

I believe the tithe was meant to be individualized. It was never intended that everyone should give the same amount; each should give according to abundance and conviction. The tenth that we are so familiar with was considered the minimum. You are in no way limited to giving only a tenth.

Anyone unable to make a commitment of a tenth of his or her resources to God should realistically examine all spending and living habits.

The thing to remember is that whatever you give probably is an indicator of your personal relationship with the Lord.

God's Word says to *"Bring the whole tithe into the storehouse, so that there may be food in My house, and test Me now in this. . . if I will not open for you the windows of heaven, and pour out for you a blessing until it overflows"* (Malachi 3:10).

Larry Burkett

Daily Scripture Reading: 2 Samuel 5:1-6:11;
1 Chronicles 11:1-9, 12:23-40, 13:1-14:17

> *"Let each one do just as he has purposed in his heart; not grudgingly or under compulsion; for God loves a cheerful giver"*
> (2 Corinthians 9:7).

GIVING ABOVE THE TITHE

In the book of Deuteronomy there are several additional offerings described as the "tithes of your increase." These were special offerings meant to care for the priests, the poor, the sick, and the elderly.

It's not possible to exact an amount except by inference, but I calculate these total "regular" gifts to be about 23 percent per year. Today it would be the equivalent of a family who is totally committed to giving.

Ask God to show you how to share in special needs above your regular giving. What worthwhile organization or ministry should you be helping to support?

The writer of Hebrews said, *"Do not neglect doing good and sharing; for with such sacrifices God is pleased"* (Hebrews 13:16).

Larry Burkett

Daily Scripture Reading:
2 Samuel 22; Psalm 18

*"Everyone who has left houses or brothers or sisters or father
or mother or children or farms for My name's sake,
shall receive many times as much, and shall inherit eternal life"*
(Matthew 19:29).

SACRIFICE

The concept of sacrifice is not popular with most Christians. Most of us like to discuss this subject in generalities, rather than in specifics.

It's all right for the pastor to mention sacrifice when he talks about missionaries or full-time Christian workers, but when he talks about giving up golf or a new car for God's work, suddenly he becomes a radical.

In this country we are not asked to sacrifice our lives, as Christians are doing in others lands.

However, if we will truly surrender ourselves to God and give Him a sacrifice of praise and thanksgiving, we will experience His faithfulness. He loves us and will never give us less than His best as long as we are surrendered to His way of living.

Ask God to reveal to you someone in need and then give sacrificially from what you have. You will be more blessed than you can imagine.

Father, stand ready to help me, because I have chosen to follow Your will.

Larry Burkett

Daily Scripture Reading: 2 Samuel 6:12-23;
1 Chronicles 15-16; Psalm 96

*"You guide me with your counsel, and afterward
you will take me into glory. Whom have I in heaven
but you? And earth has nothing I desire besides you"*
(Psalm 73:24-25 NIV).

OPEN HANDS

Recessions and natural disasters are reminders of how quickly people's money and possessions can be lost.

Fear prompts people to cling to what they have. The Rich Young Ruler had such a tight grip on his money and possessions that he missed an opportunity to follow Christ (Mark 10:17-22 NIV).

This young man's initial intentions appear to be good. He fell on his knees before Jesus and asked, *"Good teacher...what must I do to inherit eternal life?"*

The Bible says that *"Jesus looked at him and loved him."* But the young man *"went away sad"* when the Lord said, *"Go, sell everything you have and give to the poor, and you will have treasure in heaven. Then come, follow me."*

Consider the magnitude of those last four words: *"Then come, follow me."* In the process of holding on to everything this young man lost everything.

God doesn't call everyone to give all his or her wealth away, but He does test us to see if we will be faithful to Him.

Open your hands and let go of all that you think is yours. It all belongs to God. A tightly clenched fist is proof that you love things more than Him.

Chuck Bentley

Daily Scripture Reading: 2 Samuel 7;
1 Chronicles 17; Psalm 105

*"There is an appointed time for everything.
And there is a time for every event under heaven"*
(Ecclesiastes 3:1).

BUDGETING YOUR TIME

Many people think they're organized and use their time efficiently but, in reality, most of us work according to external pressures, with the most demanding things getting done first. It's called tyranny of the urgent.

Before writing one of my books I did a survey of stay-at-home moms, and one of the questions dealt with time management in their homes. The most common comment was something like, "It seems like I never get everything done now. I don't know how I was able to work and keep a home, but I did."

Not using time wisely usually results from being disorganized. Disorganization is an accumulation of little bad habits all strung together and it is the major enemy of personal success.

Sir John Lubbock said, "In truth, people can generally make time for what they choose to do; it is not really the time but the will that is lacking."

It's important to keep a good balance. As important as good organization of your time is, don't go overboard. When you budget your time, build in some slack as well.

Ask God to help you budget your time so you can keep a good balance in your everyday life. And of course, that includes spending time with Him.

"The steps of a man are established by the Lord; and He delights in his way" (Psalm 37:23).

Larry Burkett

Daily Scripture Reading: 2 Samuel 8-10;
1 Chronicles 18-19; Psalm 60

"He will call upon Me, and I will answer him;
I will be with him in trouble; I will rescue him, and honor him"
(Psalm 91:15).

DON'T PANIC, PRAY

One day I was traveling in my car and tuned to a Christian radio station that played a song with the lyric, "God said it and I believe it." That should be the standard by which we all live our lives. Unfortunately, all too often we allow doubts and fears to get in our way.

There is no problem too big for God to solve, if we believe. That doesn't mean that God will keep every problem away from us; nor does it mean He must miraculously solve every crisis, although I've seen Him do so many times.

Sometimes the problems are for our growth. Other times they are for discipline. And there are times when we simply don't know why things happen to us. But through it all, God is still there, comforting us.

I have learned that although God never promised to remove every difficulty, He has promised that we can have peace in the midst of them if we continue to serve Him.

Use the following verse as your prayer: *"O Lord, don't hold back your tender mercies from me! My only hope is in your love and faithfulness. . . . Come and help me!"* (Psalm 40:11, 13 TLB).

Larry Burkett

Daily Scripture Reading: 2 Samuel 11-12;
1 Chronicles 20:1-3; Psalm 51

*"God is not a God of confusion but of peace,
as in all the churches of the saints"*
(1 Corinthians 14:33).

LEARN TO SAY NO

We live in a time-crazy society. When you prioritize your time, be honest about it. There are only so many things you can realistically accomplish in one day. Concentrate on the important ones.

I have found that much of my own unrealistic schedule is a result of my own doing. I hate to say no to people, especially when there are so many good things to do.

Some of this tendency is probably ego: I like to be asked to do things. Some of it is naiveté. There was a time when I thought I could teach full-time, travel full-time, write full-time, and run an organization—all at the same time.

Instead, I found that the busier I was the more behind I got; the more behind I got, the more frustrated I got; and the more frustrated I got, the less productive I became.

Therefore, I have learned to say "No!" And you know what? The world just goes on turning anyway. I have long since discovered that I am not God's plan; I'm just a part of it.

Does this strike a chord in your own life?

Larry Burkett

Daily Scripture Reading:
2 Samuel 13-14

"Love the Lord your God with all your heart and
with all your soul and with all your mind"
(Matthew 22:37 NIV).

SELF-INTEREST

Some people try to manipulate God for great gain, but that doesn't work. God knows everyone's heart.

The Book of Acts tells the story of Simon, a professed convert to Christianity, who watched as Peter and John placed their hands on a group of new believers in Samaria. When those believers received the Holy Spirit, Simon offered the apostles money and said, *"Give me also this ability so that everyone on whom I lay my hands may receive the Holy Spirit." He was rebuked by Peter, who answered, "May your money perish with you, because you thought you could buy the gift of God with money!"* (Acts 8:19-20 NIV).

Today, people still seek to claim God's unique power for themselves by taking the things God has entrusted to them and using them for their own purposes. As a result, money and possessions that might have been dedicated to God's eternal Kingdom end up being dedicated to the pursuit of self-gratification in this temporary life.

Paul warned Timothy not to go near people with the wrong attitude about money. Greed is destructive. Not only does it lead people to misuse what God has freely given to them, but it also leads them to believe that what others have should be theirs. Taken to its extreme, this attitude leads to a lack of self-control and will not only harm them but others.

God warned us not to let the love of money fill up our hearts. Don't associate with people who think money is greater than God. Instead, anticipate Christ's return and keep God, not money, first in your heart.

Chuck Bentley

Daily Scripture Reading:
2 Samuel 15-17

"The lovingkindness of the Lord is from everlasting to everlasting on those who fear Him, and His righteousness to children's children, to those who keep His covenant, and who remember His precepts to do them"
(Psalm 103:17-18).

A DECISION MUST BE MADE

All parents need to ask themselves how they want to be remembered by their children.

If you are a parent, ask yourself whether you want to reinforce your own children, instill in them your beliefs, and bring them up in the way they should go. Or do you want to let someone else do it for you?

Obviously, many mothers have found ways to do this, even while working outside their homes. But, in large part, the majority of working mothers sacrifice some or all of their family goals in order to work.

It's a tough world for kids, and it's going to get a lot tougher. They will need all the support they can get to avoid the pitfalls Satan has skillfully laid for them.

My advice for anyone who is thinking about becoming a stay-at-home mom: When you are sure, do it! When you are in doubt, pray about it!

Positive self-worth and godly character are very important to your children. Maybe they will get this outside the home, but are you willing to take the chance? Your children only have one childhood and you only get one chance.

If you aren't a parent, you may know someone who is struggling with this issue and you can encourage and pray for that parent today.

"Teach me to do Thy will, for Thou art my God; let Thy good Spirit lead me on level ground. For the sake of Thy name, O Lord, revive me. . . . For I am Thy servant" (Psalm 143:10-12).

Larry Burkett

Daily Scripture Reading:
2 Samuel 18-19; Psalm 3

"Honor your father and your mother, as the Lord your God has commanded you, . . .that it may go well with you in the land which the Lord your God gives you"
(Deuteronomy 5:16).

MOTHERS

God commanded us to give honor to our mothers. What is a mother? She's the one person who knows us best and loves us in spite of it.

The most famous mother in the Bible, outside of Mary the mother of Jesus, was a woman by the name of Hannah. She suffered ridicule because she was barren; during her generation that was considered a curse from God.

Hannah made a promise to God that if He would give her a son she would dedicate him totally to God. He answered her prayer and Samuel was born. Hannah was a mother like all mothers, and to give up her son was a sacrifice, but when Samuel was 3 years old she left him with the prophet Eli.

The books of Samuel in the Old Testament are about the life of Samuel: Hannah's love for her son, how she prayed for him regularly, and how she visited him every year to bring him clothing and food. Can you imagine giving birth to a son, having him for only three years, and then only seeing him once a year? But Hannah had made a vow to God and she kept her promise.

If you have children, love them dearly, pray for them regularly, and at some point surrender them to God.

We'll be celebrating Mother's Day soon. If your mother is still living, call her and tell her how much you love and appreciate her—every day.

Larry Burkett

Daily Scripture Reading: 2 Samuel 20-21, 23:8-23;
1 Chronicles 11:10-25, 20:4-8

*"We are the temple of the living God; just as
God said, 'I will dwell in them and walk among them;
and I will be their God and they shall be My people' "*
(2 Corinthians 6:16).

HASTY DECISIONS

Often Christians rationalize hasty, even foolish, decisions on the basis of "God told me to do it."

If God tells someone to do something, He will provide for that person's needs.

The evidence that God hasn't directed everyone who says He has is the fact that sometimes the situations actually get worse.

Kenneth Wuest said, "When we have limitations imposed on us we do our best work for the Lord, for then we are most dependent on Him."

God has an individual plan for everyone. It has been my observation that this sometimes involves allowing us to work our way out of a situation of our own making—because of a hasty decision.

Ask God to show you His plan for you today. Be sure you know He is guiding you before you make any decision.

"I have chosen to do right. I cling to your commands and follow them as closely as I can. Lord, don't let me make a mess of things. Just tell me what to do and I will do it, Lord. As long as I live I'll wholeheartedly obey" (Psalm 119:30-31, 33-34 TLB).

Larry Burkett

Daily Scripture Reading: 2 Samuel 23:24-24:25;
1 Chronicles 11:26-47, 21:1-30

*"Give and it will be given to you; good measure, pressed down,
shaken together, running over, they will pour into your lap.
For by your standard of measure it will be measured to you in return"*
(Luke 6:38).

WHAT DOES IT MEAN?

Few verses are quoted more than today's Scripture regarding the principle of giving and receiving. When I first read this verse, shortly after committing my life to Christ, I pondered it for many weeks.

Did God really mean what this verse says? To me, there were some seemingly obvious difficulties with the principle that receiving was a matter of having to give first.

After many hours of contemplation and study, my conclusion was that when we give we should expect but never demand. Even if God blesses us far beyond our expectations, both materially and spiritually, our giving must be out of a desire to please God, not to profit from the relationship.

Giving is a material expression of a deeper spiritual obedience to God.

What is your motive for giving? Is it from a heart of love? Do you expect to receive from God? Pray that you will give in the right spirit.

Larry Burkett

Daily Scripture Reading:
1 Chronicles 22-24

"Better the little that the righteous have than the wealth of many wicked"
(Psalm 37:16 NIV).

DISCONTENTMENT

One of the primary symptoms of discontentment is that you're unable to experience peace living on what God has provided. You're restless, you feel that you have a void inside, and it seems you're always yearning for more.

In addition, discontentment causes you to make poor financial decisions. You buy into the philosophy that you always need more, better, faster things. You compare the things you have to the things you could have. Therefore, what you currently have is never good enough.

But more money and more things will never bring you satisfaction. *"Whoever loves money never has money enough; whoever loves wealth is never satisfied with his income. This too is meaningless"* (Ecclesiastes 5:10 NIV).

It's not wrong to have nice things, but you need to remember that true satisfaction comes from contentment with God.

Psalm 118:1 tells us, *"Give thanks to the LORD, for he is good; his love endures forever"* (NIV). Before you start your day, verbalize your contentment to God in a brief prayer thanking Him for everything in your life and for being with you no matter what.

This is not about denying the reality of life and trying to cover it up with a positive attitude. It's about living the truth of God's presence in your life.

"But because of his great love for us, God, who is rich in mercy, made us alive with Christ even when we were dead in transgressions—it is by grace you have been saved. And God raised us up with Christ and seated us with him in the heavenly realms in Christ Jesus, in order that in the coming ages he might show the incomparable riches of his grace, expressed in his kindness to us in Christ Jesus" (Ephesians 2:4-7 NIV).

Chuck Bentley

Daily Scripture Reading:
1 Chronicles 25-26; Psalm 30

"You are from God, little children, and have overcome. . . because greater is He who is in you than he who is in the world"
(1 John 4:4).

DEPRESSION

Only once in my life was I genuinely depressed. It was due to what I would call burnout. I was traveling, doing 50 to 60 seminars a year, and I had let my spiritual life run down. I got so busy for the Lord I didn't have time to spend with the Lord.

Ironically enough, this is something many full-time Christian workers experience; they are so busy serving God there's no time to spend with Him.

I didn't have time to study, to pray, to read the Bible. Everywhere I went I was giving, giving, giving, because that's what people expected.

Everyone gets down from time to time, but this time it really frightened me to realize I didn't have any control over it. I was in a downward spiral and couldn't eat, couldn't sleep, couldn't think straight, couldn't work anymore.

I had lost my direction, so I stopped, confessed it to the Lord, canceled everything, and determined to reestablish my relationship with the Lord.

I stayed with a friend until I regained my focus. I decided to resign as manager of the universe. God made it abundantly clear to me that He didn't give me that job in the first place.

Don't get so busy serving God that you don't have any time for Him. Spend time in prayer and meditate on His Word. And when you lack peace in your life, stop!

Larry Burkett

Daily Scripture Reading:
1 Chronicles 27-29

*"Behold the eye of the Lord is on those who fear Him,
on those who hope for His lovingkindness"*
(Psalm 33:18).

STRONG OR WEAK

One thing I've found after many years of counseling is that even the strongest of Christians have their weaknesses; and there is nothing unspiritual about admitting them. In fact, few people will seek counsel from "perfect" individuals. Real-life situations need real-life people to appreciate and understand them.

I find that the vast majority of people can handle the situations they face if they understand them, know the limits they can expect, and trust the Lord for His lovingkindness.

Are you trusting the Lord to help you face some situation in your life? Without a doubt, He will provide.

"Bless the Lord, O my soul, and forget none of His benefits; . . . who satisfies your years with good things, so that your youth is renewed like the eagle. . . . For He Himself knows our frame; He is mindful that we are but dust" (Psalm 103:2, 5, 14).

Larry Burkett

Daily Scripture Reading:
Psalms 5-7, 10-11, 13, 17

*"Do not work for food that spoils, but for food that
endures to eternal life, which the Son of Man will give you.
On him God the Father has placed his seal of approval"*
(John 6:27 NIV).

YOUR NEXT JOB

Do you have an idea of what your next job might be like? Are you imagining something that will lead you to retirement or to a life of comfort? Those things may be appealing, but do they fulfill God's purpose for your life?

Is that where God wants you to represent Him, serve Him, and take care of your family? That's an important question, because you may not have as much time as you think. God wants us to fulfill His plans with the resources He's given us.

If you're between jobs or about to search for a new job, now could be a great time to open yourself to however God wants to use you—even in a different field. It's a four-step process.

1. Ask God to direct you and put you where He wants you to be. Open your heart to Him, actively pray, and ask Him to counsel you as you read His Word.

2. Don't presume upon God. You need to humble yourself and be open to where, how, and when He directs.

3. More isn't always better or God's will. Be open to options and alternatives to your own preferences.

4. Act on the God-given dreams and desires of your heart. When you hear God calling you to do something, obey.

I have found that if His will is still not clear, a time of private prayer and fasting is very beneficial.

Chuck Bentley

Daily Scripture Reading:
Psalms 23, 26, 28, 31, 35

"You are worried and upset about many things,
but only one thing is needed. Mary has chosen
what is better, and it will not be taken away from her"
(Luke 10:41-42 NIV).

WORKING AT GOD'S WORK

I once heard someone laughingly say, "I'm not physically able to be a Baptist."

Christians who apply themselves to fruitless effort in the name of the Lord busy themselves to the point of exhaustion, going to conferences and countless church activities and serving on many committees. However, they are rarely, if ever, quiet enough for the Lord to direct them. They are irritable and often envious of others. They are truly working at God's work and not in it.

When Jesus was visiting Martha's home, she complained to the Lord that she was stuck doing all the "important" work while Mary was just sitting and listening to Him. We see what Jesus replied in today's Scripture verse.

How many of us have taken on a life of meaningless works to avoid the reality of serving God according to His will?

"Cease striving and know that I am God; I will be exalted among the nations, I will be exalted in the earth" (Psalm 46:10).

Larry Burkett

Daily Scripture Reading:
Psalms 41, 43, 46, 55, 61, 62, 64

"Get behind me, Satan! You are a stumbling block to me;
for you are not setting your mind on God's interests, but man's"
(Matthew 16:23).

WHY THE DISHONEST PROSPER

"My people did not listen to My voice. . . . So I gave them over to the stubbornness of their heart, to walk in their own devices" (Psalm 81:11-12).

There is no doubt that many dishonest people prosper and gain material things. Why? Because Satan, in his limited authority over us, can provide riches.

However, the problem with Satan's supply is that it's accompanied by fear, anxiety, anger, greed, resentment, and one day judgment.

Christians, on the other hand, must accept God's Word as the only standard for honesty and integrity. Only the Lord's provision is accompanied by peace and contentment.

Many Christians conform to this world and, as a result, they fail to experience God's blessings.

God has the power and the desire to grant material blessings to those who faithfully follow His directions.

"I would feed you with the finest of the wheat; and with honey from the rock I would satisfy you" (Psalm 81:16).

Larry Burkett

Daily Scripture Reading:
Psalms 69-71, 77

*"In the house of the wise are stores of choice food and oil,
but a foolish man devours all he has"*
(Proverbs 21:20 NIV).

DELAYED GRATIFICATION

Being able to delay gratification is a sign of contentment. For example, if you have worn carpet but can wait to replace it until you've saved the money, you are delaying gratification.

Another example is the Marshmallow Test. Give a marshmallow to a child and offer more marshmallows on the condition that she will wait 20 minutes before eating the first one. Most children don't pass the test and eat the first marshmallow before the time is up.

The world convinces us that if we desire something, we should have it now. If you buy into this philosophy, you won't be content until you have a particular item in your possession—even if it means buying it with credit. But having a relationship with God should give you contentment regardless of your circumstances.

The apostle Paul wrote, *"I have learned to be content whatever the circumstances. I know what it is to be in need, and I know what it is to have plenty. I have learned the secret of being content in any and every situation, whether well fed or hungry, whether living in plenty or in want. I can do everything through him who gives me strength"* (Philippians 4:11-13 NIV).

When you're having difficulty delaying gratification, remember that whatever you buy will only be new for a short time. And, in a matter of weeks, you'll probably be thinking about buying something else.

Things quickly lose their significance and their luster. It is better to be content with knowing Christ because *"Jesus Christ is the same yesterday and today and forever"* (Hebrews 13:8 NIV).

Chuck Bentley

Daily Scripture Reading:
Psalms 83, 86, 88, 91, 95

*"Do not judge lest you be judged. For in the
way you judge, you will be judged"*
(Matthew 7:1-2).

JUDGING OTHERS

I think this is one of the most misunderstood areas of God's Word—not to judge others.

This doesn't mean that we are not to exercise any judgment or discipline. To do so means that the whole structure of society and Christianity would fall apart.

When God's Word says to not judge others, lest we be judged, it means don't hold a standard up against somebody that is different from what God would establish.

However, we are told that when we see people living in sin we're to go to them, correct them, and win them over; so there's got to be a fine balance.

We are to execute judgment based on God's Word in a loving and kind way, to restore someone, not to condemn that person.

Luke wrote, *"Jesus is ordained of God to be the Judge of all—living and dead"* (Acts 10:42 TLB).

Larry Burkett

Daily Scripture Reading:
Psalms 108-109, 120-121, 140, 143-144

*"Choose for yourselves today whom you will serve. . .but as
for me and my house, we will serve the Lord"*
(Joshua 24:15).

POSITIVE ATTITUDES

According to God's Word, having a positive attitude simply means that we trust God, we are thankful for whatever He provides, and we seek His help in knowing how to use what we have.

Not only should we be positive about what is going on in our lives, but we should be able to praise God when He benefits someone else.

If we can praise God when someone else is prospering, we will have positive attitudes about whatever we are experiencing. Then, in God's timing, our lives will be blessed according to His riches in glory.

Lord, help me to be renewed in the spirit of Your mind. (Read Ephesians 4:23.)

Larry Burkett

Daily Scripture Reading:
Psalms 1, 14-15, 36-37, 39

> *"No soldier in active service entangles himself in the affairs of everyday life,*
> *so that he may please the one who enlisted him as a soldier"*
> (2 Timothy 2:4).

TAKING RESPONSIBILITY

I fear we are seeing an anemic generation of Americans, Christians included, who've had everything done for them and handed to them.

We grow strong physically, mentally, and spiritually through struggles, but this is impossible when parents shelter their children and never make them accountable for their decisions.

Government and society add to the problem by promoting the "victim" mentality and labeling overindulgence as "illness" or "addiction."

With these excuses to fall back on, people refuse to take responsibility for their actions and their own destinies. Instead of persevering, they wimp out. What an effective tool for Satan to stifle the work of the church!

We're in God's Army, and He requires commitment from His recruits. To fulfill that commitment, we must surrender our all to Him and separate ourselves from the world's system.

When we are tempted to see ourselves as victims, we should instead take full advantage of the golden opportunities we have to work for Christ and become victors.

Larry Burkett

Daily Scripture Reading:
Psalms 40, 49-50, 73

"He who prepared us for this very purpose is God, who gave to us the Spirit as a pledge. Therefore, being always of good courage, and knowing that. . .we walk by faith, not by sight"
(2 Corinthians 5:5-7).

DON'T QUIT

Thomas Edison was born into a world that had changed little in 200 years. The horse was the primary means of transportation, gas lights were the latest rage since coal lamps, and electricity was a novelty in college labs.

By his early 20s, Edison's driving motivation was to create a light source powered by electricity. After three years and over 250 failures, he discovered that a string impregnated with carbon and enclosed in an airless jar would glow twice as brightly as the best gas lamp.

Many years later, a reporter asked him how he found the motivation to keep going after so many failures. Edison replied, "I guess I never considered them failures. I just found a lot of things that didn't work."

Like Edison, other men and women throughout history persevered in the face of overwhelming odds, and many of these were Christians.

William Tyndale was determined to enlighten the people of England by translating the New Testament from Greek into English. He knew his activities were unpopular among leaders of the established church in that day, but he persevered, even in the face of death. He was burned at the stake as a heretic in 1536.

No matter what your mission is, facing opposition, becoming discouraged, or getting sidetracked are not valid reasons for quitting.

Larry Burkett

Daily Scripture Reading:
Psalms 76, 82, 84, 90, 92, 112, 115

*"The steps of a man are established by the Lord; and
He delights in his way. When he falls, he shall not be
hurled headlong; because the Lord is the One who holds his hand"*
(Psalm 37:23-24).

PERSISTENCE

The apostle Paul persevered even to the point of giving his life for the cause of Christ. His persistence will benefit all generations until the Lord returns.

If you did a study of the men and women that God has used, I believe you'd find that this attribute is a common thread among them. They have been doggedly persistent in what they were called to do.

Consider Joseph. He could have hanged himself in prison after he was sold into slavery in Egypt and then falsely accused of attempted adultery, but he persevered and became second in command to Pharoah.

Likewise, David was determined not to give up in the face of adversity. God chose him to subdue Israel's enemies and clean up the camp, which he did until the end of his life.

Remember the widow in Luke 18 who kept coming to an unrighteous judge asking for protection? She pestered him so much that he eventually did what she asked. Jesus used that parable to demonstrate that we should pray and not give up.

Persistence is an attitude that Christ desires in His followers. If you quit because things get difficult in your Christian walk, you might as well not start, because if you serve the Lord it probably will get tough.

Larry Burkett

Daily Scripture Reading:
Psalms 8-9, 16, 19, 21, 24, 29

"The fear of the LORD is the beginning of knowledge,
but fools despise wisdom and discipline"
(Proverbs 1:7 NIV).

WISDOM FROM ABOVE

Never make the mistake of believing that you can handle money well using your common sense instead of biblical wisdom. God knows more about your money than you do, and He wants to be part of your life and your finances.

Psalm 14:2 says, *"The LORD looks down from heaven on the sons of men to see if there are any who understand, any who seek God"* (NIV).

Do you seek God's wisdom? *"The wise in heart accepts commands, but a chattering fool comes to ruin"* (Proverbs 10:8 NIV).

Those seem like strong words, but not if you're in the habit of seeking God's financial wisdom and have seen the consequences suffered by those who have gone their own way.

Believers who dig deep into the Scriptures realize there's much more to learn, but a fool gets caught up in himself and thinks he knows everything.

The only reliable source of wisdom is the Word of God, and only by going back to this source can you hope to find counsel that you can place your total confidence in.

"The ordinances of the LORD are sure and altogether righteous. They are more precious than gold, than much pure gold; they are sweeter than honey, than honey from the comb. By them is your servant warned; in keeping them there is great reward" (Psalm 19:9-11 NIV).

Chuck Bentley

Daily Scripture Reading:
Psalms 33, 65-68

*"[Christ] did not come to be served, but to serve,
and to give His life a ransom for many"*
(Matthew 20:28).

SURRENDER

Christ's willingness to sacrifice on behalf of others may seem far beyond our reach. We want to be more like Him, but to do so we must cross the hurdle of surrendering everything to God.

It is at this point that Satan warns us about all the things we might lose. But all that we have belongs to God anyway. The important thing is that we learn obedience.

When we study the lives of the greatest people in the Bible, we find that they did not demand and direct. They followed, just like Shadrach, Meshach, and Abednego did when they refused to bow before the golden image of a pagan king. (Read the story in Daniel 3.)

They understood God's power, they knew their right to petition God, they accepted God as the final authority, and they surrendered themselves to Him.

We would do well to follow the example of Shadrach, Meshach, and Abednego.

Larry Burkett

Daily Scripture Reading:
Psalms 75, 93-94, 97-100

"Let each one do just as he has purposed in his heart;
not grudgingly or under compulsion; for God loves a cheerful giver"
(2 Corinthians 9:7).

CHEERFUL GIVING

Trusting God is one of the first steps toward overcoming Satan and becoming the cheerful giver the apostle Paul spoke about in today's Scripture verse.

Trust stems from love toward God, which produces love toward others. Love toward others produces giving.

The great American minister, Jonathan Edwards, said, "Love will dispose men to all acts of mercy toward their neighbors when they are under any affliction or calamity. . .for we are naturally disposed to pity those we love when they are afflicted. It will dispose men to give to the poor, to bear one another's burdens, and to weep with those that weep, as well as to rejoice with those that rejoice."

This giving spirit was evident in the Philippians, who faithfully supported the ministry of the apostle Paul. By their support, these people were counted as fellow laborers in Paul's work.

By the same token, everything we do for others we also do for Christ.

Larry Burkett

Daily Scripture Reading:
Psalms 103-104, 113-114, 117

"It is more blessed to give than to receive"
(Acts 20:35).

PURPOSEFUL GIVING

If we allow Satan's tools of fear, doubt, and selfishness to prevent us from surrendering all to God, we never can enjoy the rewards that await us when we serve, share, and give.

But if we seek God's will in giving, give only to please Him (not to impress others), and give cheerfully, we won't have to worry about our needs.

This may mean giving up having the world's "best," but that's a very small sacrifice compared to those being made by Christians in countries where professing faith in Christ means death.

God's Word says, *"Do not neglect doing good and sharing; for with such sacrifices God is pleased"* (Hebrews 13:16).

We forget that each of us has been called to suffer for Christ. For most of us, our service has not required material or physical sacrifice. However, it does require an understanding that our abundance is intended to further the kingdom of God. It is not a reward for being "nice."

How purposeful or sacrificial is your giving?

Larry Burkett

Daily Scripture Reading:
Psalm 119:1-88

"When you make a vow to God, do not be late in paying it,
for He takes no delight in fools. Pay what you vow! It is better
that you should not vow than that you should vow and not pay"
(Ecclesiastes 5:4-5).

HONORING A VOW

A principle that has been greatly overlooked in our generation is that of making a vow. A vow is literally a promise.

When someone borrows money, he or she makes a promise to repay according to the agreed-upon conditions of the loan (no matter whether it's a bank loan, personal loan, or use of a credit card). Once an agreement is sealed, repayment is not an option. It's an absolute as far as God is concerned.

As representatives of Jesus Christ before the world, Christians are admonished to think ahead and consider the consequences of their actions.

Once a Christian borrows money, the vow must be honored and the money repaid. If you can't keep your vows, don't make them.

Larry Burkett

Daily Scripture Reading:
Psalm 119:89-176

*"Do not merely look out for your own personal interests,
but also for the interests of others"*
(Philippians 2:4).

A SPIRITUAL INDICATOR

God's Word teaches that how we handle our money is the clearest reflection of our spiritual value system. Excessive debts, even bankruptcies, are not our problems; they are the external indicators of internal spiritual problems. Literally, they are a person's attitudes being reflected in actions.

I received a call from a pastor who was considering filing for bankruptcy because of a very heavy debt burden. He was fearful of his creditors obtaining judgments or even garnishments against him. "It's not fair that they can attach my salary," he said. "I won't be able to feed my family." I asked if they had tricked him into borrowing. They had not.

I asked him to consider what Christ would do if He were in his position. After all, isn't that what we're instructed to do as Christ's followers? We are to be imitators of Christ. *"Therefore be imitators of God, as beloved children"* (Ephesians 5:1).

This pastor stood up to his burden, asked for the forgiveness of his creditors, and cut up all his credit cards. He confessed his error before his church and found several kindred spirits in the congregation.

We are a generation of "quick-fix" attitudes, and the idea of absolutes has not been taught for a long time, even in Christian living.

Larry Burkett

Daily Scripture Reading:
Psalms 112, 124, 133-136

"The time will come when they will not endure sound doctrine; but wanting to have their ears tickled, they will accumulate for themselves teachers in accordance to their own desires"
(2 Timothy 4:3).

AN EASIER GOSPEL

Paul's letter to Timothy outlines the fact that trials are normal for the dedicated believer and, as a result, many fall away and seek an easier Gospel.

This easier Gospel teaches that Christ provides a buffer from all problems and provides unlimited prosperity and the freedom to spend profits as desired. In other words, God is so blessed to have us on His team that He is forced to intercede for fear that we will get discouraged and quit (as a great many do).

The truth is, God doesn't promise to buffer us from all difficulties for two basic reasons.

First, anyone would have to be simpleminded not to follow Christ if He buffered His followers from every problem. Instead, as Paul said, our faith must be tested by fire—in other words, faith for sustaining us through trials, not paving a path around them.

The second reason for not buffering a believer from all problems is so others will witness God's peace in the midst of turmoil. The unsaved can rely on money and position during good times, but during bad times emotional chaos usually reigns.

The Lord has promised a "crown of life" to those who persevere under trial and learn to love Him even more.

Larry Burkett

Daily Scripture Reading:
Psalms 138-139, 145, 148, 150

> *"A fool shows his annoyance at once,*
> *but a prudent man overlooks an insult"*
> (Proverbs 12:16 NIV).

AVOIDING CONFLICT AT WORK

One of the most important job skills you can have is being able to get along with others. If you don't develop this skill, you're headed for a long, difficult journey in the workplace.

Being easily agitated, critical, and a perfectionist can make you undesirable to be around. This could result in going through jobs fairly quickly. And, if you're an employer, you may have trouble keeping employees.

Displaying this type of character results in loss for you and suffering for others. I'm reminded of the story of Abigail and Nabal, found in 1 Samuel 25. The Bible describes Abigail as *"an intelligent and beautiful woman,"* but Nabal was *"surly and mean in his dealings"* (1 Samuel 25:3 NIV). Nabal insulted and refused to help David, Israel's future king, even though David and his men had faithfully guarded Nabal's flocks. Abigail did what was right and provided the assistance David had requested.

Shortly after this incident, *"the LORD struck Nabal and he died"* (1 Samuel 25:38 NIV). As for Abigail, she became David's wife.

Nabal could have helped David and enjoyed the satisfaction of knowing he had assisted Israel's future king. He could have lived and enjoyed the benefits of his wise and beautiful wife. But his attitude caused him to miss these things, and much more.

Overlook offenses and get along with others. If you become angry, don't lose it altogether, because you also could lose your job, your employees, or your relationships with family and friends.

"A fool gives full vent to his anger, but a wise man keeps himself under control" (Proverbs 29:11 NIV).

Chuck Bentley

Daily Scripture Reading:
Psalms 4, 12, 20, 25, 32, 38

"Just as the sufferings of Christ are ours in abundance, so also our comfort is abundant through Christ"
(2 Corinthians 1:5).

ABUNDANT COMFORT

Often those God has used most effectively are the ones who have suffered the greatest trials.

Perhaps no principle in God's Word is less understood than that of brokenness. Brokenness does not mean broke financially; it's a condition during which God allows circumstances to control our lives to the point that we must totally depend on Him.

It seems the greater God's plan for a person, the greater the brokenness. The life of the apostle Paul reflects both great power and great brokenness. Yet Paul never considered his personal circumstances as punishment. He consistently asserted that his sufferings were a direct result of service to Christ.

Dear Lord, I am totally dependent on You. Please help me in all the circumstances over which I have no control. I ask you in Jesus Name. Amen.

Larry Burkett

Daily Scripture Reading:
Psalms 42, 53, 58, 81, 101, 111, 130-131, 141, 146

*"Consider it all joy, my brethren, when you encounter various trials,
knowing that the testing of your faith produced endurance"*
(James 1:2-3).

THE PURPOSE OF BROKENNESS

"The Lord is near to the brokenhearted, and saves those who are crushed in spirit" (Psalm 34:18).

In God's wisdom, He realizes what it takes to keep us attuned to His direction: We must read His Word, accept His teachings, and be completely dependent on Him. Once we make a total surrender of ourselves to God, then, and only then, can He begin to use us.

No matter how many times we think we have surrendered ourselves to Him, we find ourselves falling into old habits and we have to try again.

Many times, as Christians, we pray, "God mold me into a vessel you can use," and then when God's work begins and things don't happen just like we had planned we are ready to call "time out."

When things are going well, we seldom complain, but when our goals are blocked—even temporarily—we become frustrated or irritated—a bit like spoiled children when they don't get their way.

If you set your mind on your own desires and not on God's will or His timing, you will not attain the happiness or satisfaction you seek.

If you want the perfecting of your faith, it comes by way of following God's leading and being in His will.

I pray that the God of peace will *"equip you in every good thing to do His will,"* working in you what is pleasing in His sight (see Hebrews 13:20-21).

Larry Burkett

Daily Scripture Reading:
Psalms 2, 22, 27

146

*"They are surprised that you do not run with them into
the same excess of dissipation, and they malign you; but they
shall give account to Him who is ready to judge the living and the dead"*
(1 Peter 4:4-5).

DIVORCE FROM THE WORLD

This principle is easier to talk about than to live. The teaching is very clear in the lives of those whom God has chosen to use throughout the Bible.

The more success you have in your service for God, the greater the potential for ego and self-centeredness. Thus, the greater the necessity for you to maintain a "God-first" spirit. The process of being molded into Christ's image must be continual.

Clearly, the purpose of being totally dependent on God is so you will be divorced from a marriage to this world and all it has to offer.

The world has its way of doing things; but, as a Christian, you should have an entirely different agenda.

Paul wrote to the Christians in Rome, *"Do not be conformed to this world, but be transformed. . . that you may prove what the will of God is, that which is good and acceptable and perfect"* (Romans 12:2).

John wrote that the world is passing away, *"but the one who does the will of God abides forever"* (1 John 2:17).

Larry Burkett

Daily Scripture Reading:
Psalms 45, 47-48, 87, 110

> *"I ask you not to lose heart at my tribulations*
> *on your behalf, for they are your glory"*
> (Ephesians 3:13).

RUN OR RELAX?

Our first reaction to the pressures of life is to run. It's simply easier to withdraw and feel sorry for ourselves than it is to stand against the enemy.

No one can question Elijah's courage or commitment to God. He regularly risked his life to deliver God's messages. And yet, right after he had called down God's fire from heaven and had destroyed the prophets of Baal, he ran when Jezebel threatened him.

In 1 Kings 19:4 he is found under a juniper tree, asking God to let him die. Instead, God comforted him, fed him, and told him to relax and rest. Later when Elijah was refreshed, God sent him back into the battle.

Then there's the apostle Paul: He must have had some real doubts about the difficulties he faced while serving the Lord. But the overwhelming characteristic we see in Paul's letters is the ability to relax and enjoy life—to be content—regardless of external circumstances.

When you are in the midst of difficult circumstances, can you say that you—like Paul—are relaxed? Or do you—like Elijah—run?

To honor God, we must be more like Paul: relaxed and content with our circumstances.

"I call upon the Lord, who is worthy to be praised, and I am saved from my enemies" (Psalm 18:3).

Larry Burkett

Daily Scripture Reading:
2 Samuel 23:1-7; 1 Kings 1:1-2:12

*"Whoever has the world's goods, and beholds his brother in need
and closes his heart against him, how does the love of God abide in
him? . . .Let us not love with word or with tongue, but in deed and truth"*
(1 John 3:17-18).

CARING ABOUT EACH OTHER

God is in control. If we are serving Him, nothing can befall us unless He allows it. It will rarely seem beneficial at the time, but if we believe God's Word we must believe He will ultimately receive the glory.

One important aspect of living for the Lord is to love and care about each other. When Christians are suffering from a financial disaster, the last thing they need is an accusation: "Well, she wasn't very careful with her money." or "He could have gotten a better job if he had really tried." or "Have you seen the car they drive?"

In fact, when people need help, they need your help. You must show compassion during their time of testing, and God's Word admonishes us to show our love with deeds.

Whatever you have is not intended solely for your personal enjoyment. God intends for you to give to others the way He has given to you—in love. What if God withheld blessings from you because you had made unwise decisions or had been careless?

People usually make their decisions based on whatever information or motivation they have at the time. It's not for us to judge their behavior. Rather, we are to care enough to help, knowing that some day we might be on the receiving end.

Larry Burkett

Daily Scripture Reading:
1 Kings 2:13-3:28; 2 Chronicles 1:15-17

"[Their] seed was sown among the thorns;
these are the ones who have heard the word, and the worries
of the world, and the deceitfulness of riches, and the desires for other things
enter in and choke the word, and it becomes unfruitful"
(Mark 4:18-19).

SOCIAL GOALS

Christians get trapped into a discontented life by adopting world goals. These goals always boil down to more, bigger, best. Scripture defines them as indulgence, greed, and pride.

Often successful Christians come to the Lord out of desperation when they realize that their lives are characterized by fear and anxiety, and the accumulation of assets has neither alleviated the fear nor provided happiness.

For a while after accepting Christ as Savior, there is peace and a real desire to commit everything to God. Unfortunately, many Christians continue to live in the natural, and the tendency is for them to fall back into the same old routine. They only go through the motions of serving the Lord.

The evidence to the contrary is a lack of peace, a lack of spiritual growth, and a growing doubt about God.

Satan's ploy is to use the riches of the world to keep you away from God's salvation and His blessings. If that fails, he will simply use riches to steer you away from God's path.

Don't let Satan get the upper hand in your life by adopting worldly goals.

The apostle Paul wrote, " 'Come out from their midst and be separate,' says the Lord. 'And do not touch what is unclean; and I will welcome you' " (2 Corinthians 6:17).

Larry Burkett

Daily Scripture Reading:
1 Kings 5-6; 2 Chronicles 2-3

"Righteousness exalts a nation, but sin is a disgrace to any people"
(Proverbs 14:34).

MEMORIAL DAY

We should honor those who died to ensure our freedoms. It seems to me that we take these freedoms for granted, but I can guarantee you that our forefathers didn't.

Ben Franklin, Alexander Hamilton, Thomas Jefferson, George Washington, and other men met in 1774 to pledge their fortunes, their lives, and their good names to secure our right to decide our own destinies.

We owe these men, but we have an even greater debt to our fallen soldiers. Every one of the original "generals," whom Christ chose and called apostles, gave his life to ensure that we would have a right to decide our eternal destinies and a right to tell others about it.

George Washington had been a wealthy man, but he was willing to pledge everything he had—fortune, fame, good name, family, even his life—for a cause he really believed in.

When people in the armed forces go to war, they must lay aside their families, businesses, and their own selfish desires and surrender themselves to the ones who have enlisted them.

The apostle Paul said that, as believers, we must do the same thing. He wrote, *"No soldier in active service entangles himself in the affairs of everyday life, so that he may please the one who enlisted him as a soldier"* (2 Timothy 2:4).

That's an important principle to remember. I encourage you to give thanks for all the fallen Americans who have preserved our freedom and our right to hear, teach, and spread the Gospel of our Lord Jesus Christ.

Larry Burkett

Daily Scripture Reading:
1 Kings 7; 2 Chronicles 4

*"Do not be anxious about anything, but in everything,
by prayer and petition, with thanksgiving, present your requests
to God. And the peace of God, which transcends all understanding,
will guard your hearts and your minds in Christ Jesus"*
(Philippians 4:6-7 NIV).

NO PEACE, NO PURCHASE

Advertisers are good at creating a sense of need and urgency. They offer an endless parade of "once-in-a-lifetime" deals. The pitch is normally to convince you that you'd better buy now because prices may never be this low again.

Even if you're seeking to be a good steward of God's resources, you may be tempted by some of these deals from time to time. The key is to be immersed in God's Word and aware of His presence.

If you don't have peace, don't buy. If a quick decision is required, don't get involved. Even if you have a legitimate need, take the time to think and pray about a prospective purchase, because God may have an alternative means of providing for you.

Decisions made on the spur of the moment often lead to regrets. Determine that you absolutely will not make buying decisions under pressure.

Waiting before you buy may cost you a few good deals. That's a small loss compared to freedom from stress and anxiety.

Chuck Bentley

Daily Scripture Reading:
1 Kings 8; 2 Chronicles 5:1-7:10

"It is vain for you to rise up early, to retire late, to eat the bread of painful labors; for He gives to His beloved even in his sleep"
(Psalm 127:2).

FATHERS

The following definition of a father was in a letter I received. "My father is the one who slips me an extra $10 for a really big date, the one who never misses my ball game even though we are 0 and 12 for the season, and the one who punishes me but always defends me against everyone else, because he's my dad, and he's my best friend."

It is customary to honor fathers at this time of year, but I want to address fathers. I encourage you not to invest in the urgent things of today, while letting the important things slip by. I've talked to so many people who look back and say, "If I could just live my life over again I'd spend more time with my children while they were growing up."

There are three important investments we have to make in our families. The first is time. God used the Scripture verse for today in my life many years ago when I was working 12 to 16 hours a day. Spend time with your children.

Second, give them your attention. Sometimes, even when we are at home, our minds are elsewhere. Nothing is worth the consequences later.

Third, give them discipline. The proverbs say that poverty and shame will come to them who lack discipline. I don't mean punishment; I mean setting an example for them to follow so you can mold them into God's image.

If your father is still living, tell him how much you love and appreciate him.

If you are a father, be the very best one you can be—with God's help.

Larry Burkett

Daily Scripture Reading:
1 Kings 9:1-10:13; 2 Chronicles 7:11-9:12

"Godliness actually is a means of great gain,
when accompanied by contentment"
(1 Timothy 6:6).

ATTITUDE EXTREMES

There are many people who seemingly have little or no regard for material possessions. They accept poverty as a normal living condition, and their major concern is where they will sleep each night.

Are they living lives of contentment? Hardly so, because that description aptly fits the homeless people found in the cities of our nation. That is one extreme.

In contrast are the affluent who have the best our society has to offer at their disposal. Their homes are the community showplaces, their summer cottages are actually small hotels, and their automobiles cost more than most families' houses. But does their abundance guarantee contentment?

Considering the amount of alcohol many of them consume, the therapists they see, and the tranquilizers a lot of them take, it's hard to imagine this group is any more content than the one I first described.

If poverty doesn't provide it and money can't buy it, how can you be content?

"Give me neither poverty nor riches; feed me with the food that is my portion, lest I be full and deny Thee and say, 'Who is the Lord?' Or lest I be in want and steal, and profane the name of my God" (Proverbs 30:8-9).

To be content is to know God's plan for your life, have the conviction to live it, and believe that God's peace is greater than any problem.

Larry Burkett

Daily Scripture Reading: 1 Kings 4, 10:14-29;
2 Chronicles 1:14-17, 9:13-28; Psalm 72

*"It is time for judgment to begin with the household of God;
and if it begins with us first, what will be the outcome
for those who do not obey the gospel of God?"*
(1 Peter 4:17).

LIFE'S STRUGGLES

All of us struggle with one thing or another in our lives. I remember the struggles I had when I was growing up in a poor family. Our family was philosophically poor—they thought "poor."

My mother and father came through the Great Depression, and my father didn't work regularly for about eight years, and it left a great impression on him. So, from that time we always lived poorly and never spent money—even on a decent house.

Every discussion I can remember about money was, "We can't afford it." So, that has haunted me all of my life. But even negative circumstances can bring positive results, because I determined I would never be poor.

Over the years, I've had the opportunity to make a lot of money—in business and from writing. The Lord has convicted me to give my surplus away, because if I didn't I would never trust Him. If we have more than we need, there isn't much need to trust in Him, is there?

We will be judged for the way we have used our resources: Have we hoarded them for ourselves or have we given to those with needs?

The first generation church set an example for us, so the question is whether we will be doers of the Word instead of hearers only.

"I delivered the poor who cried for help, and the orphan who had no helper" (Job 29:12).

Larry Burkett

Daily Scripture Reading:
Proverbs 1-3

*"[B]ut speaking the truth in love, we are to grow up
in all aspects into Him who is the head, even Christ"*
(Ephesians 4:15).

DEALING WITH A NEGLIGENT HUSBAND

Recently, Crown received a letter from a wife whose husband had worked on and off throughout their 18-year marriage. When he was employed, he wanted to spend. When he was not working, he and his wife depended on help from relatives. They had filed bankruptcy twice, and at the time of this letter, he was out of work again and didn't plan to look for a job. However, his wife had a desire to stay home and care for their children and to get out of debt.

My heart went out to this woman. This man was responsible to work and provide for his family whether he was in a high-paying or low-paying job. Here's some advice if you're facing a similar situation.

First, ask your husband to pray out loud with you every day. This will tell you a lot about what's in his heart.

Second, ask him if he's willing to approach finances God's way. Tell him you think God's way is better than man's way. Don't condemn him or make him feel like a failure. Just ask him to join you in discovering and following God's way.

Third, let him know you'll help in any way possible because you don't want to live in violation of God's principles. Even if he doesn't want to, he may let you manage the budget if you ask respectfully.

Speak the truth in love to your husband. Man is prideful and doesn't want to feel like a failure. Nagging won't be successful. Women often see the truth clearly, but they must share that truth in love. Affirm your love for your husband and ask him to work with you. In the meantime, pray regularly for patience and for wisdom as you ask the Lord to change his heart.

Chuck Bentley

Daily Scripture Reading:
Proverbs 4-6

"Blessed is the man who walks not in the counsel of the ungodly"
(Psalm 1:1).

CHOOSING GODLY COUNSEL

People have often asked me, "Should a Christian ever use non-Christian counselors, such as lawyers, doctors, accountants?" I believe the answer to that question is in today's verse.

God's Word teaches that we should seek our counsel from other Christians—godly men and women who understand and try to obey God's Word.

For example, if you are going to choose a doctor, you want to know that the person who is going to take care of you has God's wisdom, as well as being skilled in the medical profession.

If you have a non-Christian counselor (doctor, dentist, attorney), God's Word teaches that you should not get rid of that person. That can be a bad witness to an unsaved person. Perhaps God put you with that person for the purpose of leading him or her to the Lord. If these counselors have been wise, ethical, and honest, then stick with them.

I counseled a Christian businessman who had a non-Christian accountant and attorney. For about 10 years this businessman had been doing unethical, dishonest practices, at the encouragement of his accountant, in order to save taxes. His attorney kept him from being caught.

As this man's relationship with God grew, it became evident that he couldn't continue these business practices. He had to stop the dishonest practices and make restitution. The accountant and attorney quit; he has since made restitution and now has godly counselors.

Read today's verse over again. Do you need to make any changes in your own life?

Larry Burkett

Daily Scripture Reading:
Proverbs 7-9

"Our struggle is not against flesh and blood, but against the rulers, against the powers, against the world forces of this darkness, against the spiritual forces of wickedness in the heavenly places"
(Ephesians 6:12).

POWER OVER SATAN

We are told that Satan is a defeated foe. He was defeated from the beginning of eternity; he just didn't realize it. Satan thought he had won when Christ was crucified, but when Christ arose from the grave, Satan realized what a mistake he had made.

The only threat Satan has over God's creation is the threat of death. Once the threat of death was removed by the resurrection of Jesus, Satan's hold over us was lost.

Those who have accepted Jesus as Lord know that death has no meaning because we pass from life in this world to an eternity with God.

Satan may try to influence our minds, but God's Word says for us to *"Take up the full armor of God, that you may be able to resist in the evil day, and having done everything, to stand firm"* (Ephesians 6:13).

Larry Burkett

Daily Scripture Reading:
Proverbs 10-12

"Let not your adornment be merely external"
(1 Peter 3:3).

CHRISTIAN LOGOS AND SIGNS

I received a letter that said, "I'm a Christian businessman and I love the Lord, but I am really turned off by these people who display Christianity on their cards and have signs on their trucks. Either they are trying to sell Christianity or they are trying to use God to increase their business. What do you think?"

I know a lot of people who use Christian logos on their business cards and on their vehicles, and unfortunately some are phony. Some people use this means to proselytize customers. But I believe that for everyone who is phony there are a hundred more who are sincere, born-again believers, trying to serve God in a real way.

I caution everyone I come in contact with to be sure they know what that means. It doesn't just mean being a better businessperson. It means being a different businessperson because of the principles he or she is committed to live by.

Read today's verse again. In other words, don't just show your Christianity on the side of a truck or a logo on a business card. Let your behavior show that you are committed to Christ.

How can you do that? By being honest, treating your customers fairly, and by always giving them the better deal than you do yourself. You also do that by paying your employees a fair wage and treating them with honor. Then your adornment is not only external, it is internal.

If you display Christ by using symbols, live by what you are displaying. Hold up the standards of the Lord before others.

Larry Burkett

Daily Scripture Reading:
Proverbs 13-15

June 8

*"I have chosen him, in order that he may command
his children and his household after him to keep the way
of the Lord by doing righteousness and justice"*
(Genesis 18:19).

ACADEMIC ACHIEVEMENT

Samuel Johnson said, "Knowledge always desires increase; it is like fire, which must first be kindled by some external agent, but which will afterward propagate itself."

The homeschooling movement has literally exploded because of the steady deterioration of our public schools and the soaring costs of private schools. Parents are desperate to insulate their children from the permissive attitudes taught in public schools, declining achievement scores, and the total denial of basic religious values at any level in public education.

In order for our children to have good futures, we must give them the best training possible, both academically and spiritually.

In his article for Home School Researcher, Richard Medlin noted that homeschooled children are "not educationally disadvantaged" and that their achievement scores are, in fact, "above average."

The success or failure of homeschooling depends on parents' willingness to do their jobs, and only parents who are seriously committed to teaching their children at home should try it.

Ask God to bless the parents who are homeschooling their children, and pray for the children as they learn in a home environment.

Larry Burkett

Daily Scripture Reading:
Proverbs 16-18

160

"Whether then you eat or you drink, or whatever you do,
do all to the glory of God"
(1 Corinthians 10:31).

HOW TO CHEAT

I heard of a Christian couple who, in order to qualify for a low-income, subsidized government loan, had the wife's employer reduce her working hours. Because she made too much money to qualify for the loan, she reduced her working hours from 40 to 20, which also dropped her salary enough to help them qualify for the loan.

Then, after getting the loan, she went back to working her original hours. They believed there was nothing wrong with doing this since they actually didn't have too much income when they qualified for the loan.

This couple lost the concept of being able to be honest and also failed to trust the Lord for their needs. In order to get the loan they thought they needed, they relied on human devices, trickery, and deceitfulness.

If I could have talked to this couple I would have asked them to consider what God thought of what they had done. He knew all about it, of course.

Our purpose in life is to serve God. The government may never find out what this couple did; but, let me assure you, we all have to answer to a higher power than the government.

We are told in God's Word that if we regard iniquity in our hearts, God will not hear us.

No matter what other people are doing, do not conform to the image of this world.

Larry Burkett

Daily Scripture Reading:
Proverbs 19-21

*"Without faith it is impossible to please Him. . . He
is a rewarder of those who seek Him"*
(Hebrews 11:6).

YOU MUST BELIEVE

We must believe God in order to receive His best. As our Scripture verse for today says, it is impossible to please Him unless we have faith—unless we really believe what He says in His Word and act accordingly.

Most Christians say they believe God, but their lives don't show it. They can exercise discipline in their lives, but they don't exercise faith. They don't step out beyond their own boundaries.

The Pharisees were very spiritual men from outward appearances: They tithed, fasted, and prayed, but it was always with a self-motivated attitude. They tithed but expected to get money back. They fasted but wanted everyone to know it, so they made a show of looking very pitiful. That is exercising discipline—not faith.

Luke 18:1 says to pray and not to lose heart. You have to believe that God hears you. A lack of faith keeps the majority of Christians from ever receiving what God promised them.

Envision God sitting on the throne in Heaven and Jesus sitting at His right hand. They are looking down on you. God says, "I want to bless that person but she doesn't act like she believes my Word. She never gives more than she thinks she can afford. She never helps unless she thinks she can get something in return. Doesn't she know that I can bless her abundantly if she will only trust in me?"

God does want to bless us. We are His children and He loves us. He can't bless us unless we are able to come to Him unreservedly and believe His Word and His promises.

Larry Burkett

Daily Scripture Reading:
Proverbs 22-24

*"Wives, submit to your husbands as to the Lord. ...Husbands, love your
wives, just as Christ loved the church and gave himself up for her"*
(Ephesians 5:22-25 NIV).

FINANCIAL DISAGREEMENTS
IN MARRIAGE

When you or your spouse seek to have your own way about money in your marriage,
your inability to get what you want is bound to cause disagreements.

The solution for these disagreements is to turn to God and ask Him for help.
You don't have all the answers. And, following God's plan for managing money and
possessions will give you and your spouse a framework for being unified about finances.

If your spouse is not a believer, don't resort to divorce. As a believer, you've been
sanctified (set apart) for the Lord, and the family is blessed by your relationship with
Him.

Paul noted in 1 Corinthians 7:14 that *"the unbelieving husband is set apart (separated,
withdrawn from heathen contamination, and affiliated with the Christian people) by union
with his consecrated (set-apart) wife"* (AMP).

The Bible says to submit to your husband, which may not sound appealing to you at
this time. However, submission usually melts the heart of a proud man.

In the meantime, turn to God and ask Him to help you reconcile your differences.
And, as always, share the truth in love.

Chuck Bentley

Daily Scripture Reading:
Proverbs 25-27

"Are you willing to recognize. . .that faith without works is useless?"
(James 2:20).

PUT FAITH TO WORK

Many Christians don't like to hear that they must put faith to work. I've even heard the comment, "I thought faith was a free gift from God." No, grace—unmerited favor—is a free gift of God. Faith requires action.

Hebrews also says that faith is the assurance of things hoped for. If you already have it, you don't need faith to receive it. It's putting something to work that says, "I believe God's plan, and I'm going to exercise God's plan."

Our responsibility is to put faith to work. Unless you live by the principles in God's Word, He can't bless you. He is bound by the same principles we are.

If we really trust God's Word, we will step out in faith. Once we add action to our faith, then things will begin to change, but we do have to be "doers" as well as "hearers."

Think of something you have been praying about but you have never applied the corresponding actions. Take that first step. Add actions to your faith.

Larry Burkett

Daily Scripture Reading:
Proverbs 28-29

"The steadfast of mind Thou wilt keep in perfect peace,
because he trusts in Thee"
(Isaiah 26:3).

STEPS TO FREEDOM

Just as the plans we make for ourselves sometimes cause frustration and worry, God's plans always provide peace and freedom.

Peace and freedom show themselves in every aspect of our lives: release from tension and worry, a clear conscience, and the sure knowledge that God is in control.

We are human and, as such, subject to making mistakes, but once God is in charge of our lives His divine correction will bring every area under His control.

There are steps to achieving God's plan. For every promise He makes, He has a condition. In each case, some action is required to bring His power into focus in our lives. That might be prayer, fasting, or simply believing, but it will always require a free act of our wills.

If we are seeking God's best in this life, we must be willing to submit to His will and His direction.

Pray that you will be able to keep your wishes and desires in line with God's will for your life so that you will experience peace and freedom and will receive His best for you.

Larry Burkett

Daily Scripture Reading:
Proverbs 30-31; Psalm 127

"As for every man to whom God has given riches and wealth,
He has also empowered him to eat from them and to receive
his reward and rejoice in his labor; this is the gift of God"
(Ecclesiastes 5:19).

WHAT IS WEALTH?

How well do you understand God's attitude about wealth? There is so much religious folklore in the financial realm that few Christians understand what is from God's Word and what is not.

There are approximately 700 direct references to money in the Bible and hundreds more indirect references. Nearly two-thirds of all the parables Christ left us deal with the use of money. After studying these verses we have to conclude that God equates our use of wealth with our commitment to Him.

God gives us financial principles in His Word, and that's exactly what they are: principles, not laws. He will not punish anyone for violations. Those who fail simply will not receive His blessings in the area of finances and will suffer along with the unbeliever.

Historically, wealth has been related to ownership, but wealth is also related to our creative ability and our credit or borrowing ability: the trust others have in us. Thus wealth becomes an extension of our personalities. It can be used creatively—to spread the Gospel and build hospitals and churches—or it can be wasted on frivolous activities. It can even be corruptive—to purchase influence—or destructive—to buy guns and bombs.

Wealth is neither moral nor immoral. There is no inherent virtue in poverty or in wealth. Rather, God condemns our preoccupation with wealth.

We must learn to trust God in every circumstance, believing that He loves us and gives us only what we can handle without being tempted beyond what we can withstand.

God may use money as a testing ground of your true willingness to surrender yourself to Him. Will you pass the test?

Larry Burkett

Daily Scripture Reading:
Song of Songs

*"Enjoy life with the woman whom you love all the days
of your fleeting life which He has given to you under
the sun; for this is your reward in life"*
(Ecclesiastes 9:9).

OPPOSITES ATTRACT

I received a letter from a young lady saying, "I'm engaged to a nice man, but we are so opposite it seems we never agree on anything. Do you think we are so incompatible that we will not get along in a marriage?"

Possibly they are incompatible, but I know for a fact that if two people in a marriage are just alike one of them is unnecessary. In great part, God puts opposites together because opposites really do attract. In most marriages, one gets up early; the other prefers to stay in bed. One splashes in the sink; the other cleans up. One has a good sense of direction; the other gets lost.

All of this is so that one will offset the extremes of the other one. If we look at differences as a problem rather than as a balance, we will end up arguing a lot. By recognizing the differences as an asset, a couple can become one working unit. That is what God desires.

Unless you have an absolute commitment to make the marriage work, it won't, because when the going gets tough you'll want out.

Whether you are already married or you are about to get married, think about what you are willing to do to fulfill your commitment to a happy marriage.

If you are already married, think about what you believe has helped you to make a success of your marriage.

If you are unmarried, with no plans for such, think about a couple you know and then pray for them.

Larry Burkett

Daily Scripture Reading:
1 Kings 11:1-40; Ecclesiastes 1-2

"The peace of God, which surpasses all comprehension,
shall guard your hearts and your minds in Christ Jesus"
(Philippians 4:7).

REJECT A FEARFUL SPIRIT

One of Satan's favorite tools is to get you to question "What if?"

Dedicated Christians get trapped into hoarding because they fear the "what if" of retirement, disability, unemployment, or economic collapse.

Obviously, God wants us to consider these things and even plan for them, within reason. But when fear dictates to the point that giving to God's work is hindered, foolish risks are assumed and worry becomes the norm, rather than the exception. Then contentment is impossible.

Christians must consciously reject this attitude of fear.

To claim God's victory, it may be necessary for you to face your fear. If your fear is a lack of surplus, it may be necessary to live without it in order to conquer that fear.

But remember above all else, *"My God shall supply all your needs according to His riches in glory in Christ Jesus"* (Philippians 4:19).

Larry Burkett

Daily Scripture Reading:
Ecclesiastes 3-7

*"The thief does not come except to steal, and to kill,
and to destroy. I have come that they may have life,
and that they may have it more abundantly"*
(John 10:10 NKJV).

ABUNDANT LIFE

What does "abundance" mean to you? To most people, it probably means a large amount of money and possessions. God's perspective is different. He teaches that abundance is found in four key relationships.

The first of these relationships is with God Himself, because true wealth comes from knowing Him. Following are suggestions for developing a vibrant relationship with God.

1. Read His Word and memorize the Scripture with the mindset to know the Author.

2. Pray—Humble yourself before the Lord, confess you don't have the kind of relationship with Him that you need, and ask Him to draw closer to you, to free you from fear, and allow you to experience His abundance.

3. Fast—If you trust God and follow through with fasting, you'll discover God is ever-present, the true Master of your life.

4. Learn to be generous—Generosity shows you believe God and trust He will take care of you.

The second relationship you need for abundant life is a relationship with a community of believers. You can't experience the riches of relationships with others if you don't join a church, participate, and serve.

The third relationship necessary for abundant life is a relationship with family and friends, which you can improve through an investment of time. Offer them hospitality, kindness, grace, forgiveness, and mercy.

The fourth and final relationship necessary for abundant life is a right relationship with money. Money has a grip on the lives of many people, but only God should be your Master. He wants you to be free to serve and give, but you won't be able to do that if you're a slave to money.

Chuck Bentley

Daily Scripture Reading: 1 Kings 11:41-43;
2 Chronicles 9:29-31; Ecclesiastes 8-12

"I say to you, love your enemies, and pray for those who persecute you"
(Matthew 5:44).

RESPOND OR REACT?

When we are hurt or betrayed by friends or business associates, our initial impressions are purely emotional ones, and unless we are controlled primarily by God's Word the first impressions are rarely correct.

In fact, I have discovered that many initial impressions run opposite to God's direction. Therefore, we must turn to His Word.

The Scriptures present an interesting perspective of strength and compassion when dealing with those who cause us harm or hurt.

Read the account of David's confrontation with Nabal in 1 Samuel 25:2-39. In spite of David's noble gesture to protect Nabal's property, when David needed help Nabal refused even to acknowledge him. This obvious affront infuriated David.

In anger (sometimes our first reaction), David decided to take matters into his own hands and destroy Nabal. God used Nabal's wife to stop David from taking vengeance, and in the face of godly counsel David cooled off and withdrew.

His withdrawal could have been interpreted as weakness by others; however, the result was that God executed judgment in His own time. Thus, the use of restraint was more effective than the use of strength.

It is always better to respond to situations (with patience, prayer, understanding) than to react (with anger and retaliation).

Larry Burkett

Daily Scripture Reading: 1 Kings 12;
2 Chronicles 10:1-11:17

"The God of all grace, who called you to His eternal glory in Christ,
will Himself perfect, confirm, strengthen and establish you"
(1 Peter 5:10).

WHAT IS STRENGTH?

Even a cursory review of Scripture reveals that strength does not always mean the exercise of power. More often, it means the relinquishing of personal rights to God.

The opposite of strength is cowardice. Those who flee from any confrontation display cowardice. What's the difference? It's whether God receives honor from the action.

If you allow others to cheat and abuse you because you are fearful of any conflict, you are displaying cowardice. Cowardice is generally motivated by self-preservation—not compassion.

A classic example is found in Numbers 13 and 14. God's people refused to occupy their promised land because of the giants living there. Were they demonstrating compassion for their enemies? Hardly! They were self-motivated.

Strength is demonstrated when you exercise the proper use of power to accomplish God's assigned tasks.

God works through your life if you are surrendered to Him. Will you display cowardice or strength? It's your choice.

Larry Burkett

Daily Scripture Reading: 1 Kings 13-14;
2 Chronicles 11:18-12:16

"Jesus said to them, 'Watch out and beware of the leaven of the Pharisees and Sadducees'"
(Matthew 16:6).

AID THE ENEMY?

Loving your enemies (anyone who does you harm) is different from aiding them. Christ loved the Pharisees (He loved everyone), but He certainly did not help them.

To the contrary, as we see in today's Scripture verse, He opposed them and warned His disciples to stay away from them. They represented a counterforce that was anti-Christian.

This is not meant to imply that all our enemies fall into the same classification as the Pharisees. But when others purposely set themselves against your interests and God's, they certainly cannot be classified as friends.

God wants us to love others both prayerfully and spiritually, but that does not mean to aid what they are doing. On occasion God may direct you to aid someone who is doing you wrong, but it is so you can provide a strong and effective witness for Him.

Helping someone who has wronged you is the only type of "revenge" God would sanction.

"Vengeance is Mine, and retribution. . . . For the Lord will vindicate His people, and will have compassion on His servants" (Deuteronomy 32:35).

Larry Burkett

Daily Scripture Reading: 1 Kings 15:1-24;
2 Chronicles 13-16

*"I said to myself, 'Come now, I will test you with pleasure.
So enjoy yourself.' And behold it too was futility"*
(Ecclesiastes 2:1).

SELFISHNESS

The theology of selfishness is an easy one to promote because most of us were raised with it, and today it virtually dominates our society. It's the philosophy called "get all you can out of life today; live with gusto." This certainly is not a new philosophy. As you can see in today's Scripture, Solomon wrote about it in the book of Ecclesiastes.

Selfishness, ego, and pride are about as opposite from biblical concepts as light is from darkness.

It is important to discern the difference between the pride of wealth and the wealth itself. Christ never condemned wealth; He condemned the wealthy-minded of this world.

God has blessed many people with both spiritual and material wealth. Those who are selected by God to manage a large surplus—to feed His sheep—should manifest humility, not pride.

Dear Father, am I guilty of selfishness, ego, and pride? Help me to operate in humility and walk in the light of your Word.

Larry Burkett

Daily Scripture Reading: 1 Kings 15:25-16:34, 17;
2 Chronicles 17

*"Do not love the world, nor the things in the world.
If anyone loves the world, the love of the Father is not
in him. . . . The one who does the will of God abides forever"*
(1 John 2:15, 17).

COMPROMISE

Few Christians willfully violate the Ten Commandments. Most appear to be basically moral. But what about inward doubts, temptations, and failures? Are these sins?

Compared to overt sins (like lying or stealing), compromises don't seem so bad. If God were merely an accountant, weighing good against bad and one person against another, there would be no problem.

However, God deals in absolutes, not comparisons. His Word is straightforward and any compromises of what it says are usually just symptoms of spiritual problems.

J.R. Lowell said, "Compromise makes a good umbrella, but a poor roof; it is a temporary expedient."

As an individual, you are responsible and accountable for your own actions, regardless of what others do.

Dear Lord, forgive me if I'm guilty of compromising anything in Your Word and help me make the changes in my life that are needed.

Larry Burkett

Daily Scripture Reading:
1 Kings 18-19

*"O LORD, our Lord, how majestic is your name in all
the earth! You have set your glory above the heavens"*
(Psalm 8:1 NIV).

ARE YOU IMPRESSED?

The thing that impresses you is the clearest indication of the direction you're taking in life. Jesus was impressed by a widow who gave two coins, because it was all that she had. The widow was impressed with God, which is why she gave everything.

However, Jesus was not impressed with the temporal things of this world, which are destined to be destroyed…if they don't wear out first. The Bible tells us when the Lord returns, *"the earth and its works will be burned up"* (2 Peter 3:10).

One day, as Jesus was leaving the temple, one of his disciples said, *"Look, Teacher! What massive stones! What magnificent buildings!"* Jesus replied, *"Do you see all these great buildings? …Not one stone here will be left on another; every one will be thrown down"* (Mark 13:1-2 NIV). This prophecy was literally fulfilled in A.D. 70, when Roman forces destroyed Jerusalem and its temple, as well.

So, what should impress us as Christians in this life? God deeply desires for us to be impressed with Him, so much so that we trust Him with everything we have. There's nothing wrong with having wealth or being significant in the world, but we're not to be impressed with these things, or with anything else that isn't eternal.

Chuck Bentley

Daily Scripture Reading:
1 Kings 20-21

*"People who want to get rich fall into temptation
and a trap and into many foolish and harmful desires
that plunge men into ruin and destruction"*
(1 Timothy 6:9 NIV).

IS GREED ACCEPTABLE?

Greed has become such an accepted attitude that most major advertisements for luxury products are built around it. Many committed believers are convinced (often by other believers) that it is God's absolute responsibility to make them wealthy and successful.

Just to help Him out (in case God neglects His responsibility), they are willing to borrow large amounts of money to invest in get-rich-quick schemes, abandon their families to provide the good life for them, and rob God of His tithes and offerings. Then they rationalize their behavior under the guise of doing what they have to do to succeed.

God does have a plan for success, and although it is unique for each individual it is common in three ways.

God never provides success at the expense of serving Him first.

God never provides success at the expense of our peace.

God never provides success at the expense of the family.

Albert Einstein said, "It is high time that the ideal of success should be replaced by the ideal of service."

Larry Burkett

Daily Scripture Reading: 1 Kings 22:1-40;
2 Chronicles 18

*"Become blameless and pure, children of God without fault
in a crooked and depraved generation, in which you shine
like stars in the universe as you hold out the word of life"*
(Philippians 2:15-16 NIV).

GOD'S WAY: OPTIONAL OR MANDATORY?

It seems abundantly clear from God's Word that when we accept Christ as our Lord we are to live by a much higher standard than the rest of the world—not because as Christians we are supposed to be pious or super spiritual but simply because we are to be normal.

It is God's way that is normal and the world's way that is abnormal—not the other way around, as some would think.

We are to be lights in a dark world, for the express purpose of leading others to a saving knowledge of Jesus.

What we say is not enough. God requires that we "show and tell." When others observe our attitudes and our behavior, they will either see Christ in us or they won't. It is as clear as that.

True believers possess a serenity and joy that comes from knowing Christ and living for Him. And true believers set standards for their lives that are in tune with the Word of God.

"As for me, I shall walk in my integrity; redeem me, and be gracious to me. My foot stands on a level place" (Psalm 26:11-12).

Larry Burkett

Daily Scripture Reading: 1 Kings 22:41-53; 2 Kings 1;
2 Chronicles 19:1-21:3

*"Should a man like me run away? Or should one like me
go into the temple to save his life? I will not go!"*
(Nehemiah 6:11 NIV).

PRECONDITIONED RESPONSE

As Christians, we learn a great deal about discipline and dedication from the secular world. It is interesting that those in the secular business world are sometimes more punctual and reliable in their work than Christians are in serving God.

Sadly, some Christians apply a degree of excellence and dedication to their business careers that are woefully lacking in their walk with the Lord.

The secular business world practices what is called "preconditioned response." For instance, the airlines have found that it is not feasible to wait until inflight emergencies occur to acquaint pilots with emergency procedures. Therefore, they attempt to precondition their responses.

Even a cursory scan of Scripture will reveal that the truly successful servants of the Lord made decisions on the preconditioned belief that God's way wasn't the best way; it was the only way.

Just as Nehemiah did when he refused to compromise God's way even to save his own life, a Christian must precondition all responses to temptations and problems on the basis of what God says, not what is normal and acceptable to the world.

God promises that He will protect us so that He may receive the glory. *"Call upon me in the day of trouble; I will deliver you, and you will honor me"* (Psalm 50:15 NIV).

Larry Burkett

Daily Scripture Reading:
2 Kings 2-4

"Who, then, is the man that fears the LORD?
He will instruct him in the way chosen for him"
(Psalm 25:12 NIV).

FEAR AND WISDOM

Wise decisions lead to blessings; foolish decisions lead to suffering. The cornerstone of wise decision-making is the fear of the Lord. Fools despise wisdom and discipline and turn to sources not of God.

The final hours of King Saul present us with one of the most striking examples of seeking wisdom from a source other than God. Worried about the outcome of an upcoming battle, Saul told his attendants, *"Find me a woman who is a medium, so I may go and inquire of her"* (1 Samuel 28:7 NIV).

Saul ended up dying in the battle *"because he was unfaithful to the LORD; he did not keep the word of the LORD and even consulted a medium for guidance, and did not inquire of the LORD"* (1 Chronicles 10:13-14 NIV).

If you fear the Lord, you won't turn to sources other than Him. You'll realize your desperate need for wisdom and recognize and honor Him as the primary source of wisdom.

Christianity is a living, dynamic relationship with Jesus Christ, the living Lord who gives us guidance through His thoughts and ways. We get into trouble when we don't fear the Lord and seek wisdom from other sources.

Chuck Bentley

Daily Scripture Reading:
2 Kings 5-7

*"If our hearts do not condemn us, we have confidence
before God and receive from him anything we ask,
because we obey his commands and do what pleases him"*
(1 John 3:21-22 NIV).

GOD'S ABSOLUTES

The actual violations of God's commandments involve attitudes that develop over a period of time and are difficult to guard against. Most of us simply find ourselves doing them without realizing how or when the attitudes started.

It's apparent from God's Word that He also recognizes this and has provided an objective question we can ask ourselves to measure our internal attitudes: How do we respond to temptations?

God's minimum acceptable attitudes are developed by accepting the two conditions mentioned in the verse following today's Scripture verse: *"This is his command: to believe in the name of his Son, Jesus Christ, and to love one another as he commanded us"* (1 John 3:23).

Christ said that loving God more than anything else is a prerequisite to receiving God's best, and I believe that's what most of us want, isn't it?

Use the words of a hymn by Frances Havergal and Henry Malan as your prayer: Take my life and let it be consecrated, Lord, to Thee. Take my moments and my days and let them flow in ceaseless praise.

Larry Burkett

Daily Scripture Reading: 2 Kings 8-9;
2 Chronicles 21:4-22:9

180

"Be on guard for yourselves and for all the flock, among
which the Holy Spirit has made you overseers, to shepherd
the church of God which He purchased with His own blood"
(Acts 20:28).

WHICH SPIRIT?

I have a friend who is a missionary in South America. Several years ago, when he was visiting the U.S., one of the things he said struck me very forcefully.

He went to church with us, and a Christian semi-rock group played and sang Christian lyrics to music with a rock beat.

When we came out of that service, he said, "You know, in South America I spend my time getting those spirits out of the people that I'm ministering to, and here you are inviting them into your churches. I cannot believe this."

He went on to say that the music, the beat, and the content of what we're doing is very similar to the demonic content of what he sees in the people who believe in witchcraft.

He spends his time and energy trying to get rid of those evil spirits, and then he comes to America and sees that we've brought them into the church.

Of course, he was just expressing his opinions, but it made an impression on me.

What do you think? It's up to every church to pray about and decide what is appropriate and what will honor God.

The psalmist wrote, *"Sing for joy to God our strength; . . raise a song, strike the timbrel, the sweet sounding lyre. . . blow the trumpet"* (Psalm 81:1-3).

Larry Burkett

Daily Scripture Reading: 2 Kings 10-11;
2 Chronicles 22:10-23:21

*"Whatever you do, work at it with all your heart,
as working for the Lord, not for men"*
(Colossians 3:23 NIV).

MAKING THE MOST OF YOUR WORK

Because you spend a large part of your time at work, it's important to find contentment in this aspect of your life. If you're miserable in your current job or if you're looking for a new job, here are some tips to help you deal with job-related conflict and transition.

1. Adam was created to work before he disobeyed God, so recognize that you are working for God, not man.

2. All of your skills, talents, and even your promotions come from God, so trust Him to be in charge of your career. *"But it is God who judges: He brings one down, he exalts another"* (Psalm 75:7 NIV).

3. Work as if God were your boss, because He is. *"Whatever your hand finds to do, do it with all your might, for in the grave, where you are going, there is neither working nor planning nor knowledge nor wisdom"* (Ecclesiastes 9:10 NIV).

4. Honor your employer even if you don't like or agree with him or her. Some of the greatest spiritual leaders in the Bible served corrupt, immoral masters.

5. Develop a strength-training program. Work conflict and transition will cause a lot of stress, so get into a program that includes exercise, eating right, and getting plenty of sleep and rest.

6. Don't jump at the first job that becomes available. Take the job that is the closest match with how God wired you.

7. Never focus solely on the money. Focus on doing the task and being a great servant on the job.

8. Consider whether or not you're current on the latest trends in your field of work. Next, determine what knowledge you have that could help your company become a leader. Then, work to increase your excellence and value by becoming a continual learner in your field.

Chuck Bentley

Daily Scripture Reading:
Joel

*"We have been buried with Him through baptism
into death. . . so we too might walk in newness of life"*
(Romans 6:4).

NEWNESS OF LIFE

In many ways, I think I have a great advantage by not being saved until age 32, because I clearly recognize what newness of life is. It's being snatched out of the clutches of Satan and thrust into the Spirit of God.

The apostle Paul addressed this issue in today's Scripture verse and the surrounding verses. When you and I accept Jesus Christ and the Holy Spirit comes to dwell within us, we literally have a new life—a new spirit living within us.

God's Word tells us to be transformed by the renewing of our minds. The word transformed is a translation of the Greek metamorphosis, the process by which a caterpillar becomes a butterfly. Isn't that a beautiful picture?

Of course, this doesn't mean that we are immune to temptation or that we won't sin anymore. Quite the contrary. When we are trying to live for the Lord, Satan will try even harder to distract us or send us down the wrong road.

I can assure you that on any given day I am capable of letting my anger overwhelm me, bad attitudes override my actions, or my weaknesses influence my decisions. But I have found that the more I yield to the power of the Holy Spirit, the more God helps me overcome those things.

If you haven't experienced that newness of life, it is never too late.

Larry Burkett

Daily Scripture Reading: 2 Kings 12-13;
2 Chronicles 24

"Everyone who competes in the games exercises self-control in all things"
(1 Corinthians 9:25).

CHRISTIAN ATHLETES

Since about 1975, I have worked with Christian professional athletes on their personal finances. I've met some really neat guys and many of their wives.

One of the finest athletes was a middle linebacker with the Atlanta Falcons. He was saved shortly before I met him and was in the process of living like a professional athlete: buying the biggest house and best cars. However, after hearing the financial principles, he began to put them into action.

For a period of time I mentored him and we spent lots of time together. I can remember going into fast food restaurants with him. He would go place his order and then twist the microphone around and share Christ with everybody in the place. Not exactly the way I would have chosen, but it worked for him (he was a large man and most of the people in Atlanta knew him).

One time a young kid came up to him and said, "Man, who do you think you are sharing that Christian stuff?"

The athlete, still a relatively new Christian at the time and a bit rough around the edges, reached over and grabbed the kid by his jacket, lifted him about an inch off the ground, and said, "You want to hear about Jesus?" You should have seen the kid shaking his head and saying, "Yeah, sure! I do!"

I'm not advocating his methods, but I do suggest that you pray for Christian athletes everywhere—that they will be godly witnesses to their unsaved families, teammates, coaches, and fans.

Larry Burkett

Daily Scripture Reading: 2 Kings 14;
2 Chronicles 25; Jonah

*"Instruct those who are rich in this present world not
to be conceited or to fix their hope on the uncertainty of riches,
but on God, who richly supplies us with all things to enjoy"*
(1 Timothy 6:17).

WHAT IS WEALTH?

A missionary had been invited by a church pastor to bring a message one Sunday morning. The missionary had one married son and five married daughters, all of whom were in Christian work and present at that service. His five daughters had just finished singing a special song before the congregation.

As he rose to speak, a friend whispered, "Emil, you are a very wealthy man." The missionary didn't have much money, yet his friend considered him wealthy. Emil's friend was correct. He was truly wealthy. His trust was in God.

There are some Christians who are rich in the riches of this world, but their conceit and trust in money have robbed them of their spiritual wealth.

Your spiritual wealth is more than just possessions and money. It is all of God's blessings: family, friends, health, home, spiritual gifts, job—and much more.

How wealthy are you?

Jesus said, *"Not even when one has an abundance does his life consist of his possessions"* (Luke 12:15).

Give thanks to the Lord now for your "wealth."

Larry Burkett

Daily Scripture Reading:
Hosea 1-7

"All who are being led by the Spirit of God, these are sons of God"
(Romans 8:14).

INDEPENDENCE DAY

What does Independence Day mean to most of us? Firecrackers? Picnics? Parades? I'm afraid that's about all our children understand about it.

It's easy to look back and just assume that the Declaration of Independence from our forefathers was just one of the steps down the road to liberty. In fact, it was the break point—the final step—before war.

These men were saying, "We declare ourselves to be a free nation." They were coming against the strongest military power in that day. There was no Constitution, no Bill of Rights, no country in existence. It was a small group of men who, as the leaders of our country, said they believed it was their right to choose their own destiny. We can all praise God for their commitment.

One of the things I encourage all Christian parents to do is to check out a copy of the diary of General George Washington. He kept a fairly complete diary all during the Revolutionary War and I believe it should be required reading for all American children.

Not only was Washington a great patriot and the father of our nation, he was a born-again Christian who believed that what he was doing was God's will for this nation.

Let's give thanks for our forefathers, who were willing to confront the establishment of their day to secure the freedoms we have in this most influential nation in the world—a nation that stands as a bastion of freedom.

Larry Burkett

Daily Scripture Reading:
Hosea 8-14

"Do not put your trust in princes, in mortal men, who cannot save"
(Psalm 146:3 NIV).

THE SOLUTION TO OUR PROBLEMS

Many people have been led astray through power, praise, and humanism, the lie that humans can solve their problems without God. When people turn their backs on God, they must look somewhere for hope, and often they turn to leaders.

Isaiah 6 begins with the words, *"In the year that King Uzziah died…"* (Verse 1, NIV). Uzziah's death was so significant that it was used by the prophet Isaiah to define the year. This well-known leader started out as a great king. He became known as a warrior, builder, farmer, and inventor. He became famous and powerful, the hope of the people.

He succeeded as long as he sought God, but pride led to his downfall. Ego drove him to take the place of a priest unlawfully, and God afflicted him with leprosy. He had to live apart from the people and couldn't reenter the temple.

But even at this low point, the second half of Isaiah 6:1 tells us that the prophet *"saw the Lord seated on a throne, high and exalted, and the train of his robe filled the temple."*

Uzziah experienced the fame and power of the world and the false hope of humanism. Isaiah experienced God.

Uzziah's pride drove him to demand his way with God. Isaiah was humbled when he saw God and was aware of his own sin. " *'Woe to me!' I cried. 'I am ruined! For I am a man of unclean lips, and I live among a people of unclean lips, and my eyes have seen the King, the LORD Almighty'"* (Isaiah 6:5 NIV).

Uzziah was made large by the praise of men. Isaiah was made small by his encounter with God. Uzziah was exiled because of his leprosy. Isaiah was sent by God to point the people to the true king.

Today, we must understand the truth as Isaiah did. The world doesn't offer any solutions. God is the only solution to man's problems. Like Isaiah, we must ask God to cleanse us and use us to speak to others about turning from humanism and following the Lord.

Chuck Bentley

Daily Scripture Reading: 2 Kings 15:1-7;
2 Chronicles 26; Amos 1-4

"Eye hath not seen, nor ear heard, neither have entered into the heart of man, the things which God hath prepared for them that love Him"
(1 Corinthians 2:9).

WHAT HAS GOD PREPARED?

It was 9:00 A.M. and the doctors had just finished working frantically to save the life of an elderly woman. Several times during the operation the doctors thought they had lost her. The last time there was no breathing, her pulse had stopped, and there were no vital signs whatsoever. But death had lost and the doctors' efforts had prevailed.

The operating room was silent for a few moments; then everyone began to smile as life began to flow back into the body of the patient. In a few moments she regained a brief state of consciousness, looked at the doctor with tears in her eyes, and asked, "Why did you bring me back? I wanted to stay with Jesus!"

Too often we look at death as an end when it is only a beginning. It is not a time of sadness; it is one of gladness. We set our eyes on the things of this world—money, possessions, and good times—and the world blinds us to the things He has for us. If we walk in the Spirit, the things of this world will not have a hold on us.

And, as we walk in the Spirit, the apostle Paul's testimony—"for me to die is gain"—will become our testimony.

You will know you are walking in the Spirit when the things of this world are overshadowed by the eternal things of heaven.

Larry Burkett

Daily Scripture Reading: 2 Kings 15:8-18;
Amos 5-9

*"For all that is in the world, the lust of the flesh, and the
lust of the eyes, and the boastful pride of life, is not
from the Father, but is from the world"*
(1 John 2:16).

DUPED BY ADVERTISING

When we get caught up in the desire to satisfy our senses, we become vulnerable to a lifestyle that has as its goal the accumulation of money, because, if we are to have the things we see advertised, we will need to have money to purchase them. God equates this commitment to riches with sin.

It's not that God wants us to live in poverty; neither does He mean for us to be drawn into the allure of advertising. Our lives should not be characterized by the extravagance and foolish sensualism promoted by the mass media.

Solomon explains the result of indulgence in Ecclesiastes 2: *"And all that my eyes desired I did not refuse them. . . .and behold all was vanity and striving after wind, and there was no profit under the sun."*

We deeply desire something, work for it, finally get it, and shortly thereafter we experience boredom or emptiness. This is why God wants to fulfill the desires of our spirits—because these other desires never can be totally gratified. They always bring with them the quest for more.

But, when our spirits are satisfied, we have peace. If you haven't committed your desires to the Lord, do it now.

"Thou, O Lord, hast made me glad by what Thou hast done, I will sing for joy at the works of Thy hands" (Psalm 92:4).

Larry Burkett

Daily Scripture Reading:
Isaiah 1-4

"The end of a matter is better than its beginning,
and patience is better than pride"
(Ecclesiastes 7:8 NIV).

QUICK FIXES

Often, people in financial trouble want a quick solution to a deep problem. If God doesn't miraculously rescue them, they become impatient and make more foolish decisions.

They'll pay lip service to God but then do things their own way. That type of behavior leads to disaster.

The world offers a number of quick fixes for financial problems: credit repair, debt reduction plans, payday loans, and easy refinancing terms. But we often hear from people who were disappointed by quick fix solutions because they ended up in worse shape than when they started.

The world is determined to forget God and be its own savior. As a result, it views the Bible as impractical. But the Bible is the most practical book ever written because God's ways are proven and effective.

Patiently seeking God's wisdom in times of need, as well as living by His financial principles, leads to a life of wisdom, discipline, productivity, and integrity. The end results of these things are blessings for you and for others.

Avoid quick fixes and wait patiently on the Lord, and the end of the matter will be better than the beginning.

Chuck Bentley

Daily Scripture Reading: 2 Kings 15:19-38;
2 Chronicles 27; Isaiah 5-6

"Even Simon himself believed; and after being baptized, he continued on with Philip; and as he observed signs and great miracles taking place, he was constantly amazed"
(Acts 8:13).

NOT FOR SALE

Simon, a magician during the time of the apostle Peter, believed on the Lord Jesus and, after being baptized, went with Philip. He noticed that the Spirit was being bestowed by the laying on of hands by the apostles.

When Simon offered money to receive this authority, Peter responded by saying, *"May your silver perish with you because you thought you could obtain the gift of God with money! . . . You have no part or portion in this matter, for your heart is not right before God"* (Acts 8:20-21).

It was a terrible thing for Simon to try to buy the power of God with money. We need to realize one thing about Simon, however: He did recognize the value of God's power and was willing to spend his money to get it. Too often Christians do not value God's power at all but spend money on the power of the world.

God's power is not for sale; it is given freely by Him. He will not refuse us His power when we give ourselves completely to Him.

The apostle Paul wrote about his desire: *"That I may know Him, and the power of His resurrection and the fellowship of His sufferings, being conformed to His death"* (Philippians 3:10).

Larry Burkett

Daily Scripture Reading:
Micah

191

*"Who is the man that has built a new house and has not
dedicated it? Let him depart and return to his house,
lest he die in the battle and another man dedicate it"*
(Deuteronomy 20:5).

DEDICATE YOUR HOME

Many years ago, we arrived home to find that one of the apartments in our building
had been vandalized, and the thieves had broken three locks to get in our neighbor's back
door. Then we noticed that our back door was open.

We ran upstairs, looked throughout our apartment, but found nothing missing.
Judy then remembered that she had unintentionally failed to close the back door that
morning. Even though it was open and easily observed from the bottom of the stairs,
nothing was missing from our apartment.

Our neighbors were robbed of their TV, stereo tape deck, radio, CB, and other
valuable possessions. When they found out we had lost nothing, they couldn't understand
why the thieves had broken through three locks to get in their apartment but had not
touched ours.

However, we understood. Our apartment had been dedicated to God. Just as the
Israelites did, we dedicated our home to God. We shared this with our neighbors, but
it wasn't clear whether they believed that it was really God protecting our things. That
wasn't important; what was important was that we believed it.

If faith can move a mountain, it can certainly move a thief. Of course, we learned
a lesson from this experience. Although we trust God, we must not disregard safety
measures. We must do all we can; He will do the rest.

"He will give His angels charge concerning you, to guard you in all your ways"
(Psalm 91:11).

Larry Burkett

Daily Scripture Reading: 2 Kings 16;
2 Chronicles 28; Isaiah 7-8

"The man who lays up treasure for himself. . .is not rich toward God"
(Luke 12:21).

A REASONABLE LIVING STANDARD

Although many Scriptures teach about the dangers of material riches, God's Word does not teach that poverty is the alternative. God wants us to understand that money is a tool to use in accomplishing His plan through us.

Just having surplus does not mean that it's all right to use it as we want. It is important to develop a lifestyle based on conviction—not circumstance.

Since there is no universal plan suitable for everyone, this must be a standard established among husband, wife, and God. Obviously, God will assign Christians at every economic level.

If God's plan puts you in the upper level of income, there will be a purpose for the abundance and a ministry through it. But just having an abundance is not a sign of God's blessings. Satan can easily duplicate any worldly riches.

God's riches are without sorrow and for bringing others to salvation.

Living a disciplined lifestyle with an abundance is a much stronger witness than having the abundance ever could be.

Larry Burkett

Daily Scripture Reading:
Isaiah 9-12

> *"It is not an enemy who reproaches me, then I could*
> *bear it. . . but it is you, a man my equal"*
> (Psalm 55:12-13).

TRANSCENDING LINES

Regardless of what we might say, we seldom treat all people equally. In fact, it may not even be possible, since we all have preconditioned biases and prejudices of one kind or another.

As Christians, we must transcend lines of culture, race, denomination, or age. If we can't it's because we think more highly of ourselves than we should.

The apostle Paul said, *"I should never think of anyone as inferior"* (Acts 10:28 TLB). Everyone is of value to society and of value to the Lord Jesus Christ.

Of course, there are people we may not like to spend time with—because of their attitudes or because we enjoy doing different things. But if we avoid anyone because of a preestablished mindset, then we are bigoted.

We live in a country in which we have the freedom to worship as we please with those who believe the same as we do.

But to ignore someone or mistreat someone because that person is from a different background or skin tone, it is displeasing to God.

God does not see what shade our skin is or what nationality or denomination we are. He looks into our hearts, and it's what's in there that matters.

When Jesus gave the commandment to "love one another," He didn't add, "if everything about them pleases you." It was an unqualified commandment.

"A new commandment I give to you, that you love one another, even as I have loved you, that you also love one another" (John 13:34).

Larry Burkett

Daily Scripture Reading:
Isaiah 13-16

*"For our struggle is not against flesh and blood, but against
the rulers, against the authorities, against the powers of this dark world and
against the spiritual forces of evil in the heavenly realms"*
(Ephesians 6:12 NIV).

FIGHTING SPIRITUAL WARFARE

If you're walking with Christ and seeking to live by His financial principles, you're going to experience spiritual warfare. This type of warfare happens in your mind and is the battle between truth and lies.

1. Satan's first plan of attack is to weaken your faith in God. He wants you to doubt God and make you believe that God doesn't care about your finances and won't help you.

2. Next, he tempts you to compromise by offering you an alternative to trusting God. This alternative may involve risky, unethical, or immoral actions.

3. He masquerades as a messenger from God. When the Assyrian king Sennacherib threatened Jerusalem, he sent a message to Hezekiah, the Israelite king, which said, *"The Lord himself told me to march against this country and destroy it"* (2 Kings 18:25 NIV). Anytime someone comes to you "in the name of the Lord," compare what he or she says to the truth of God's Word.

4. Satan will attempt to focus your thoughts on your mistakes, which he will use to erode your confidence in God.

5. He will try to give you a false promise of peace and prosperity. Most people desperately desire these things, and their desire gives Satan an opportunity to deceive them.

Hezekiah, did not compromise; he tore his clothes, put on sackcloth, and went into the temple. He humbled himself and sought the Lord.

God answered.

By a miracle, equivalent to the power of an atomic bomb, 185,000 men in the Assyrian army died, demonstrating that the power of truth was greater than the power of a lie.

When you face spiritual warfare, humble yourself before the Lord and seek His help. Use His Word to win spiritual battles and put Satan on the run.

Chuck Bentley

Daily Scripture Reading:
Isaiah 17-22

"Let your light shine for all the nations to see!
For the glory of the Lord is streaming from you"
(Isaiah 60:1 TLB).

CITIZENSHIP AND CHRISTIANITY

Have you ever considered the relationship between citizenship and Christianity? Which takes priority?

As Americans, we have all the rights and privileges granted to us by the Constitution and the Bill of Rights. And, I believe we are bound according to God's Word to obey the legal authority over us, including the IRS.

"Let every person be in subjection to the governing authorities. . . . Because of this you also pay taxes, for rulers are servants of God" (Romans 13:1, 6).

Although I don't like paying taxes, and I think the amount we have to pay is unfair, I am bound by that authority and by God's Word.

But, is there any point at which I am no longer bound by government authority? In my opinion, there is when that authority violates the superior authority of the Word of God.

For example, although abortion is legal according to the law of our land, it is totally immoral and is abhorrent to the Word of God. Therefore, I must take a stand against abortion.

We haven't started euthanizing elderly people, but it's not impossible that we might find that legal in the future.

As God's people, we are also citizens and therefore we have the right to appeal any laws of this land to protect our constitutional rights.

When the laws of this land try to supersede the law of God, that's when we must take a stand, even to the point of imprisonment, if necessary.

Larry Burkett

Daily Scripture Reading:
Isaiah 23-27

"Faith comes from hearing, and hearing by the word of Christ"
(Romans 10:17).

KNOW GOD'S WORD

How can you claim God's promises? You must know what God's Word says and believe it. If you don't know what God's Word promises, you can't claim His best for you. You can't claim what you don't know.

Spend time with God to get to know about Him. Study and meditate on His Word. You must believe so thoroughly that God loves you and cares about your needs that, when you ask, you expect to receive.

Make a commitment today to spend time every day, without fail, learning what's in God's Word. Study it. Pray about it. Claim it for yourself.

Spending time in God's Word is evidence of a commitment to God's way and will open new avenues of blessings in your life.

Larry Burkett

Daily Scripture Reading:
Isaiah 28-30

"Faith, if it has no works, is dead, being by itself"
(James 2:17).

FAITH AND WORKS

I heard a Christian teacher one time say that he wished the book of James had never been written. He felt the book emphasized works and not faith. I don't agree with his conclusion at all.

If you'll read James, you'll see that the point he was making is that if you are saved you have made Jesus the Lord of your life; therefore, you will have works in your life.

After saying that faith without works is useless, James uses the example of Abraham, who was *"justified by works when he offered up Isaac his son on the altar"* (James 2:21). Abraham's faith *"was working with his works, and as a result of the works, faith was perfected"* (verse 22).

We are not saved by our works. The apostle Paul tells us in Ephesians 2:8-9 that we are saved by grace, through faith, and it is not a results of works.

Then in 2 Timothy 1:9 Paul says that the power of God has saved us and called us, *"not according to our works, but according to His own purpose and grace which was granted us in Christ Jesus."*

I believe that James was saying that if we are saved, our lives will show it by our works. The works are evidence that the Holy Spirit is residing within us.

Larry Burkett

Daily Scripture Reading:
Isaiah 31-35

*"One Lord, one faith, one baptism, one God and
Father of all who is over all and through all and in all"*
(Ephesians 4:5-6).

ONE GOD

God is sovereign. He is the omnipotent (all powerful), omniscient (all wise), omnipresent (present everywhere at once) creator of all things and the absolute authority.

Sometimes we live our lives as if God were a genie in a bottle. We go about doing what we please until we need help. Then we uncork the bottle and ask the "genie" to come out and solve our problems. Then when things are running smoothly, we just put Him back into the bottle and put the cork back in.

Unfortunately, that's not the way it works. Our responsibility as followers of the sovereign God is to obey His instructions on a day-by-day basis, knowing that He will guide us.

"You will call, and the Lord will answer; . . . 'Here I am.' . . . The Lord will continually guide you" (Isaiah 58:9, 11).

The great joy we have is that God is also a loving, caring, comforting Father. All He wants is our fellowship with Him. He likes doing good things for us.

With our finite thinking, it is hard for us to grasp the immensity of a sovereign God. When we pass from this life into the next life, we will understand the sovereignty of God and His love, because He is waiting with open arms to welcome us.

How much fellowship with the Lord do you experience? What can you do to make it better?

Larry Burkett

Daily Scripture Reading: 2 Kings 18:1-8;
2 Chronicles 29-31

"Submit therefore to God. Resist the devil and he will flee from you"
(James 4:7).

AUTHORITY OVER SATAN

When Satan was cast out of Heaven, the only authority granted to him was the authority given by God: authority over this world.

We read in the book of John that Jesus said, *"The thief* [Satan] *comes only to steal, and kill, and destroy"* (John 10:10).

As Christians we have authority over Satan. James said in today's verse that we are to "resist the devil and he will flee."

The apostle Paul wrote, *"Our struggle is not against flesh and blood, but against the rulers, against the powers, against the world forces of this darkness, against the spiritual forces of wickedness* [Satan] *in the heavenly places. Therefore, take up the full armor of God, that you may be able to resist in the evil day, and having done everything, to stand firm"* (Ephesians 6:12-13).

When the devil tempted Jesus, he fought him off with the phrase, *"It is written."* We can do the same thing. We can use God's Word to raise hedges around us.

Jesus told the disciples, *"He who believes in Me, the works that I do shall he do also. . . . And whatever you ask in My name, that will I do"* (John 14:12-13).

It seems pretty clear to me that we have authority over Satan as long as we are living in the power of the Holy Spirit, following God's Word, doing God's will, and resisting him in Jesus name.

Larry Burkett

Daily Scripture Reading: 2 Kings 17, 18:9-37;
2 Chronicles 32:1-19; Isaiah 36

"Beware, and be on your guard against every form of greed; for not even when one has an abundance does his life consist of his possessions"
(Luke 12:15).

THE DANGER OF ABUNDANCE

The majority of warnings in Christ's messages were to the wealthy, not the poor. In poverty, the issue is usually black or white—honesty or dishonesty.

In affluence, it is much more subtle. I believe that in America nearly everyone would be graded as wealthy by any biblical standard.

Our anxieties and worries are not related to the lack of things but, rather, to the loss of things. Many, if not most, Christians inwardly fear they might lose what they have acquired materially.

Therefore, they compromise God's best in their lives to hang on to the very way of life that brought so much worry and turmoil before they met the Lord.

This does not necessarily mean surrendering the assets. It means being willing to surrender them. It boils down to what your priorities are, doesn't it?

Remember the story in Acts: *"All those who had believed were together, and had all things in common; and they began selling their possessions and were sharing them with all, as anyone might have need"* (Acts 2:45).

Could you do that? How important are your possessions to you? Pray about it.

Larry Burkett

Daily Scripture Reading: 2 Kings 19;
2 Chronicles 32:20-23; Isaiah 37

*"Train a child in the way he should go,
and when he is old he will not turn from it"*
(Proverbs 22:6 NIV).

TEACHING CHILDREN ABOUT GENEROSITY AND WORK

As a parent, you want your children to be successful in life, and one area they really need to get right is handling money. Children need to learn that God owns everything and that we are His stewards. And, they must learn to serve Him, not money, and be content with what He provides.

Following are three ideas for helping your children develop an understanding of these important principles.

First, teach your children to be generous, especially toward the poor. Jesus said, *"It is more blessed to give than to receive"* (Acts 20:35 NIV). This is the greatest possible hedge against materialism, and it will bring your children priceless joy and prepare them for supporting God's work in their generation.

Second, your children need to learn the benefits of work. Proverbs 14:23 says, *"All hard work brings a profit, but mere talk leads only to poverty"* (NIV). Work is a blessing, not a curse. Model hard work and diligence for your children, and they will learn that our work gives glory to God.

Third, help your children discover the skills and talents God has given them and encourage them to excel at what they do. Excellence combined with humility will equip your children to become salt and light in the workplace. (See Matthew 5:13-16.)

Chuck Bentley

Daily Scripture Reading: 2 Kings 20;
2 Chronicles 32:24-33; Isaiah 38-39

"The mind set on the flesh is hostile toward God"
(Romans 8:7).

CARNAL MINDS

We've all heard the expression, "people with carnal minds." In Romans I believe the apostle Paul was talking about people with what we call "lower natures" and people who live only to please themselves.

He went on to say that following after the *"old nature leads to death, because the old sinful nature within us is against God"* (Romans 8:7 TLB).

Christians who continue to live in their old sinful ways cannot please God.

If we're following the Spirit of God and living by the principles of God's Word, the Holy Spirit will convict us when we are out of the will of God.

Those who set their minds on worldly things and are motivated by them, have carnal minds, and need to repent. *"Repent of this wickedness of yours, and pray the Lord that if possible, the intention of your heart may be forgiven you"* (Acts 8:22).

If you have a particular weakness, the smart thing to do is to avoid any contact with it.

A man who travels in business and finds a pornographic channel on the television in his hotel room must make a decision. Will he allow the Holy Spirit to take control of his life or give in to his carnal nature?

Airline pilots spend many hours training in a simulator for every potential problem they might face when flying an airplane. They train themselves for every contingency so they cannot be caught unaware.

We must do the same in our spiritual lives.

Larry Burkett

Daily Scripture Reading: 2 Kings 21:1-18;
2 Chronicles 33:1-20; Isaiah 40

*"Sin shall not be master over you, for you
are not under law, but under grace"*
(Romans 6:14).

LAW OR GRACE

It's interesting as we look back into the time of the apostles and see how many of the Jews who had accepted Christ tried to apply both law and grace at the same time.

They required the Jewish converts to Christianity to adhere to all the ritualistic laws of the Old Testament and, to a large degree, subjugated grace to a secondary role.

The apostle Paul writes about this issue in Romans. Following the Scripture verse for today, he said, *"Shall we sin because we are not under law but under grace? May it never be!"* (Romans 6:15).

What Paul was saying to his generation is, "We are not controlled by the law; it is not the governing force over your life. God's grace is."

However, because we are saved by grace (see Ephesians 2:8-9) and live under grace, we don't have a license to do whatever we want when we want to do it. We are bound by God's Word, and it teaches that we should abstain from anything that would bring dishonor or disservice to God's name.

Therefore, under grace we have a greater responsibility to live in a purer way than anyone ever did under the Law.

"The higher a man is in grace, the lower he will be in his own esteem." —Charles Spurgeon

Larry Burkett

Daily Scripture Reading:
Isaiah 41-43

"My kingdom is not of this world"
(John 18:36).

KINGDOM ADDRESS

When Christ was on Earth, He said, "My kingdom is not of this world." If it had been, He could have called a legion of angels to His defense and nobody could have hanged Him on Calvary's cross.

We know that Satan has power in this realm—at least for the time being. Perhaps it's to see whether we will be faithful to the Lord.

Peter wrote, *"Be all the more diligent to make certain about His calling and choosing you. . . for in this way the entrance into the eternal kingdom of our Lord and Savior Jesus Christ will be abundantly supplied to you"* (2 Peter 1:10-11).

So, Christ's kingdom is coming, and when it does it will be an absolute monarchy—a spiritual theocracy of the highest order.

I don't know about you, but I'm looking forward to spending eternity with a loving, kind, and gracious Ruler.

Maranatha!

Larry Burkett

Daily Scripture Reading:
Isaiah 44-47

"The Law is holy, and the commandment is holy
and righteous and good. . . . The Law is spiritual; . . . I agree
with the Law, confessing that it is good"
(Romans 7:12, 14, 16).

MORAL LAW/GOD'S LAW

There is no way to separate moral law from God's Law, unless it's through the situational ethics that we see in our generation.

God established the moral laws. The Ten Commandments are simple, straightforward, and absolute. If you follow those, you will follow moral law.

C. S. Lewis wrote, "Morality is indispensable: but the Divine life, which gives itself to us and which calls us to be gods, intends for us something in which morality will be swallowed up. We are to be remade."

In our society we have adopted situational ethics. Basically that means that the times and the situations dictate morality. Therefore, if everyone believes that abortion is okay, then it is. Or if everyone says that homosexuality is acceptable, it is.

When it comes to morality, God's Word is piercingly clear. Right is right, and wrong is wrong.

Clearly, our "enlightened" society could use a good dose of God's biblical absolutes. I grieve that the youth of this generation have been deceived by "situational ethics."

Pray that the Holy Spirit will guide you to be morally and spiritually pure.

Larry Burkett

Daily Scripture Reading:
Isaiah 48-51

*"Consequently they are no longer two, but one flesh.
What therefore God has joined together, let no man separate"*
(Matthew 19:6).

GOD-ORDAINED MARRIAGE

From the beginning, God designed marriage to be the ideal setting for perpetuating the human race. He developed the union to consist of a man and a woman, committed to each other for life and to raising their offspring.

God knew that a mother and a father were needed to create the best environment for children. Couples are warned in their marriage vows not to take this union lightly.

There are times in every marriage when it seems barely tolerable. I know that was true of my marriage for the first several years. Judy and I came out of non-Christian backgrounds, with little or no training for a good marriage relationship. Consequently we argued about nearly everything, and this caused hurt feelings on both sides.

We live in a generation that has not been taught the importance of keeping vows. The words "until death do us part" don't really have any significance to many couples. Marriage is entered into with the idea, "If it doesn't work out, I can always get out."

It is only when two people make an absolute commitment to each other that a marriage can function as God intended. It is unrealistic to think that conflicts won't occur. They will, but if spouses know that both of them are irrevocably committed to the marriage, the problems can be resolved.

There are steps to take to help keep a marriage strong: keep the lines of communication open and spend time together in Bible reading and prayer.

"Hear my prayer, O God; give ear to the words of my mouth" (Psalm 54:2).

Larry Burkett

Daily Scripture Reading:
Isaiah 52-57

"Who has a claim against me that I must pay?
Everything under heaven belongs to me"
(Job 41:11 NIV).

TEACHING CHILDREN ABOUT
LORDSHIP AND CONTENTMENT

If your children never understand God's lordship and never learn contentment, they stand a good chance of becoming self-focused consumers who buy first and worry about the consequences later.

You don't want to see them value money before God or end up in financial bondage, so here's some advice that you as a parent can use to help your children avoid these pitfalls.

Psalm 24:1 says, *"The earth is the LORD's, and everything in it, the world, and all who live in it"* (NIV). God is the owner of everything, and your children need to know that they are stewards, not owners, of things in this life.

When you make a wise financial decision, explain it to your children within the framework of being a good steward. Children need to learn that being more frugal or less materialistic is not the same as being a faithful steward.

In addition, Matthew 6:24 says that no one can serve two masters. You can't love God and money. Teach your children who God is and why He should be Master of their lives instead of money.

Finally, Philippians 4:11-13 teaches that you must learn to be content in any circumstance and that your true strength comes from the Lord. If you are content, your children will hear you praise God for whatever blessings He gives you, and they will learn to do the same.

Chuck Bentley

Daily Scripture Reading:
Isaiah 58-62

*"If you are living according to the flesh, you must die, but if by the Spirit
you are putting to death the deeds of the body, you will live"*
(Romans 8:13).

MORTIFY THE FLESH

Instead of saying "putting to death the deeds of the body," the King James version of the Bible uses the term "mortify the deeds of the body."

I think what the apostle Paul was saying is that if you're living according to your fleshly desires, just doing whatever you happen to think is right, you're going to die—physically and spiritually.

Then he goes further and says, *"All who are being led by the Spirit of God, these are sons of God"* (Romans 8:14).

Paul was giving his generation (and now ours) a spiritual attitude check. If you are living in the flesh and doing all the things the world around you is doing, you'd better check your spiritual condition.

Personally I don't want to be a part of the group identified in verse 13. I prefer the group he wrote about in verse 14.

Think about this: *"Those who are in the flesh cannot please God. However, you are not in the flesh but in the Spirit, if indeed the Spirit of God dwells in you. But if anyone does not have the Spirit of Christ, he does not belong to Him"* (Romans 8:8-9). *"It is the Spirit who gives life; the flesh profits nothing"* (John 6:63).

Father, I ask in Jesus' name that you will help me to put to death the fleshly desires in my life.

Larry Burkett

Daily Scripture Reading:
Isaiah 63-66

"So shall My word be which goes forth from My mouth; it shall not return to Me empty, without accomplishing what I desire"
(Isaiah 55:11).

THE POWERFUL WORD

We know that God is all powerful (omnipotent), and His Word is as powerful as He is.

The Bible says that Christ spoke the world into existence, so we know how powerful the voice of God (His Word) is. The apostle Paul tells us, *"He [Jesus] is the image of the invisible God, the first-born of all creation, for by Him all things were created. . . all things have been created by Him and for Him"* (Colossians 1:15-16).

God says that His Word will not return to Him without accomplishing what it says it will.

If you are just beginning to read the Bible, you have a great treat ahead. If you've read it for years, you can testify to how rich it is and what a comfort. If you don't read it every day, you are cheating yourself (that's my opinion, of course).

When David wrote about God's Word he said, *"The precepts of the Lord are right, rejoicing the heart; the commandment of the Lord is pure, enlightening the eyes. . . . The judgments of the Lord are true. . . . They are more desirable than gold. . . sweeter also than honey. . . . In them is great reward"* (Psalm 19:7-11).

Martin Luther said, "The Bible is alive, it speaks to me; it has feet, it runs after me; it has hands, it lays hold on me."

How much does your Bible mean to you?

Larry Burkett

Daily Scripture Reading: 2 Kings 21:19-26;
2 Chronicles 33:21-34:7; Zephaniah

*"Do not go on presenting the members of your body
to sin as instruments of unrighteousness to God"*
(Romans 6:13).

UNRIGHTEOUSNESS

There were very few moral absolutes during the dark days of the Roman empire. It appears to me that our generation has gotten so caught up in the same relativism as the first century people were.

The apostle Paul addressed the basic sins and abominations of his society when he wrote, *"Consider yourselves dead to sin, but alive to God in Christ Jesus. Therefore do not let sin reign in your mortal body that you should obey its lusts"* (Romans 6:11-12).

When you look around today, there is very little that is considered immoral, unethical, or illegal. We have moralized homosexuality, sexual promiscuity, filthy movies, and pornographic magazines. The government even hands out condoms in the public schools. We accept, and even reelect immoral, degenerate politicians. And the list goes on.

Christians are to be examples of righteousness in a sinful world—lights in the darkness.

A fallen, dying generation does not need more tolerant Christians; they need more lights in their dark world.

Read the eighth chapter of Romans. Then ask the Holy Spirit to reveal to you how you can help make a difference.

Larry Burkett

Daily Scripture Reading:
Jeremiah 1-3

*"Walk in a manner worthy of the calling
with which you have been called"*
(Ephesians 4:1).

HOLINESS

D. L. Moody said, "Next to the might of God, the serene beauty of a holy life is the most powerful influence for good."

The scribes and Pharisees of Jesus' day were hypocrites who concentrated on appearing holy, even though they were neglecting real holiness: of their hearts.

There's a saying that sometimes people are so busy being religious they fail to be spiritual. Outward acts of goodness can never make up for hearts that are cold or empty.

"Whoever believes in Him should not perish, but have eternal life" (John 3:16). After we accept Jesus as Lord and Savior of our lives, how can we have clean hearts? *"If we confess our sins, He is faithful and righteous to forgive us our sins and to cleanse us from all unrighteousness"* (1 John 1:9).

To be holy, we must have pure hearts. James says *"Purify your hearts. . . . Humble yourselves in the presence of the Lord"* (James 4:8, 10).

Oswald Chambers said, "Holiness is not only what God gives me, but what I manifest that God has given."

Have you had your heart checked lately? Imagine you are strapped into a machine that can see into your heart and measure the holiness there. What would the diagnosis be?

Holiness just means being separated to God. It's what you do with your life every day; it's ordering your conduct according to the Word of God and being of one mind with God. No one ever said it would be easy. But it is possible.

Larry Burkett

Daily Scripture Reading:
Jeremiah 4-6

*"Hagar bore Abram a son; and Abram called the
name of his son, whom Hagar bore, Ishmael"*
(Genesis 16:15).

RUNNING AHEAD

Have you ever run ahead of God because you became impatient with His timing? You probably know how much pain that can bring and you quickly learned why it is so important to do things in God's timing.

God's covenant with Abraham included the fact that he would be the father of nations. God took him outside, showed him the heavens, and told him to see how many stars there were. Then He said, *"So shall your descendants be"* (Genesis 15:5).

But perhaps childless Sarah got impatient, or maybe she didn't have Abraham's faith. She suggested that Abraham go in to her handmaiden; he did and Hagar bore him a son. As a result, Hagar's son grew up to be in competition with Isaac, Sarah's son and rightful heir of the covenant.

God did bless Abraham and Sarah, but they always remembered that they had attempted to go around His plan.

If or when you have that kind of experience—of running ahead of God—you should realize that you've made a mistake and ask God's forgiveness. Since you can't undo what has been done, forgiveness is the most important thing—not guilt.

Ask God to help you know His timing in everything you do. *"The Lord is not slow about His promise, as some count slowness, but is patient toward you"* (2 Peter 3:9).

Larry Burkett

Daily Scripture Reading:
Jeremiah 7-9

"Blessed is the man who fears the LORD,
who finds great delight in his commands"
(Psalm 112:1 NIV).

PROMISES IN PROVERBS

When it comes to financial principles, one of the richest books in the Bible is Proverbs. This book contains two important promises that are very helpful in our efforts to handle our money in a way that pleases the Lord.

Promise 1—Wisdom and discipline can be acquired.

We all make mistakes, but the wisdom found in Proverbs can help us change and become wise and disciplined in our behavior. This is critical; because when we're undisciplined we stumble through life, pay penalties for our behavior, and end up in serious trouble.

Symptoms of a lack of discipline include believing advertising. You think you need what you see, hear, and read about. But you don't realize that advertising is designed to create needs in your mind.

You struggle to live within your means and become trapped in a cycle of debt. You fail to accomplish your life purpose and achieve your potential. You want to accomplish things the easy way.

Promise 2—The fear of the Lord is the beginning of knowledge.

Proverbs links the fear of God with ending foolishness. A life of wisdom and discipline begins with fearing God (i.e., giving God the respect and position in our lives He deserves). Most people believe it begins with bettering themselves, but we must see ourselves as smaller than God in order to acquire what He has for us. We must acknowledge that we need Him and that He has a better way and plan.

True wisdom starts with having an awe of God. You can't have wisdom without humility. Where you turn for wisdom shows where your heart is, and if you're not turning to God, you're headed for trouble.

If you've become self-reliant, confess that attitude and repent before God. He will teach you His ways, and through following them you will be blessed by knowing Him better.

Chuck Bentley

Daily Scripture Reading:
Jeremiah 10-13

*"In Him we have redemption through His blood, the forgiveness
of our trespasses, according to the riches of His grace"*
(Ephesians 1:7).

NO ONE IS PERFECT

Committing sin has its consequences. One of the best examples of that is the story of David and Bathsheba. They committed adultery and a child was born. However, the child didn't live, even after David pleaded with God to spare the life of his baby.

David knew he had sinned and he was consumed with guilt and remorse. He didn't try to deny his sin or make excuses for it by claiming the temptation was too great. Instead David owned up to his sin and sought God's forgiveness.

Because you are human, you are going to sin, but you don't have to live with your guilt. If you truly repent of your sin, God will readily forgive you and restore you to His favor. That's what grace is all about.

Just open your heart to His forgiveness and allow Him to deal with you right where you are. What we have done isn't as important as what we are going to do about it.

God knows you aren't perfect and He doesn't love you any less when you sin. When Jesus shed His blood on the cross and died in our place, He opened the door to full redemption. The only criteria for forgiveness is true repentance.

"Our Redeemer, the Lord of hosts is His name" (Isaiah 47:4).

Larry Burkett

Daily Scripture Reading:
Jeremiah 14-16

*"The God of peace, who brought up from the dead the great
Shepherd. . . even Jesus our Lord, equip you in every good thing
to do His will, working in us that which is pleasing in His sight"*
(Hebrews 20-21).

COMMUNING WITH GOD

Oswald Chambers says that when you stay in contact with God so much that you never need to ask Him to show you His will, you have gotten close to the final stages of being disciplined in the life of faith.

When you stay in constant communion with God, you develop a delightful friendship with Him. You read His Word, pray without ceasing; then go ahead and make the everyday, commonsense decisions, assured that He will let you know if what you plan to do isn't what is best for you.

Have you ever decided to do something but felt a sort of scratchy feeling in your spirit? That's a sure sign you may not have made the right decision. Listen to that inner voice. It can save you a lot of heartache.

God never gets tired of hearing you call out to Him. He promises good things for those who seek Him. Your fellowship with Him through your faith in Jesus Christ opens the door to communication.

Father, thank You for being so accessible to me at all times.

Larry Burkett

Daily Scripture Reading:
Jeremiah 17-20

"I have known you by name, and you have also found favor in My sight"
(Exodus 33:12).

ONLY YOU WILL DO

Did you ever audition for a play or for a chorus? Usually you have to do a bit of acting or singing—whatever is required—and then leave, hoping to get chosen and called back. You have to be absolutely perfect for the role you tried out for.

You have a role in life that only you can fill. You don't have to audition for it, because you are the only one who can do exactly what it calls for. God has chosen you to do a specific thing. And, the best part is, you aren't in competition with anyone else for the "part." No one could be as good a YOU as you can be.

You could follow Billy Graham around for weeks or months, study his preaching, mannerisms, talents, and learn to sound just like he does. But you could never be a better Billy Graham than he is. That's because God called him to be just who he is.

The same is true of you. You don't need to be jealous of anyone else, because when God calls for you there is nobody else who can answer your call. You have no contenders. You are the "star." You won the "audition."

You are a unique individual. God's Word says, *"The very hairs of your head are all numbered"* (Matthew 10:30).

If God calls you to the task that is specifically yours and you don't accept His call, your blessings will go to someone else. Pay close attention to the prompting of the Holy Spirit so you won't miss your blessings.

Larry Burkett

Daily Scripture Reading: 2 Kings 22:1-23:28;
2 Chronicles 34:8-35:19

"It is vain for you to rise up early, to retire late, to eat the bread of painful labors; for He gives to His beloved even in his sleep"
(Psalm 127:2).

OBSESSED WITH WORK

If God were to call you home today, would you leave with regrets? Would you have missed His best for your family, your career, and your life because you were too busy pursuing success?

Success is a good thing, but like everything else, it needs boundaries. When the pursuit of success dominates your life, you've allowed it to go too far.

Workaholics attempt to justify their behavior on the grounds of doing their best and providing for their families—even if it leaves them exhausted and their families frustrated.

But what would the outcome be if you allowed your family to vote on your work habits? Most spouses and children would vote for more time with you, not more success.

Like every other believer, you're God's servant. And, when you're bound by the pursuit of success, you can't fulfill your function in God's Kingdom. That function includes walking in a manner worthy of the Lord, pleasing Him in all respects, bearing fruit in every good work, increasing in the knowledge of God, and being a dedicated spouse and parent.

A workaholic lacks faith, and is often controlled by fear—especially fear of failure. If you truly believe that God is in control, you should be able to rest from your work and keep everything else in balance.

Chuck Bentley

Daily Scripture Reading: Nahum; 2 Kings 23:29-37;
2 Chronicles 35:20-36:5; Jeremiah 22:10-17

*"If anyone would come after me, he must deny himself
and take up his cross daily and follow me"*
(Luke 9:23 NIV).

"MATERIAL" WITNESS

God has placed us in a materialistic world, not only to witness to the unsaved but also for the purpose of examining our relationship to Him.

There can be no clearer reflection of the true value system of a Christian than the way he or she handles money and the way others are treated when a profit or loss is concerned.

Can Christians be honest in our society? To experience the fullness of God's power and love, we must be honest. There will be times when it will seem that others take advantage of that honesty. The Lord knew that would happen; that's why He admonished us to take up our crosses daily and follow Him.

There is often a price to be paid for following in the path of Christ, but there also is a great reward as a result of doing so.

We must decide whether to build on the solid rock of God's Word or on the shifting sands of society.

The decision to behave by the world's normal standards is a decision to deny Christ. What is your decision?

Larry Burkett

Daily Scripture Reading:
Jeremiah 26; Habakkuk

*"Go to the ant, you sluggard; consider its ways and be wise!
It has no commander, no overseer or ruler, yet it stores
its provisions in summer and gathers its food at harvest"*
(Proverbs 6:6-8 NIV).

SAVING MONEY

By saving money, we can be prepared for God to use us to serve others in times of plenty and in times of need.

If you haven't saved money in the past, start now by setting money aside for emergencies. Your first goal should be a $1,000 emergency fund that will allow you to pay cash for unplanned expenses.

Your savings goal should increase to one month's living expenses, then three to six months of living expenses.

Savings should become a way of life for you, and you can avoid hoarding by giving along the way. If your job is volatile, if you have health issues, or if a major expense is upcoming, you'll need more savings.

Every time you save money, you take a step back from the cliff. If you're living without margin, you're on the cliff's edge, and one gust of wind will push you over.

A key to being successful at saving is to develop a spending plan, which helps you spend on purpose. You need to stop spontaneous and needless spending, which consumes the money you should be saving.

As you develop your plan, focus on cutting expenses. Set limits for spending, then faithfully live within those limits every month. Reducing excess consumption will help you create financial margin, and as a result, you will have more money to save.

Chuck Bentley

Daily Scripture Reading: 2 Kings 24:1-4;
2 Chronicles 36:6-7; Jeremiah 25, 35, 46-47

"No one, after putting his hand to the plow and looking back, is fit for the kingdom of God"
(Luke 9:62).

SERVING THE MASTER

Our motives about earning a living are encompassed within our service to the Lord.

Many times our commitments will break down when they require sacrifices that may include a career change.

I met a Christian who was a hotel chain executive. The company he worked for had made a decision to include a pornographic cable system in its guest's rooms. After complaining as loudly as he could about it, he determined that as a Christian he could no longer be associated with them.

At almost 60 years of age, he knew his decision was clearly one of deciding which master he must serve. He went on to be a successful real estate salesman who sought to put the Lord first in everything.

The decision of choosing which master to follow is one that each of us must make every day. Are we willing to weigh every decision against God's Word and follow the narrow path God requires?

Larry Burkett

Daily Scripture Reading:
Jeremiah 36, 45, 48

*"Forgetting what lies behind and reaching forward to what
lies ahead, I press on toward the goal for the prize
of the upward call of God in Christ Jesus"*
(Philippians 3:13-14).

BEING IN GOD'S WILL

Even with the best discernment, it's possible, and even probable, that we will do things that are out of God's will.

How can you know God's will for your life? God's Word, the Bible, tells us what His will is. "If anyone is God-fearing, and does His will, He hears him" (John 9:31).

One sure way to step out of God's path is to compromise His Word or His will for us and justify it by the obvious success it brings. Satan is quite willing and able to bless any plan that serves his purpose rather than God's. Only by staying in God's Word, praying, and seeking godly counsel can we avoid Satan's traps.

Thomas Guthrie wrote, "If you find yourself loving any pleasure better than your prayers, any book better than the Bible, any persons better than Christ, or any indulgence better than the hope of heaven—take alarm."

If you find yourself outside of God's will and are experiencing a lack of peace (spiritual deadness), you must be willing to abandon everything and seek God's path again—reaching toward the "goal for the prize of the upward call of God."

Larry Burkett

Daily Scripture Reading:
Jeremiah 49:1-33; Daniel 1-2

"But among you there must not be even a hint of sexual immorality, or of any kind of impurity, or of greed, because these are improper for God's holy people. ...For of this you can be sure: No immoral, impure or greedy person—such a man is an idolater—has any inheritance in the kingdom of Christ and of God"
(Ephesians 5:3, 5 NIV).

GREED

Greed is the insatiable desire to have more and demand only the best for yourself.

Greed is actually idolatry, as noted by Paul in Ephesians 5:5. It also leads to destruction. *"People who want to get rich fall into temptation and a trap and into many foolish and harmful desires that plunge men into ruin and destruction"* (1 Timothy 6:9 NIV).

God does not prohibit us from enjoying the benefits of our own labors—after all, we are told to work and provide for our needs. But we are not to become entangled in the desire for more or the best of everything. When greed rules in our hearts, we're no longer able to fulfill our primary purpose: to serve God.

We all have an inborn attitude of greed, always desiring more. The Lord gave direct instructions not to get caught up in this natural desire. He identified greed as the "storing up of temporal treasures."

"Do not store up for yourselves treasures on earth, where moth and rust destroy, and where thieves break in and steal. But store up for yourselves treasures in heaven, where moth and rust do not destroy, and where thieves do not break in and steal" (Matthew 6:19-20 NIV).

To overcome greed, change the goal of your efforts to store up eternal treasures. That is the only real cure for idolatry.

Chuck Bentley

Daily Scripture Reading: 2 Kings 24:5-20; 2 Chronicles 36:8-12; Jeremiah 22:18-30, 24, 29, 37:1-2, 52:1-3

"He who conceals his transgressions will not prosper, but he
who confesses and forsakes them will find compassion"
(Proverbs 18:13).

CORRECTING DECEPTION

Lord Denman wrote that "deception is a delusion, a mockery, and a snare."

Whenever you detect a deception in your own life, large or small, stop what you're doing and confess it immediately. This means to confess not only to God but also to the others who are involved.

There are many rationalizations for not doing this, but there really is only one reason: pride. You must resolve not to be deceptive before the situation presents itself or it will be impossible for you to do the right thing when you are faced with a decision.

You can't assume that the victims of your act of deception will understand or accept an apology either. But, the apology is not for them; it's for you, because if you don't confess your transgression (deception) you will not prosper.

However, just as today's Scripture verse says, when you confess your sins you will find compassion.

Larry Burkett

Daily Scripture Reading:
Jeremiah 23, 27-28

"My God, My God, why hast thou forsaken Me?"
(Matthew 27:46).

QUESTIONING GOD

The question in today's Scripture verse is one of the most poignant questions ever asked in history. It makes me wonder what I would say if I could ask God one question?

If we are made in God's image, as the Bible says we are, that means that we think, to some degree, like Him. Now, if I were God and saw all the ungodliness and sin, I would have destroyed all of creation. I would have just wiped it out and started all over again. At some point, why didn't He just start over?

Yes, I know that at one point He did wipe out all but Noah and his family. But I would have taken the "modeling clay," rolled it into a ball, and said, "Okay, we'll try this thing again. And, remember that angel that was such a bother to me? I'll just do away with him too."

All the angels in Heaven would have been a witness to that and would have left God's creation alone.

Think of all the grief that has been caused and is being caused as a result of God allowing Satan to infect the earth.

It seems that the mess we are making of things just keeps getting worse. Of course He has a reason for it, because He's God. He can do whatever He wants.

He gave us the ability to think on our own (another thing I'm not sure about). He gave us the ability to make decisions. He gave us the ability to love; and He longs for us to love Him and fellowship with Him. What we do is left up to us.

"The Lord is the portion of my inheritance and my cup. . . . I will set the Lord continually before me" (Psalm 16:5, 8).

Larry Burkett

Daily Scripture Reading:
Jeremiah 50-51

"No one can serve two masters; for either he will hate the one and love the other, or he will hold to one and despise the other. You cannot serve God and mammon"
(Matthew 6:24).

FINANCIAL DISCOURAGEMENT

Perhaps the most consistent area of discouragement for most people is financial failure. Not only are our egos involved with our ability to provide, but our security also is threatened.

Quite often the demonstration of our stewardship is not how much we give but how we react when there isn't much to give.

With many, if not most Christians, their faith at any given time seems proportional to their material resources. Obviously this is not true for everyone. Some Christians find that in the midst of their most difficult times their faith grows and matures, which is exactly what James says it will do if we abide in Christ (see James 1:2-3).

God's Word teaches that it is impossible for a Christian to divide loyalties. We can serve but one God. We must decide where our hearts are.

Sometimes God will allow financial crises to come into our lives to give us the opportunity to decide where our loyalties are.

Larry Burkett

Daily Scripture Reading:
Jeremiah 34:1-22, 49:34-39; Ezekiel 1-3

*"So if you have not been trustworthy in handling
worldly wealth, who will trust you with true riches?"*
(Luke 16:11 NIV).

TRUE RICHES

What are the "true riches" that Christians receive for being faithful in handling money and possessions?

After the fall of mankind in Genesis 3, humans began to view things as more important than God—even though He was their only hope of salvation.

Mark 8:36 says, *"What good is it for a man to gain the whole world, yet forfeit his soul?"* (NIV). No amount of money or possessions is more valuable than your soul, and nothing on earth can replace the riches of knowing Jesus Christ.

We chase after things in life that we believe are going to make us rich, but the grace, mercy, forgiveness and blessings that come from God are the true riches. God raised you up from your sins to know Him. All other things pale in comparison.

God challenges us to see the truth—that He is greater than all other things. There are no exceptions for anything we think is valuable. We are to love Him with all we have.

If you're faithful to God and wisely manage what He entrusts to you, He will reveal more of Himself to you. You will begin to experience the true riches.

If you don't know God, pray and invite Jesus to come into your life as Savior and Lord so that you, too, can begin to experience the "true riches."

Chuck Bentley

Daily Scripture Reading:
Ezekiel 4-7

"Concerning spiritual gifts, brethren, . . . There are varieties of gifts, but the same Spirit. . . . and there are varieties of effects, but the same God who works all things in all persons"
(1 Corinthians 12:1, 4, 6).

BE THE BEST

Noah was told to build a ship; Abraham was instructed to leave his home for a strange land; David came to be known as Israel's finest king; Daniel was appointed to interpret dreams; Saul (later called Paul) was called to become the church's first missionary/evangelist/pastor.

When I was very young, I decided that, no matter what, I was going to be better at one thing than anybody else. That made many decisions much easier, because when I got in a job I knew I wasn't good at I would leave.

In college, I changed my major from engineering to business because I realized I never would be the best engineer.

I tried a lot of things: I was an electrician; in electronics in the Air Force; an electrical engineer at the Space Center, involved with an experiments ground station, but every day I was there I knew I was working around people who were better at what we were doing than I was.

At one point in my life—after I got into what I do now—I felt that in the area of biblical finances I knew more about it than anyone else. Perhaps other people have passed me now, and that's okay, but at that point I was functioning at my best and I knew I was where God wanted me to be. There's nothing better than that!

If I could emphasize one thing for my grandchildren—outside of a love for the Lord and a personal relationship with Him—I'd tell them to find out what they are good at, what they enjoy, and be the best they can be, with the Lord's help.

"I will instruct you and teach you in the way which you should go" (Psalm 32:8).

Larry Burkett

Daily Scripture Reading:
Ezekiel 8-11

"Behold, the day of the Lord is coming, cruel, with fury and burning anger, to make the land a desolation; and He will exterminate its sinners from it"
(Isaiah 13:9).

END TIMES

There are many views on end-time prophecy. My philosophy is twofold. I got part of it from my former pastor, who said, "Live like you're going through the tribulation, and pray that you don't have to."

Will we or won't we go through the tribulation? I can't honestly say. I've heard some intelligent people argue, very convincingly, in any number of positions—at least three: premillennial, amillennial, and postmillennial. All of them were convincing.

My other philosophy was set by John Wesley. Someone asked him what he would do if he knew the Lord was coming back tomorrow. He said, "If I were a gardener, I'd go out and plant another tree today." I agree with that.

The apostle Paul, in his early ministry, wrote like he expected the Lord's return any day and stressed the urgency of being ready. After he had lived many years and knew that he was going to die, you can see the shift in his writing, placing the emphasis on maintaining the church (the body of Christ).

My closing thought would be that we should live as if Christ were coming back tomorrow.

"The nations of the world will see me arrive in the clouds of heaven, with power and great glory" (Matthew 24:30 TLB).

Larry Burkett

Daily Scripture Reading:
Ezekiel 12-14

*"Be diligent to present yourself approved to God as a workman who does
not need to be ashamed, handling accurately the word of truth"*
(2 Timothy 2:15).

GOD'S WORD

I read the Bible in my private devotion time. I don't actually study during those times. Rather, I'm looking to see if God might reveal something to me out of a passage of Scripture that I might have already read many times but had missed. Often you'll do that, because at different stages of your life you're more open to specific things.

Sometimes when I study the Bible I am looking for something—a particular word—and I'll look up all the verses that deal with that word or subject.

I use different translations: the New International Version in my private devotions or when I'm just reading the Bible. If I'm studying, I use the New American Standard version, and that's primarily because I grew up using it. Once you've used one translation that long, it's hard to change.

If I ever find what I think is a discrepancy in one translation, I'll look that up in several translations or I'll get out a lexicon and see if that determines for me the root meaning of a word. If that doesn't work, I'll go to someone who knows the root languages of Greek and Hebrew. Whatever they say pretty well settles it for me.

Unless we read God's Word, we cannot know what God is saying to us. His Word is full of rich history, exciting events, instruction for daily living, encouragement, and strength.

When we pray we talk to Him. When we read the Bible, He is talking to us.

Larry Burkett

Daily Scripture Reading:
Ezekiel 15-17

"Food is for the stomach, and the stomach is for food;
but God will do away with both of them"
(1 Corinthians 6:13).

EATING HABITS

The majority of Americans have poor eating habits. I think the problem we're having with food is the same problem we have with almost every other thing we do: We tend to overindulge and not be very discerning.

When I think back to when I had my heart attack (eight years before I was diagnosed with cancer), I remember what changes had to be made. I changed my diet—drastically! I got busy and lowered my cholesterol from about 245 down to 90, and I kept it there or below for eight years.

Looking back, and having read a lot more about it, I believe that I might have overreacted. That drastic measure could possibly have contributed to my having cancer.

After both illnesses, I knew that to do what God wanted me to do, which is to teach and to write, I had to make some fundamental decisions, either in treatment or in diet.

After researching many diets, some of which were so rigid I knew I would never stick to them, I decided I would have to establish my own regimen—one that would not prohibit my work for the Lord.

We are responsible for the way we take care of our bodies. Being a good steward is not limited to how we manage our money. It also includes taking care of the "temple."

The apostle Paul wrote, *"Do you not know that you are a temple of God, and that the Spirit of God dwells in you?"* (1 Corinthians 3:16).

Larry Burkett

Daily Scripture Reading:
Ezekiel 18-20

"*Shout joyfully to the Lord, all the earth; break forth
and sing for joy and sing praises*"
(Psalm 98:4).

JOYFUL NOISE?

Everyone has his or her own opinion about what music is approved by God. Is some music bad?

Well, from a humanistic perspective, we know that children who have been raised hearing quality music—that's music with good rhythm, harmony, and balance—will have more intelligence and be more well-rounded. It has been proven that music somehow affects brain development.

From a personal perspective, I love all music. I can listen to anything from the classics to country to 50s music, which is what I grew up on. I do not like hard rock or heavy metal; the music's consistent beat agitates my spirit somehow.

As Christians, we can pray about what kind of music is honoring to God and what is displeasing to Him. As in all other areas of life, we must follow our convictions. What is all right for someone else may not be right for you. Pray about it.

"*Praise Him with trumpet sound; praise Him with harp and lyre. Praise Him with timbrel and dancing; praise Him with stringed instruments and pipe. Praise Him with loud cymbals*" (Psalm 150:3-5).

Reread today's Scripture verse.

Larry Burkett

Daily Scripture Reading:
Ezekiel 21-23

*"One man gives freely, yet gains even more; another withholds
unduly, but comes to poverty. A generous man will prosper;
he who refreshes others will himself be refreshed"*
(Proverbs 11:24-25 NIV).

SIX WAYS TO BE GENEROUS

Our generosity as the Body of Christ has been tested in the past, and it will be tested more in the future. We need to decide now to be generous in every possible way.

Following are six ways you can be generous today.

1. In Genesis 12, God told Abram to go to a new land. Abram obeyed and took his nephew, Lot, with him. Lot's father had died, and this was an incredible act of generosity on Abram's part. God may be leading you to care for people, such as elderly parents or a family in crisis, in the same way that Abram cared for Lot.

2. Abram showed generosity by giving Lot the first choice of the land. Has God called you to be generous with another member of your family as you divide an estate? Or, are you being called to forgive someone who took advantage of you in a past estate settlement?

3. When Lot was captured, Abram rescued him. Lot's foolish behavior had cost him everything, but Abram loved him anyway. We should be willing to serve, help, and be generous to those in need—even those who have been foolish.

4. As a result of rescuing Lot, Abram and his servants captured treasures that had been stolen. From these treasures, Abram gave a tithe to Melchizedek, king of Salem, who was a *"priest of God Most High"* (Genesis 14:18 NIV). He knew that everything he had came from God. Has God called you to have a greater focus on supporting His Kingdom?

5. Abram gave back all the captured treasures except what his men needed for refreshment. If you're an employer, be generous to your employees. Share your company's victories with them, and let them know you couldn't make it without them.

6. Abram gave back all the captured treasures to the King of Sodom. Has God called you to be generous even with those who don't deserve your generosity?

Remember Abram's model for generosity in these days. And, be listening for the Lord to prompt you to be generous.

Chuck Bentley

Daily Scripture Reading: 2 Kings 25:1; 2 Chronicles 36:13-16;
Jeremiah 21:1-22:9, 32:1-44, 52:4; Ezekiel 24

*"If I go and prepare a place for you, I will come again,
and receive you to Myself; that where I am, there you may be also"*
(John 14:3).

I SHALL RETURN

"I shall return" is a quotation that was made famous during the years of World War II. Gen. Douglas MacArthur visited the people of the Philippine Islands while they were under enemy occupation, and when he left he promised them he would return.

We have that same promise from Jesus, and that should counteract any gloom, confusion, disappointment, sadness, or lack of hope we might have in this life.

We get so Earth-bound that we forget that this earth is not our home; we are just visitors here. Our real home is with Jesus Christ in Heaven, if we have accepted Him as Lord and Savior of our lives.

We should be looking forward to that day when His promise is fulfilled and He comes back to receive us unto Himself.

"The Lord Himself will descend from heaven with a shout, with the voice of the archangel, and with the trumpet of God; and the dead in Christ shall rise first. Then we who are alive and remain shall be caught up together with them in the clouds to meet the Lord in the air, and thus we shall always be with the Lord" (1 Thessalonians 4:16-17).

We should do what verse 18 says, *"Comfort one another with these words."*

Larry Burkett

Daily Scripture Reading:
Jeremiah 30-33

"Because of the proof given by this ministry they will glorify God
for your obedience to your confession of the gospel of Christ"
(2 Corinthians 9:13).

RECOGNIZING GOD'S WILL

It seems evident that many Christians fall victim to worldly success motivation. They have a lot of drive and ambition, but they fail to recognize God's will for them and, thus, they submit to the world's will.

Often they spend too much time asking someone else about God's will for their lives, when it is God they should be asking. Ask those who are truly living God's plan how they found it, and usually they will say "God just revealed it to me."

Many times other people helped to point them in the right direction, but just as many tried to talk them out of doing God's will. God will reveal His plan to those who seek him diligently.

The difficulty is that although Christians sense God's will for them it may not agree with what they had in mind, particularly in regard to income and ego, so they rationalize their way out of it.

For a while there will be feeling of loss, but with time it passes. The next time, the direction is not quite as strong and it's easier to ignore. Eventually, God's call just fades away and the thorns choke out any further direction.

Once a Christian examines his or her life and discovers that the fruitfulness is gone (regardless of income), it is certain that God's will has been bypassed and another master has become Lord.

There are no quick, simple solutions to resolving this condition. Only earnest, honest prayer and petition will restore that sensitivity to the Holy Spirit's guidance.

Larry Burkett

Daily Scripture Reading:
Ezekiel 25, 29:1-16, 30-31

"Let another praise you, and not your own mouth;
a stranger, and not your own lips"
(Proverbs 27:2).

PRIDE OR CONFIDENCE

Our society has taught us that if we don't show self-confidence others won't have confidence in us either. We live in a time when a great deal of emphasis is placed on personal credentials.

Qualifications are based on personal achievements, education, and experience. And, when viewed in the right perspective, these things are good; but, when they produce pride, they lose their value from a godly perspective.

There is no doubt that we should work with all our might in whatever we do; but, the presence of pride indicates confidence in self rather than in Christ, who enables us.

Pride is an enemy of God, the cause of the fall of both Lucifer and of man. The attitude God wants us to have is demonstrated by the story of a convicted prisoner.

With Napoleon's permission, a Russian prince was allowed to pardon one convict in a French prison. As he talked with the prisoners, each one professed innocence and said they had been unjustly punished. Finally, he found a man who sorrowfully confessed his guilt and acknowledged that he was deserving of the punishment. To this man the prince said, "I have brought you pardon in the name of the emperor."

Isn't this the way we receive our salvation? And isn't it the way we live our Christian lives? The next time you are tempted to "watch out for number one," remember that Number One (Jesus) died nearly 2,000 years ago and now lives in the hearts of the humble.

Larry Burkett

Daily Scripture Reading:
Ezekiel 26-28

*"Who regards you as superior? And what do you have
that you did not receive? But if you did receive it, why
do you boast as if you had not received it?"*
(1 Corinthians 4:7).

PROUD OR PLEASED?

There was a time when I found it difficult to accept that everything I possessed was not a direct result of my hard work and superiority. I often observed those who had less than I did, and I concluded that their lack was because they didn't work as hard as I did.

On the other hand, I looked at others who had more and calculated that I needed to work harder and become wiser in order to have what they did.

After reading today's Scripture verse I had to change my thinking.

Consider the farmer. He prepares the ground and plants and waters the seed, but God gives the increase. To say that the farmer grew the crops would be incorrect. He only harvested the crops that God grew. There's no question that the farmer had to be faithful in doing his part; however, the farmer can't boast in the crop that is harvested. He can only be thankful that God blessed the work of his hands.

Don't discount your efforts completely, though. Faithfulness is required. God doesn't honor slothfulness; He honors faithfulness. And the most significant thing about faithfulness is that even the most untalented or unskilled person can be faithful.

Pride says, "Look what I did." Humility says, "Look what God did through me."

Father, thank You that everything good and perfect comes to us from You, the Creator of all things.

Larry Burkett

Daily Scripture Reading: 2 Kings 25:2-21;
2 Chronicles 36:17-21; Jeremiah 37:3-39:10, 52:5-30

*"He who is spiritual appraises all things,
yet he himself is appraised by no man"*
(1 Corinthians 2:15).

JUMPING THE GUN

Several contestants entered a race, which was to start with the firing of a gun. But, in anticipation, one of the contestants started before the gun fired. He "jumped the gun."

Christians can be guilty of spiritually jumping the gun. The apostle Peter was guilty of this more than once but the Lord just said, "Get thee behind me, Satan."

Jumping the gun can be a conditioned response from Satan. The Scriptures clearly demonstrate that God is patient, and everything He does is thought out in advance.

God does not anticipate. He prepares. The Christian also should prepare, through appraisal or investigation. The spiritual person investigates first—then acts. The natural man simply reacts, almost always resulting in disaster.

How many times have you jumped into a conversation impulsively, to add your two cents, only to regret it later? Remember, *"He who gives an answer before he hears, it is folly and shame to him"* (Proverbs 18:13).

It is vitally important in everything to allow the Lord to prepare your heart. An immediate response or quick reaction is rarely ever from the Lord.

Pray before you act, or speak, or react. Jumping the gun can result in all manner of problems.

Lord, in Your Word, James said that if I could control my tongue it would prove that I have perfect control over myself in other ways. Help me, Lord!

Larry Burkett

Daily Scripture Reading: 2 Kings 25:22;
Jeremiah 39:11-40:6; Lamentations 1-3

*"Yours, O LORD, is the greatness and the power and the glory and the
majesty and the splendor, for everything in heaven and earth is yours. . . . In
your hands are strength and power to exalt and give strength to all"*
(1 Chronicles 29:11-12 NIV).

A BIBLICAL VIEW OF SUCCESS

One of the greatest mistakes humans make is to define success based on what they
can do without God. Even Christians can allow their thinking to become tainted by
humanism, which is the view that they are the cause and creator of their own success.

We celebrate human achievement and think that everything good in our history
is a result of our own brilliance. However, if you truly know God and have a biblical
worldview, you'll see Him as the sole source of success. And, you'll want to do everything
on His terms.

One example of this is Nehemiah, who had the task of rebuilding Jerusalem. He
knew he couldn't do this on his own, so he cried out to God for help. Satan loves to mock
and ridicule those who walk by faith, and Nehemiah met with tremendous resistance. But
like him, we must remain faithful to God despite the difficulties of life. Nehemiah did his
part and trusted God to give him success.

Later, Nehemiah was able to write, *"So on October 2 the wall was finished—just fifty-
two days after we had begun. When our enemies and the surrounding nations heard about it,
they were frightened and humiliated. They realized this work had been done with the help of our
God"* (Nehemiah 6:15-16 NLT).

"Have a dream and make it happen" is a lie. Your dream should be to do the Lord's
will. When you are faithful to this dream, you will experience success on God's terms, not
your own.

Chuck Bentley

Daily Scripture Reading:
Lamentations 4-5; Obadiah

*"Keeping faith and a good conscience, which some have rejected
and have suffered shipwreck in regard to their faith"*
(1 Timothy 1:19).

FAITH AND CONSCIENCE

Our Scripture verse likens faith to a ship. The conscience can be likened to the hull of that ship. When the conscience (hull) gets a hole in it, faith (the vessel) can become shipwrecked and sink.

Picture a ship sailing down a channel. The ship is faith and the channel is love. If the ship (faith) gets outside of the channel (love) it will run aground, puncture the hull (conscience), and sink.

When we operate our lives outside of love, we will cause our consciences to become defiled and suffer shipwreck with regard to our faith. And we know from God's Word that without faith it is impossible to please God.

Augustine said, "The words of God come like fire, so that when your heart is cleared, Christ can be built in you."

How can we clean up an evil conscience and restore faith in a ship-wrecked condition? Through confession of sin.

A very practical and easy way to do this is to ask God to reveal the things in our lives that aren't pleasing to Him. Write them down, repent of them, receive His forgiveness, and then destroy the list. After you've been forgiven, the list no longer exists, because God's Word promises, *"Their sins and their lawless deeds I will remember no more"* (Hebrews 10:17).

Pray a prayer of thanksgiving for this very special blessing as God's child.

Larry Burkett

Daily Scripture Reading:
2 Kings 25:23-26; Jeremiah 40:7-44:30

"Commit thy works to the Lord, and your plans will be established"
(Proverbs 16:3).

ELIMINATE FAILURE

Jim operated a business with another man who was both his friend and partner. When the business began to generate losses, rather than profits, Jim called and shared his concern with me, stating that they were losing up to $1,000 a day.

As I reviewed the nature of the business, I learned that it was a liquor store. Jim hadn't wanted to go into this particular business, but he did so because of his friendship with his partner.

I asked Jim is he had dedicated his business to God, and he said that he hadn't. I explained that before God can establish our plans our works must first be committed to Him. But could the sale of beer and wine be dedicated to God? Jim and I agreed— probably not.

The verse for today is a guide to help us to begin eliminating some of our failures. If we are going to commit our works to God, there are prerequisites that must be met.

First, is the nature of our work honoring to God? Second, what is the purpose of our efforts? In 1 Peter 4:11 we read that the purpose is that *"in all things God may be glorified through Jesus Christ."*

Jim's liquor business was really a "planned failure" from God's viewpoint. In all good conscience, he could not ask God to bless the business, because the works couldn't be committed to the Lord.

Remember, works committed to God will be supported by God.

Larry Burkett

Daily Scripture Reading:
Ezekiel 33:21-36:38

"Each of you should look not only to your own interests,
but also to the interests of others"
(Philippians 2:4 NIV).

IT'S JUST ENTERTAINMENT

Some people say gambling is just entertainment, like fishing, seeing a movie, or going to a baseball game. But when you win at gambling, you do so at many other people's expense.

Gambling really boils down to self-gratification. It's the thrill that you could hit the jackpot at any time. And, if you win, you don't have to look at all those other people who lost.

Another myth regarding gambling is that you're doing it to become rich so you can give more to the church. But our focus should be on good stewardship of the money we currently have, not on dreams of what we might win at gambling. *"Whoever can be trusted with very little can also be trusted with much, and whoever is dishonest with very little will also be dishonest with much"* (Luke 16:10 NIV).

Be faithful with what you have and trust God to multiply your efforts, no matter how small, for His glory. Focus on laying up treasures in heaven, not on earth (Matthew 6:19-21).

Don't believe the lie that gambling is good for society. If you invest in a successful company that's making advances in medical technology, you're putting your money into something that has intrinsic value. Jobs are created, you receive returns on your investment, and patients benefit from the products that the company creates. It's a win-win situation. But if you invest in gambling and hit the jackpot, it's a winning situation for you and a losing situation for all the others.

What about the argument that money from lotteries goes to support education? Let's go back to the example of the medical manufacturer cited above. Products that help others have intrinsic value. But there is no intrinsic value in the act of taking money that people lost and making ourselves feel better about it by putting it into education.

It would be much better to fund education by investing in a product with intrinsic value—something that would benefit others in the process of providing for educational needs.

Chuck Bentley

Daily Scripture Reading:
Ezekiel 37-39

"The plans of the diligent lead surely to advantage, but everyone who is hasty comes surely to poverty"
(Proverbs 21:5).

HASTE MAKES WASTE

Bill and Jayne were seminar sponsors for their city. Bill, as usual, took little interest and left the preparation to Jayne. However, in addition to coordinating the seminar, Jayne also had her family obligations, which often caused her to make last-minute plans. They were habitually late and Bill continually remarked about Jayne's poor planning.

Some people seem to constantly have emergencies or are always in a frantic rush to get things done. This is the result of failing to plan, which indicates something important: Usually there's a failure to pray.

If Bill and Jayne had recognized the principle of stewardship, they would have realized that Jesus is Lord and that we are His stewards. And, as His stewards, we should seek His direction through prayer.

When we think of being good stewards, often we think only of how we use our money. But being good stewards involves far more than money; we are to be good stewards of our time.

Prayer is the instrument for planning. If we will start the day with prayer and then spend more time in prayer throughout the day, there will be better planning, and proper planning will eliminate most emergencies and haste.

Ask the Lord to reveal to you how you can be a better steward of your time. If you already have that under control, pray for someone else you know who has more than he or she can handle.

Larry Burkett

Daily Scripture Reading:
Ezekiel 32:1-33:20; Daniel 3

"We are ambassadors for Christ,
as though God were entreating through us"
(2 Corinthians 5:20).

THE KING'S BUSINESS

A businessman was summoned before England's queen. When he appeared, she requested that he represent England as one of the country's ambassadors.

He expressed his delight and appreciation for the honor, but he told of his reluctance to leave his own business, which demanded most of his time and attention. If he were to leave for two years of service to England and the queen, his business surely would fail.

The queen said, "You take care of England's business, and England will take care of yours."

After his tenure of service, the man returned to find his business had doubled in size. What if you were given the same offer? Well, you have been! Today's Scripture verse says that we are ambassadors and God has given us the privilege of attending to His business. He, in turn, will take care of us.

However, God has no obligation to anyone who neglects His business in pursuit of his or her own.

As long as we have our priorities right, we have an unfailing guarantee of success from God's Word: "Commit your work to the Lord, then it will succeed" (Proverbs 16:3 TLB).

Father, help me find balance between "taking care of business" and being Your ambassador.

Larry Burkett

Daily Scripture Reading:
Ezekiel 40-42

*"Give to him who asks of you, and do not turn away
from him who wants to borrow from you"*
(Matthew 5:42).

LENDING TO OTHERS

Does it bother you when someone wants to borrow something that belongs to you? I suppose we all have had bad experiences and don't want to be "taken" again.

But there is an attitude problem in the hearts of Christians who have difficulty lending, and God will deal with that attitude.

Personal attachment to the things of this life is contrary to Scripture. Anyone who loves the world and what it offers doesn't have the love of God abiding in him or her.

God may allow us to lose an item just to show us how much we love the things of this world. Lending grudgingly or refusing to lend should be seen as a red light of warning by a Christian. Also, demanding replacement of a lost item should be an indicator of attachment to things.

Our Scripture verse for today may be difficult to live by, but it is not impossible or Jesus wouldn't have expected it of us.

God can help us overcome the attitude of greed (an attitude that makes us think our possessions actually belong to us).

Even though we may have worked hard for what we have, the truth is that God has provided our material blessings. They are all from Him, and it is not a matter of ownership; it is a matter of stewardship. Being a good steward is miles apart from being a concerned owner.

Recognize the true ownership of your possessions and transfer ownership to Christ.

Think of what all you "own." Then acknowledge God's ownership by turning it all over to Him.

Larry Burkett

Daily Scripture Reading:
Ezekiel 43-45

"Then He said to them, 'Watch out! Be on your guard against all kinds of greed; a man's life does not consist in the abundance of his possessions' "
(Luke 12:15 NIV).

FINANCIALLY ASSISTED SUICIDE

The most common group that commits suicide is adult males. And a common source of pain in their lives is their finances. I have known six men who completed this horrifying act of self-destruction.

I have come to term this tragedy as a "Financially Assisted Suicide."

Satan works hard to cause all of us, especially men, to derive our identity from work or financial success. When a man is out of work or has a reversal of financial success, he senses a loss of identity and purpose. This loss leads him to embarrassment and despair.

It is so important to base our identity on God's truth, not in our work or money or possessions. The Lord warns us to be careful that we never define our life by our possessions. It is a dangerous and potentially destructive path.

Romans 12:1-2 is the solution to free ourselves from conformity to the patterns of this world. When freed of placing our identity in money and possessions, we are also protected from Satan's lies.

These tragic suicides are always a reminder to me to take God's Word seriously and encourage men to renew their minds on His truth that will set them free.

Chuck Bentley

Daily Scripture Reading:
Ezekiel 46-48

*"Whatever is born of God overcomes the world; and this
is the victory that has overcome the world—our faith"*
(1 John 5:4).

THE LAW OF FAITH

Prayer is probably one of the most talked about and least understood topics in the Bible. How does prayer really work? Many Christians say that they pray, but they seldom get an answer. Have you ever felt that way?

The reason prayer goes unanswered is because God answers prayer based on faith. Romans 3:27 tells us that faith is a law—just like gravity. You can't jump off the top of a building and ignore the law of gravity without suffering a grave consequence.

However, many of us ignore the law of faith, expecting God to violate His own principle.

Since faith works by love (see 1 Corinthians 13:1-3), all prayers must be based on love.

Any time we pray, we should search our hearts for the true motives behind our requests. Are our prayers motivated by greed or by love? Without love, prayer will not be answered, because it is not according to faith. Faith works through love, which pleases God. He then rewards that faith.

How can you be sure your prayers are according to faith and will please God and evoke His response? Weigh your motives. Is the prayer for selfish benefit, or will it benefit someone else?

Look up James 4:3 and write it down. Continue to read it over until you know you have come to terms with what it says. What about your motives? God wants to give you His best, but you must follow the teaching in His Word.

Larry Burkett

Daily Scripture Reading: 2 Kings 25:27-30; Psalm 44;
Jeremiah 52:31-34; Ezekiel 29:17-21; Daniel 4

"Rest in the Lord, and wait patiently for Him: fret not
yourself because of him who prospers in his way"
(Psalm 37:7).

THE "KEEPING UP WITH" DISEASE

Do you worry or become overworked because someone else is prospering and you aren't? This is caused by a malady called "keeping up with the Joneses," and there are many Christians who have this disease in its final stages.

There is a cure; it's called patience. The prescription is faith, and it can be obtained from your Great Physician.

In trying to keep up with the Joneses, we suffer an "attack" of money shortages. However, for too many Christians with this disease the "infection" of impatience is severe. Many cannot wait for God to act; they must put a "bandage" on the shortage now. This might be done by taking a second mortgage, a second job, a get-rich-quick scheme.

The Great Physician doesn't administer human salve. The answer to money problems isn't more money. We wouldn't give more sugar to a diabetic. Instead He prescribes a "double dose" of patience, the very deficiency that brought about the "keeping up with" disease.

More work to meet higher financial demands may keep us from the Lord's rest and bring on fatigue. If we refuse His "treatment," we will take our own medicine.

How can you avoid catching this dreaded disease? Avoid contact with others who have the disease, and read Psalm 37:1-7. Confess your envy and ask for the Lord's "treatment."

Larry Burkett

Daily Scripture Reading:
Psalms 74, 79-80, 89

"Plans fail for lack of counsel, but with many advisers they succeed"
(Proverbs 15:22 NIV).

COUPLES AND RISK

As an investor, you'll have to deal with the issue of how much risk you can take. If you're married, an equally important issue is how much risk your spouse can take. Chances are your opinions will be different.

Spouses have personality differences that cause them to approach matters in different ways. But differences can strengthen a marriage if they are accepted as beneficial to each other.

When husbands and wives are able to listen to each other and cooperate in meeting each other's needs, the differing viewpoints of a husband-wife team contribute to a balanced life together. They learn how to complete, rather than compete.

If your investment strategy is worlds apart from that of your spouse, be willing to compromise and seek peace from the Lord. He will confirm your plans and unite your hearts.

However, if you're unable to agree, seek competent outside help from a financial adviser who has the experience you lack.

When selecting an adviser, be sure that he or she is a committed Christian. As Psalm 1:1-2 says, *"Blessed is the man who does not walk in the counsel of the wicked or stand in the way of sinners or sit in the seat of mockers. But his delight is in the law of the LORD, and on his law he meditates day and night"* (NIV).

Chuck Bentley

Daily Scripture Reading:
Psalms 85, 102, 106, 123, 137

*"Seek first my kingdom and my righteousness,
and all these things shall be added unto you"*
(Matthew 6:33).

PUT GOD FIRST

It's a simple thing to say, "I do put God first." But, is He the first thing on your mind in the morning and the last thing on your mind at night?

What if God looked at the use of our time during any given day? How much time do we really put into the study of His Word or talking with Him? If He is first, we should be studying the handbook of life, the Bible, and spending time in prayer.

The man who invented most of our road grading equipment in America was R.G. LeTourneau, an uneducated man with a sixth-grade education. He was told by his own college-graduate engineers that the equipment he designed wouldn't work.

What they didn't know was that every evening before he went to bed he would study God's Word thoroughly and spend the last 30 minutes of his evenings in prayer before going to sleep. When he awoke in the morning, he had a fully formed design for a new piece of equipment, given to him by God, with an absolute assurance from God that the piece of equipment would work.

LeTourneau designed some truly remarkable equipment. In fact, long after his death, that equipment is still operating and, in great part, no one has ever improved on the initial design. Why? Because LeTourneau put God first in his life.

Not only did he give God a portion of his money (90 percent!), but he gave God a portion of his time. He made it clear that God was first in his life.

Where does God rank in your schedule for the day?

Larry Burkett

Daily Scripture Reading:
Daniel 5, 7-8

"If anyone serves me, let him follow Me; and where I am, there shall My servant also be; if anyone serves Me, the Father will honor him" (John 12:26).

BE A GOOD FOLLOWER

Would you rather be a follower or a leader? Leaders earn more money, get more recognition, and are more popular. Who wouldn't rather be a leader?

God didn't call us to be leaders. He called us to be followers, and as followers we honor others and build them up.

I truly believe with all my heart that one of these days we are going to show up in Heaven at the judgment seat of Christ, and when He calls all the nations of the world together we will be working for some little white-haired lady we never heard of during our lifetime. She never received any recognition, never received any great rewards in this life, but she was doing what God called her to do.

As a result, God blessed her and gave her a number one position in the kingdom of God, along with other deserving followers.

Are you a leader or a follower?

Larry Burkett

Daily Scripture Reading:
Daniel 6, 9

*"Many who are last in this kingdom shall be
first in the kingdom of God, and many who are first
in this kingdom shall be last in the kingdom of God"*
(Matthew 19:30).

SERVING OTHERS

At the Last Supper, when Jesus went into the upper room He took off His clothing, except for a loin cloth, put a towel over His shoulders, and then, as His apostles came into the room, He began washing their feet.

When He came to Peter, who was more impetuous than the others, *"Peter said to Him, 'Never shall You wash my feet!'"* (John 13:8). Why do you think he said that? What would you have said?

There was a hierarchy in Jerusalem at the time, and at the bottom of the system were the people Jesus called His disciples: workmen, fishermen, carpenters, and laborers. Below them were slaves, and at the lowest level of slavery was a foot servant—someone who washed other people's feet.

When Peter refused to let Jesus wash his feet, the Savior said, *"If I do not wash you, you have no part with me"* (John 13:8). Then he went on to say (in verses 14-15), *"If I then, the Lord and the Teacher, washed your feet, you also ought to wash one another's feet. For I gave you an example that you also should do as I did to you."*

Jesus was on His way to being the most exalted person in the kingdom of God; therefore, he had to show them that He was willing to take the very least position in the kingdom. He wanted to be the least glorified before He became the most exalted.

Jesus set a perfect example of how to put others before self.

Could you humble yourself to wash someone else's feet like Jesus did?

Larry Burkett

Daily Scripture Reading:
2 Chronicles 36:22-23; Ezra 1:1-4:5

*"Does any one of you, when he has a case against
his neighbor, dare to go to law before the unrighteous?"*
(1 Corinthians 6:1).

SUING CHRISTIANS?

A lawsuit is nothing more than a legal recourse for an assumed loss. Suing is not a new concept. The apostle Paul wrote about it almost 2,000 years ago. He said it is better to be defrauded and lose everything you have than to take a fellow Christian to court and present a poor witness to an unsaved world. There are alternatives to suing available to us.

God cannot bless our attitudes until we forgive the ones we feel like we have the right to sue. No matter what wrong they have done, we must forgive them, because the principles of God's Word are for restoring people—not punishing them.

The next step is to go to the guilty party and confront that person face to face. If this doesn't do any good, then you are to take the person before the church.

God's Word teaches restoration—not vengeance.

Is there someone you need to forgive? A relationship that needs to be restored?

Larry Burkett

Daily Scripture Reading:
Daniel 10-12

*"Give to everyone who asks of you, and whoever takes
away what is yours, do not demand it back"*
(Luke 6:30).

SUING NON-CHRISTIANS

We know from reading Paul's writings to the Corinthians that we are not to sue Christians, but what about non-Christians? The Bible is not quite as specific, but just because God didn't make it a "thou shalt not," that doesn't mean you should sue non-Christians.

The Scripture verse for today is a strong statement about how we are to treat other people.

I'm not saying that you have to let people take things away from you that belong to God or that you should loan them things and never try to recover them. But there are ways to recapture things without taking someone to court.

God is quite competent to protect His own business and His own people.

I know of instances in which a person was saved because of the actions of a Christian not being willing to sue a non-Christian.

However, this means giving up our "rights" rather than pursuing vengeance.

Only God can tell you what is right for you to do in any given situation. Pray fervently.

Larry Burkett

Daily Scripture Reading:
Ezra 4:6-6:13; Haggai

"He who walks with the wise grows wise,
but a companion of fools suffers harm"
(Proverbs 13:20 NIV).

SELECTING THE RIGHT COUNSEL

If you're looking for an investment adviser, try to find someone who's a committed Christian.

Psalm 1:1 says we should avoid ungodly counsel. So, when you meet with a prospective adviser, test his or her value system. Advisers who will cheat for you will also cheat you. And, advisers who will bend the rules on your behalf against someone else will do the same thing to you. If a person's counsel runs contrary to God's Word, discount it as worthless.

Proverbs 13:20 says we should look for wise counsel. You want someone who earns you more money than he or she costs you. When you first meet with an adviser, ask questions about a particular investment that you're knowledgeable about. Do research beforehand, if necessary. Then, if the adviser doesn't impress you with his or her answers, look elsewhere for advice.

Proverbs 15:22 says we are to have multiple counselors. Don't rely solely on the advice of one person. Ask trusted friends for their input. If you're married, seek the advice of your spouse.

Finally, check a prospective adviser's references and ensure that he or she has integrity. Your spouse should have input into the selection of any prospective adviser. God may give sensitivity and discernment to one of you that the other does not have.

Chuck Bentley

Daily Scripture Reading:
Zechariah 1-6

"Since his days are determined, the number of his months
is with Thee, and his limits Thou hast set"
(Job 14:5).

DIFFERENT METHODS

Like many people, I have thought through the message of eternal life in Jesus many times. Thoughts of facing death can cause one to examine his or her faith.

I think of a story you've probably heard about the man who was trapped on his roof during a flood. While clinging to the chimney, he was praying that God would rescue him. A fellow came by in a boat and asked if he could help. The man said, "No, that's okay. God's going to rescue me."

The water continued to rise and another fellow came by, paddling a skimpy little raft. He offered help to the man on the roof but was told, "No, thank you. God is going to rescue me."

The water rose higher and higher and then a helicopter hovered over him. The pilot offered to lower a rope, but the man said, "No, God has this under control. He's going to rescue me." As the water continued to rise, the man was swept to his death.

When the man reached heaven he asked St. Peter why God didn't rescue him. Peter smiled as he said, "Well, my friend, He sent three people by to pick you up and you turned them all away. What did you expect?"

Though it is a fictitious story, the principle cannot be lost. Often God uses natural things to rescue His people. They are not always instantaneous, miraculous answers.

We should always be open to what God is trying to do for us.

Larry Burkett

Daily Scripture Reading: Ezra 6:14-22;
Psalm 78; Zechariah 7-8

*"In the early morning, while it was still dark, He arose and went
out and departed to a lonely place, and was praying there"*
(Mark 1:35).

A NEW APPRECIATION

I've always been a late-night person, but following my cancer surgeries sleep was particularly hard to come by. Because the pain prohibited sleep, one of the great blessings for me personally was to turn on my local Christian radio station and listen to the comforting music.

With so much time on my hands, I really began to focus in on the music—probably more than at any other time in my life. I was amazed at how much Christian music truly centers on the theme of the death and resurrection of Jesus Christ.

Not only did His resurrection take place, but our resurrection—the future for those who trust Jesus as Lord and Savior—to eternal life. What a comfort that message was, reasserting that death is not a curse but a reward—for God's people.

We have an enormous number of Christian radio stations throughout America. They are the best resource available to God's people to communicate quickly with one another and as a means of ministering to one another.

I pray you will help me protect the medium of Christian radio as a sacred trust from the Lord. That means, if you listen to Christian radio, you should support it. If we ever lose access to Christian radio, there will be a great gap in spreading the Gospel across the world.

Jesus told the disciples: *"You shall receive power. . . and you shall be My witnesses both in Jerusalem, and in all Judea and Samaria, and even to the remotest part of the earth"* (Acts 1:8).

Larry Burkett

Daily Scripture Reading:
Psalms 107, 116, 118

*"The earth is the Lord's, and all it contains,
the world, and those who dwell in it"*
(Psalm 24:1).

MINE OR GOD'S?

When my children were young I shared with them the importance of recognizing that everything we have is from God and that we should transfer ownership back to His care and protection.

Years ago two friends and I purchased a chain saw for a project on which we were working. After using the saw, it was placed in what we thought was a safe place. But, a day or two later, we discovered it was missing.

My oldest son asked if I had turned over ownership of the saw to God. I had forgotten to do this. I immediately asked my two friends if they had committed the saw to God and they hadn't either.

This made me sure of two things: my son had learned the scriptural lesson I had wanted to teach him, and I needed to practice what I had preached to my family.

Keep in mind that God isn't responsible for what we do not give to Him.

How do we protect what we have? Make a list of your possessions and give them all to God. He will protect what has been committed to Him.

Larry Burkett

Daily Scripture Reading:
Psalms 125-126, 128-129, 132, 147, 149

"For as he thinks within himself, so he is"
(Proverbs 23:7).

IT'S A HEART THING

The Bible makes it clear that the battle to live godly lives is won or lost first in our hearts—long before we actually make a decision or follow a certain course.

In every area of our lives, we must determine to follow God's way, whatever the cost. Then when our old sinful nature tries to surface and take control, we have the grace to resist our natural impulses and are given strength through Christ to live lives pleasing to Him.

Open your heart to Him and allow Him to deal with you right where you are in your life. Remember, our lives are not who we are—they are who we are becoming.

Elisabeth Elliot, widow of slain missionary Jim Elliot, wrote, "[Lord] remind us that it is in losing ourselves that we find You."

If there is an attitude hidden in your heart that is contrary to God's plan for you and it is hindering your spiritual growth, get rid of it by planting God's Word there instead. Confess it to the Lord now.

Larry Burkett

Daily Scripture Reading:
Zechariah 9-14

*"The righteous cry and the Lord hears, and delivers them
out of all their troubles. The Lord is near to the brokenhearted,
and saves those who are crushed in spirit"*
(Psalm 34:17-18).

EMOTIONAL SUFFERING

Mental suffering revolves around our attitudes and thought patterns; emotional suffering reflects the pain we experience in our feelings. In our culture, many equate emotional struggles with spiritual weakness or even mental disturbances.

The vast majority of human beings struggle from time to time with depression. We call it "feeling blue," or "being down." Some of the great saints of the Bible struggled with these same kinds of feelings. Read about Elijah in 1 Kings 19 or about Moses in Numbers 11. Or read through the Psalms and hear the pain and despair in King David's heart from time to time.

The difference between those times and now is the way the church, in general, condemns or makes the battle against depression a moral issue. The general comments might be "You just need to pray more" or "You must have some unconfessed sin somewhere in your life." Such comments usually evoke more guilt, shame, or inadequacy, which only makes the problem worse, leaving the person in an even deeper tailspin.

I'm telling you that God expects more out of His church than those kinds of responses. Emotional pain and suffering are very real. Unfortunately, rather than helping people see God as their merciful Father, eternally filled with compassion and care, often our responses drive people further away from Him by heaping on guilt or shame.

The Scriptures indicate that God desires for us to draw near to Him in our time of need. It also says that we are to help those in need—whatever the need.

Larry Burkett

Daily Scripture Reading:
Esther 1-4

"Be imitators of God, therefore, as dearly loved children and live a life of love, just as Christ loved us and gave himself up for us as a fragrant offering and sacrifice to God" (Ephesians 5:1 NIV).

PERSONALITIES IN MARRIAGE

With rare exception, couples have different personalities, and as a result, they have different habits, abilities, and preferences.

Opposites do attract, but couples sometimes approach their marriages as combatants because of their different personalities. They may forget that they were originally attracted to each other because of their differences.

Personality differences don't have to be a source of conflict in your marriage. Compromise is the key, but how do you get there?

First, speak the truth, but consider the other person's side. A good marriage is built on a foundation of trust, and it doesn't take a lot of lying to destroy that foundation.

Second, don't keep things bottled up until you explode. Settle differences before you go to bed so the Enemy does not get a foothold.

Third, learn to work on the problem, not the person. Step back into a third-party position and seek a solution rather than trying to make a "point."

Fourth, develop an understanding of why your spouse responds the way he or she does. A good personality assessment (a free one is offered through Crown) can give each of you a better understanding of the other's personality.

By understanding each other's personalities, a couple can understand why they approach the same problem in different ways. This can give them a head start on anticipating and dealing with conflicts before they occur.

Chuck Bentley

Daily Scripture Reading:
Esther 5-10

"Bear one another's burdens, and thus fulfill the law of Christ"
(Galatians 6:2).

CHURCH ASSISTANCE

There will be times when Christians in need should approach their church families for financial assistance. That's totally biblical, and the precedent is seen clearly in Scripture.

Although most churches can help a family in need with daily living expenses, few are prepared to help with major, catastrophic medical bills. They just don't have the resources. Of course, we would have more available if the church would obey God's command of bringing the tithes into the storehouse.

The reason needs go unmet is because we, God's people, are mismanaging what God has provided, spending it on our own desires.

God has no shortage of funds in His economy. Rather, there is a shortage of vision among His people today. In Haggai 1:4-6 the prophet had stern words for the people of Judah because they put their own selfish needs ahead of the work within God's house. These words serve as quite a challenge to the American church today.

Ironically, by putting our own priorities first, we never have enough. Conversely, when we sacrificially obey God's commands, He will supernaturally multiply our resources, providing nothing less than an abundance.

It is the story of the five loaves and two fishes all over again. That should not take us by surprise, since God has already told us that He would respond to our faith and obedience in this manner.

Lord, show me how to help someone who is in need—either through my church or individually.

Larry Burkett

Daily Scripture Reading:
Ezra 7-8

*"It is the blessing of the Lord that makes rich,
and He adds no sorrow to it"*
(Proverbs 10:22).

OUR SECURITY

As we fight against the rampant materialism in our society, the serious danger our world is in becomes more obvious to me daily.

The goal of our lives, according to society, is to be rich or at least to live like we are. Without a doubt, even the poor in our country would not be considered impoverished when compared to most Third World countries.

And yet, in the U.S. there are children who are going to bed hungry tonight. I believe that the materialism and monetary poverty in this country are just symptoms of a great problem: emotional and spiritual poverty.

As a culture, because we are searching for significance and security in our lives, we put a high value on having things, on making lots of money, and on getting all we can.

As Christians, our significance comes from being the children of God—equals with Jesus, the Son of God! In John 17:21 Jesus prayed, *"That they may all be one; even as Thou, Father, art in Me, and I in Thee, that they also may be in Us; that the world may believe."*

As His children, God wants us to serve Him by loving those around us and revealing His nature to them by the way we live our lives.

Our security comes from knowing that God loves with an unlimited love—not from our income or the amount of money we have in the bank. Our significance comes from being His children.

Thank You, God, for being my loving Father.

Larry Burkett

Daily Scripture Reading:
Ezra 9-10

*"As obedient children, do not be conformed to the former lusts
which were yours in your ignorance, but like the Holy One
who called you, be holy yourselves also in all your behavior"*
(1 Peter 1:14-15).

Purposeful Obedience

Sometimes it can be difficult to do the things we want to do. When we became Christians, God began to change us from the inside, as the Holy Spirit began moving in us, creating new hearts with new desires.

As a new Christian, I surprised myself with the longing to be obedient to God in ways I'd never considered before. These longings changed the way I thought, and those new thoughts began to change the way I lived.

Often, though, I found myself, like Paul, doing the things I didn't want to do and not doing the things I did want to do. My behavior frustrated and disappointed me, and I think many people are feeling the same frustration.

One area is in stewardship. The Holy Spirit has placed a longing in our hearts to become good managers of what God has given us. We truly want to control our spending, give more to help others, get out of debt, and bring a balance into our financial lives. However, we find that the path to stewardship is difficult, and it's easy to stumble.

I've learned that it's okay to stumble, because when we are aware of our shortcomings and turn to Him, He can work more powerfully through us. Being obedient means being willing to do what God's Word says—regardless.

Are there ways you have failed to be obedient to God that you want to confess? Pray about it now.

Larry Burkett

Daily Scripture Reading:
Nehemiah 1-5

*"It is vain for you to rise up early, to retire late, to eat the bread
of painful labors; for He gives to His beloved even in his sleep"*
(Psalm 127:2).

BALANCING HOME AND WORK

It's difficult to maintain the correct balance between work, family, and other important things if you're working more than 60 hours per week. There may be occasional periods when excessive hours are necessary, but even in those times relationships suffer.

If you're a business owner, your actions affect a far greater range of people than just you and your family. When a business owner adopts an excessively long workday that seldom provides time for relaxation and other outside activities, he or she establishes an unwritten policy: "If you don't work long hours, you won't get ahead in this company." This puts the employees (particularly managers) under great stress and eventually makes them less productive.

Turnover in such companies is usually enormous, and they need high salaries to attract workers. The owners believe that if they pay their employees enough, they'll be able to retain them. But money is only a temporary motivator. It's true that too little pay will usually force good people out, but too much pay won't keep them on a job that totally dominates their lives.

When it comes to matters of work and life, strive to shine like a slowly burning candle in the darkness, not flame out like a shooting star. The number of hours you devote to your career can have severe implications for your children.

Remember, the Lord commanded that we rest from all work at least one day for every six that we work. Resting can be a testimony of faith.

Chuck Bentley

Daily Scripture Reading:
Nehemiah 6-7

"Hope does not disappoint, because the love of God has been poured out within our hearts through the Holy Spirit who was given to us"
(Romans 5:5).

HOPE FOR THE FUTURE

As we read our daily newspapers and watch the local and national news on television, we are disturbed by the violence, bloodshed, chaos, strife, and international unrest.

For unbelievers the future must look pretty dark. However, Christians know what is ahead and can have hope. In the Bible we read about the evidences of the fulfillment of biblical prophecy.

John Baillie wrote that "the future is in the hands of One who is preparing something better than eye hath seen, or ear heard, or has entered into the heart of man to conceive."

The psalmist says that the Lord is our light and salvation and that we should have no fear (see Psalm 27:1).

And, as Christians, we know that we are promised life in a happy place where we won't have hardships and casualties. We have an assurance that life there will be happiness, joy, and peace. This blessed hope allows us to look forward to that day.

"You have need of endurance, so that when you have done the will of God, you may receive what was promised" (Hebrews 10:36).

Larry Burkett

Daily Scripture Reading:
Nehemiah 8-10

"The effectual prayer of a righteous man can accomplish much"
(James 5:16).

EFFECTUAL PRAYER

All through the Bible we read about what was accomplished through prayer. When Elijah prayed, God sent fire from heaven. When Daniel prayed for his and his companions' lives, the hungry lions were unable to hurt them.

When the Assyrian army was advancing, Hezekiah prayed and his nation was spared for another generation.

In the New Testament we have example after example of the power of prayer. Peter prayed and Dorcas was brought to life. Paul prayed and many churches were established in Asia Minor and in Europe.

Seventeenth century theologian John Owen once said, "He who prays as he ought will endeavor to live as he prays."

The problems of our society could be resolved if our national leaders would go to God in prayer. Can you imagine what would happen if every session of Congress was begun with the representatives on their knees in prayer?

Our nation was founded by people who believed in prayer. Benjamin Franklin knew that there was only one power that could redeem the course of events: the power of prayer.

Abraham Lincoln said, "I have been driven many times to my knees by the overwhelming conviction that I had nowhere else to go."

How wonderful it would be if our nation's leadership lived by those values!

Have you made prayer a part of your daily schedule?

Think of several people and situations you will pray for today.

Larry Burkett

Daily Scripture Reading:
Nehemiah 11-13

"By this all men will know that you are my disciples,
if you have love for one another"
(John 13:35).

THE TEST OF DISCIPLESHIP

The message the Lord Jesus Christ gave His disciples just before going to be with the Father in Heaven is recorded in John 13 and 14. He announced His betrayal, His departure, and His return to receive His disciples unto Himself. For three years Jesus had ministered to them and taught them His way. These last words with His disciples would be vital in reinforcing all He had taught them.

There are many vital parts of the Christian's life. Caring for and witnessing to the lost is one part. Prayer, Bible study, and gathering together as a body for fellowship are all very essential to Christian growth. But caring for one another is the test of a disciple, because that, according to Jesus, is how everyone will know that we belong to Him.

We demonstrate the degree of our love for Christ by the way we give to other Christians. Giving to the needs of another demonstrates the sincerity of our love.

Remember, the household of faith is built on the foundation of brotherly love.

How do you think Christ views us if we show little concern for the needs of others? Can you pass the test of discipleship?

Larry Burkett

Daily Scripture Reading:
Malachi

"Be devoted to one another in brotherly love.
Honor one another above yourselves"
(Romans 12:10 NIV).

TREAT EMPLOYEES FAIRLY

I once asked Larry Burkett for his best advice for leading a ministry. I remember he did not even hesitate one second as he looked me in the eye and said, "Treat all people the same. Don't consider one better than the other. That approach has served me well whether in business or ministry." Larry was a true example of one who believed and practiced this principle.

Sometimes, people in authority are quick to criticize but slow to reward the work of their subordinates. Often, they are simply too busy to notice the achievements of the people they supervise. This will never pay long-term dividends on any level.

Negative consequences result from supervisors who look down on lower-strata workers. That attitude will be transmitted and received, and a barrier will be built between the two sides.

Instead, those in authority need to recognize that all people are important, regardless of income or education. If they find that they can't give the same honor and regard to all ranks within their business, they need to examine their heart and resolve the issue in a meaningful demonstration of respect.

When it comes to dealing with subordinates, there's no room for ego, because there is no self-made businessperson. Only God's blessing, and the combined efforts of a great many people, make anyone a success.

Chuck Bentley

Daily Scripture Reading:
1 Chronicles 1-2

*"If you then, being evil, know how to give good gifts
to your children, how much more shall your Father who is
in heaven give what is good to those who ask Him!"*
(Matthew 7:11).

THE GUILT TRAP

We sometimes fail to trust God because, inwardly, we believe that God wants to deprive us and punish us. It is important to remember that God does not punish us, His children; He chastens us. Chastening is always directed toward correction, which is always for the benefit of the person being chastened.

Through the Holy Spirit, our Father convicts of wrong actions. On the other hand, Satan accuses. Correction of our errors is what the Lord wants; Satan's desire is that we become depressed and despondent, convinced of our unworthiness to serve God. The Lord seeks to improve our service for Him, but Satan wants our guilt to paralyze us into idleness.

We must never forget that God loves us as His children, and what He does is always for our benefit. We must never allow difficulties to keep us from our Heavenly Father.

In Hebrews we read that Jesus is sitting at the right hand of the Father, making intercession for us.

God loved us when we were sinners. He will not stop loving us now if we sin.

"Commit your way to the Lord, trust also in Him. . . . He will bring forth your righteousness as the light, and your judgment as the noonday" (Psalm 37:5-6).

Larry Burkett

Daily Scripture Reading:
1 Chronicles 3-5

*"All that my eyes desired I did not refuse them. I did not
withhold my heart from any pleasure, for my heart was pleased
because of all my labor and this was my reward for all my labor"*
(Ecclesiastes 2:10).

ACCUMULATING THINGS

The tendency expressed in today's verse is what prompted Karl Marx to comment that capitalism destroys itself because it is humanistic and feeds its own greed.

Christianity in America has been the controlling influence on capitalism, because we practice self-control and moderation. But now we have become caught up with everyone else in the race to see who can accumulate the most things. As a result, we have lost our witness in that area.

A Christian businessman and his wife were asked to go on a trip to Haiti with a missionary group. It was their first trip into an impoverished culture and it was a life-changing experience.

The husband said, "I had always assumed we were helping a few ignorant natives who were really too lazy to do better. But instead, we saw fellow human beings who had been born into total poverty. Twice we were offered babies by women who desired, above all else, that their children be given a chance to live."

When we recognize that these kinds of needs exist, it should become easier to curb our temptations to accumulate things.

Remember what Peter said: *"In your knowledge, self-control, and in your self-control, perseverance, and in your perseverance, godliness"* (2 Peter 1:6).

Is your focus on accumulating more things or on what you can do for someone in need?

Larry Burkett

Daily Scripture Reading:
1 Chronicles 6

*"The flesh sets its desire against the Spirit, and the Spirit
against the flesh; for these are in opposition to one another,
so that you may not do the things that you please"*
(Galatians 5:17).

WANTS OR NEEDS

Balance and moderation are the keys to determining what is a need, want, or desire. How can you tell when your life is indulgent?

One sign is that you or your family must always have "better" than before. This could be cars, clothes, houses, or recreation equipment. Another sign is that you must always have better than others and find yourself trying to top their lifestyles.

Also, you find that you have a lot of things that you feel embarrassed about around other people.

Many people struggle with discerning between need and greed. The decision is not related to what we buy but, rather, to our attitude about things in general.

Without a doubt, it is easier in the short-run to give in to indulgence than it is to control it. I say short-run because in the long-run the result is a growing sense of restlessness and distance from God.

If you have experienced this, you are the only one who can do anything about it. It's your decision to make changes. If you want to, God will supply the power.

Once we recognize the need to control indulgent spending, something else becomes obvious: The money we don't spend on ourselves is now available to help someone else's need.

"Let everyone see that you are unselfish and considerate in all you do. Remember that the Lord is coming soon" (Philippians 4:5).

Larry Burkett

Daily Scripture Reading:
1 Chronicles 7:1-8:27

"Pray without ceasing"
(1 Thessalonians 1:17).

PRAYER HABITS

It's good to set aside a particular time or times each day for prayer. But, instead of being in prayer at just those times, we should be in an attitude of prayer all day—wherever we are.

Of course, I don't mean to pray aloud all day; that wouldn't be practical or reasonable. I have found, however, that it's easy to pray as you drive your car—just thanking the Lord for all you have or asking guidance for what you are about to do. If your particular job allows it, pray during your work time.

Your prayers must mean something to you if they are going to be effective. Without prayer, your life will be empty and discouraging. However, if you do pray "without ceasing," you'll find a peace that truly does pass all understanding.

If you try to make decisions without praying about them first, you'll be operating in your own strength and, in large part, just cheating yourself.

Prayer brings the blessings of God's will to your personal life and helps to keep you within God's plan. Pray when you are in trouble; pray when things are going well. Pray for forgiveness; ask for an outpouring of the Holy Spirit in your life. Pray for the salvation of others; pray for God's continued protection and grace. Pray sometimes when all you do is praise God for His goodness and faithfulness.

Make a list of some other things you can pray for, put it in your Bible, and then read Mark 11:24 as confirmation that your prayers will be answered.

Billy Graham wrote that "Heaven is full of answers to prayer for which no one ever bothered to ask."

Larry Burkett

Daily Scripture Reading:
1 Chronicles 8:28-9:44

"A good man leaves an inheritance for his children's children,
but a sinner's wealth is stored up for the righteous"
(Proverbs 13:22 NIV).

LEAVING A LEGACY

Certainly this proverb makes it clear that a good man thinks well beyond his own needs and makes plans for an inheritance that will extend to his grandchildren.

I have always admired the philosophy of R.G. and Evelyn LeTourneau, who were more concerned with leaving their children to meet the needs of the world than leaving the world to meet the needs of their children. Often we fail to realize that an inheritance can be so much richer than the passing on of money to the next generation. Allow me a few other possible "inheritances" for your consideration:

1. Leave a legacy of righteousness in the way you conduct your life;
2. Leave a legacy of love in the way you treat others;
3. Leave a legacy of grace in the way you forgive faults;
4. Leave a legacy of faithfulness in the way that you love God;
5. Leave a legacy of joy in the way you endure hardships;
6. Leave a legacy of generosity in the way you liberally give;
7. Leave a legacy of character in the way you live out biblical values;
8. Leave a legacy of servanthood in the way you humbly care for others.

I had the privilege of attending Larry Burkett's memorial service. It was there that I was struck by the real legacy of this godly man. Not a person expressed gratitude for his financial wisdom or expansive ministry. Each person who spoke referenced a legacy that sounded much closer to the qualities listed above.

Yes, leave your children and grandchildren an inheritance, one that will endure far longer than a deposit in their bank account.

Chuck Bentley

Daily Scripture Reading: Matthew 1:1-17;
Mark 1:1; Luke 1:1-4, 3:23-38; John 1:1-18

"You shall not covet your neighbor's wife or his male servant or his female servant or his ox or his donkey or anything that belongs to your neighbor"
(Exodus 20:17).

COVETOUSNESS

Covetousness is desiring to have what belongs to others. This is a characteristic that rears its head when we begin to compare ourselves with others and see what they have that we don't have—but would like to.

We tend to measure our successes against the achievements of friends or family or even fellow church members. Often career choices are made, based on gaining the status, income, or prestige others have, rather than what is truly best.

To avoid covetousness, take the long-term view: Understand that God has a unique plan for you. Fulfillment comes by seeking His will and His way and following His plan. You'll only reap frustration when you covet someone else.

Remember, *"This you know with certainty, that no immoral or impure person or covetous man, who is an idolater, has an inheritance in the kingdom of Christ and God"* (Ephesians 5:5).

Lord, show me if there is any covetousness in me.

Larry Burkett

Daily Scripture Reading:
Luke 1:5-80

"Create in me a clean heart, O God,
and renew a steadfast spirit within me"
(Psalm 51:10).

A CLEAN HEART

We read in Jeremiah 17:9 that our hearts are desperately wicked. Our hearts need the changes that come from receiving grace, which is a free gift from God. Grace is literally the divine influence on our hearts and is reflected in the lives we live.

The heart wants its way, but there are many times when we should not follow the leading of our hearts.

Having a clean heart will come from praying for the Holy Spirit to guide you in all your attitudes and actions.

"[Jesus] *said, 'Not all of you are clean'"* (John 13:11).

Larry Burkett

Daily Scripture Reading:
Matthew 1:18-2:23; Luke 2

"We can make our own plans, but the LORD gives the right answer. People may be pure in their own eyes, but the LORD examines their motives. Commit your actions to the LORD, and your plans will succeed"
(Proverbs 16:1-3 NLT).

THE RIGHT MOTIVE FOR BEING FINANCIALLY FREE

You can make great financial decisions in life, but unless your motives are aligned with God's purposes, those decisions have no eternal value.

For example, getting out of debt is biblical. But if your motive for getting out of debt is to be your own master or to live at a higher standard than your neighbors, recognize that this is pride.

Your motive for getting out of debt should be centered on God, not yourself. The Bible says that you are to have only one Master. You are never to claim that you have no Master, even when you are debt free and have sufficient money to do whatever you dream of doing.

Your motivation for getting out of debt should be to become free from your false Master, the Lender, and become a slave only to Christ. This will allow Him total freedom to use you according to His will.

True stewardship is ordering your life in such a way that God can freely spend you, not so that you can freely spend whatever you want. That motive will enable you to resist pride and be used for eternal purposes.

Chuck Bentley

Daily Scripture Reading: Matthew 3:1-4:11; Mark 1:2-13; Luke 3:1-23, 4:1-13; John 1:19-34

"A man with an evil eye hastens after wealth,
and does not know that want will come upon him"
(Proverbs 28:22).

GET RICH QUICK

The basic premise of all get-rich-quick schemes is to make a lot of money with very little effort—fast! A typical get-rich-quick "opportunity" involves investing in an area you know little or nothing about. It leads you to risk money you can't afford to lose and forces you to make snap decisions. Most of the time this leads to "get-poor-quicker" instead of get-rich-quick.

You can avoid falling into a get-rich-quick snare if you will set a minimum time to pray and seek God's direction, never risk money you can't afford to lose, never become involved with things you don't understand, demand enough information for a thorough evaluation, and seek counsel from knowledgeable and impartial Christians.

Be a good steward of what God has entrusted to you.

"Let no man deceive himself. If any man among you thinks that he is wise in this age, let him become foolish that he may become wise. For the wisdom of this world is foolishness before God. For it is written, 'He is the One Who catches the wise in their craftiness'" (1 Corinthians 3:18-19).

Larry Burkett

Daily Scripture Reading:
John 1:35-3:36

278

"My dishonor is before me, and my humiliation has overwhelmed me, because of the voice of him who reproaches and reviles"
(Psalm 44:5-16).

CHRISTIAN TESTIMONY

I met a man years ago who was using some very unethical practices in his life. In fact, I met him as a result of counseling another Christian who had just finished a real estate transaction with this man and had been cheated.

In the course of having lunch one day with the man who had cheated, I challenged him, telling him that I knew what he'd done and asking why, as a Christian, he would willfully deceive another Christian.

"Well," he said, "that's just a bad habit of mine, but I don't let anyone know I'm a Christian, because I don't want to reflect my bad image on Jesus Christ." In other words, he thought it was all right to be dishonest and deceitful as long as no one knew he was a Christian.

It is not all right for any Christian to do that. God requires us to be honest and tell the truth, with no exaggerations and without leaving out any pertinent details.

A Christian testimony is necessary, in every aspect of our lives, if God is going to be able to use us in an effective way.

"He who walks in a blameless way is the one who will minister to me" (Psalm 101:6).

Lord, help me to walk daily in a blameless way so that I can be a Christian witness for you.

Larry Burkett

Daily Scripture Reading: Matthew 4:12-17;
Mark 1:14-15; Luke 4:14-30; John 4

"Because you. . . did not ask for riches, wealth, or honor. . . but you have asked for yourself wisdom and knowledge. . . wisdom and knowledge have been granted to you. And I will give you riches and wealth and honor"
(2 Chronicles 1:11-12).

TWO WAYS TO VIEW WEALTH

To most people being wealthy means having an abundance of money. However, this falls short of what God's Word describes as true wealth.

The worldly view of money is temporal. The biblical meaning is not restricted to money and earthly possessions. It goes far beyond the temporal values to include heavenly and eternal riches.

In Acts 5 we read about Ananias and Sapphira, short-sighted Christians who failed to realize the meaning of wealth and allowed Satan to fill their hearts with evil. As a result of their actions, they died.

On the other hand, Solomon wasn't concerned with earthly wealth and, instead, asked for wisdom to rule God's people. Because he wasn't greedy, God gave him what he didn't ask for—riches and wealth.

True wealth is never obtained by greed or selfishness; only the world's wealth is achieved that way. God's wealth is gained through ministering to others, and it lasts forever.

If you were given the choice between wisdom and wealth, which would you choose? How wealthy are you? What is the source of your wealth?

Larry Burkett

Daily Scripture Reading: Matthew 4:18-25, 8:2-4, 14-17;
Mark 1:16-45; Luke 4:31-5:16

"Be still before the LORD and wait patiently for him"
(Psalm 37:7 NIV).

GETTING OUT OF DEBT

Once you've established the right motive for getting out of debt, which is to be free and ready to serve God, pick the first debt you want to pay off. A high-interest debt is always a good one to tackle first. Or, pick the one that's troubling you most—one that never seems to go away.

Select a realistic date for when you can pay off this debt and make a commitment to someone regarding your goal. Choose someone who will hold you accountable, and ask that person to check in with you and be an encouragement to you—not to embarrass you but to love you when the going gets tough.

Adjust your lifestyle to your goal and eliminate any nonessential spending that could hinder your success. Then, get started.

Make your repayment process "visible" by putting marbles in a jar or using a "countdown" paper chain or placing notes on your bathroom mirror. This will constantly remind you of your progress.

Set target dates for paying off portions of the debt, and when you reach those milestones, give yourself an inexpensive reward.

Don't be discouraged. Repayment goes faster than you think, and people frequently share stories of how God shortened the time they thought it would take to eliminate their debt. So, stick with it!

Finally, remember that God owns everything. We are only stewards of the resources He entrusts to us. So, be generous and give back to His Kingdom.

Chuck Bentley

Daily Scripture Reading: Matthew 9:1-17;
Mark 2:1-22; Luke 5:17-39

*"Do nothing from selfishness nor from empty conceit,
but with humility of mind let each of you consider
other people as more important than yourself"*
(Philippians 2:3).

GIVE HONOR

If you are an employer, do you give honor to those who work for you? Or does your employer give honor to you as an employee?

I'm afraid we believe that unless we elevate ourselves above others we are failures. The "Indian/Chief" principle was not established by God. There is no caste system in God's family.

If you are a supervisor or manager, are you building up or tearing down people? Are you trying to honor them? The word honor means to give a position of worth. That doesn't mean you have to pay them as much as you make. The amount is between you and the Lord.

What it does mean is that you honor them by showing the people who are making lower salaries that they are as important to the success of the business as the salespeople who are generating $1 million a year in income.

Another way to give honor is by controlling your tongue. For every fault you find in a person, you should look for two positive characteristics to build that person up. God says to give honor to those below us and above us.

God wants us to have compassion on the people around us, to care about them and to love them. There is no greater testimony a Christian can have in business than to show honor toward others.

Do you show honor to your employer (or to your employees)? Pray about what changes you can make in this area.

Larry Burkett

Daily Scripture Reading: Matthew 12:1-21;
Mark 2:23-3:12; Luke 6:1-11; John 5

"The Lord said to [Ananias], 'Go, for he is a chosen instrument of Mine, to bear My name before the Gentiles and kings and the sons of Israel' "
(Acts 9:15).

THE APOSTLE PAUL

My favorite person in the New Testament, outside of the Lord, is the apostle Paul. He's my kind of guy. I think Paul probably had the same personality type I do: "D," dominant, decision maker. It could be said of us both: "often wrong, but never in doubt."

Paul was impetuous and charged ahead, and whatever God told Paul to do, he did it.

On his last journey into Jerusalem, the Christians begged Paul to stay because the prophet Agabus said Paul was going to be bound and cast into prison.

Paul's response was, "Why do you break my heart so? Don't you know that God has also told me this. I must do what God has told me to do."

I admire Paul for his boldness, his ability to speak up for the Lord but, also, for his humility. He never thought more highly of himself than he should have.

I believe all of his characteristics made him useful to the Lord. I love the concise writings of Paul, which fill a large part of the New Testament.

He was a man who liked to pay his own way and was willing to suffer whatever it took to serve the Lord.

Paul said of himself, *"I can do all things through Christ who strengthens me"* (Philippians 4:13). Are you claiming this for yourself?

Larry Burkett

Daily Scripture Reading: Matthew 5;
Mark 3:13-19; Luke 6:12-36

*"He also forced everyone, small and great, rich and poor,
free and slave, to receive a mark on his right hand or on his
forehead, so that no one could buy or sell unless he had the mark,
which is the name of the beast or the number of his name"*
(Revelation 13:16-17 NIV).

THE FINAL CHOICE: MONEY OR GOD

Now I have no interest in predicting the End Times or debating Eschatology. This is not my calling or reason for this statement. But the Bible says we must choose between two masters, God or money, and a day will come when people will be given a final choice between these two.

Revelation 13 is known for the first reference to the "mark of the beast," but it is often overlooked as a passage about money. Here is what the final choice will be:

1. Accept Satan's mark and have "security" to be able to buy and sell in the marketplace of man's economy, or

2. Choose what will then appear to be the less secure path of trusting God, knowing you will be shut out from the marketplace where you buy food, clothing, and housing and transact business. Furthermore, persecution will immediately follow those who do not comply.

Let's recognize that the choice presented here hits at our core need for "security." So, let's trust God now as our only Master and make the choice that we will derive our security from Him and not money or possessions.

In Matthew 6:31-33 Jesus said, *"So do not worry, saying, 'What shall we eat?' or 'What shall we drink?' or 'What shall we wear?' For the pagans run after all these things, and your heavenly Father knows that you need them. But seek first his kingdom and his righteousness, and all these things will be given to you as well"* (NIV).

Chuck Bentley

Daily Scripture Reading:
Matthew 6-7; Luke 6:37-49

"Commit your works to the Lord, and your plans will be established"
(Proverbs 16:3).

WHY SOME CHRISTIANS FAIL

Many people believe that whatever they can conceive and believe they can achieve. This kind of positive thinking and success motivation require goal setting, to which those people attribute the successes in their lives.

However, all too often these goals are centered on personal success, and the plans to accomplish them become selfish and ultimately self-defeating.

In 1 Corinthians 13, God tells us that whatever is done for self is profitless, and only that which is done out of love will benefit self. This creates a paradox: to be successful we must make someone else successful; to be leaders, we must be servants.

In order for our plans to be established, our works must be committed to God. It is evident that selfish goals cannot be committed to God—only unselfish ones.

Therefore, the prerequisite for receiving God's help in our planning is the commitment of the end result to God. The problem is that many works cannot be committed to God because of their very nature. At that point, Christians rob themselves of God's help. To paraphrase James 4:3: We ask and don't receive because we ask with wrong motives.

The answer to whether you will succeed or fail is found in today's Scripture verse. Read it prayerfully.

Larry Burkett

Daily Scripture Reading:
Matthew 8:1, 5-13; 11:2-30; Luke 7

285

"Blessed is the nation whose God is the Lord,
the people whom He has chosen for His own inheritance"
(Psalm 33:12).

CHRISTOPHER COLUMBUS

Historically we have celebrated Columbus Day to honor Christopher Columbus as the explorer who is credited for having discovered America.

If you read your history books, however, you'll find that long before Columbus arrived America had been discovered by the Nordic tribes who visited America regularly—as far back as about A.D. 1000.

You probably learned the same rhyme in school that I did: "In 1492 Columbus sailed the ocean blue" but do you remember why he faced peril to discover another continent? We are told that he was searching for a new, shorter trade route to the Dutch West Indies.

However, I've read parts of the reprint of Columbus' diary and it reveals something else. He had heard reports from some of the other navigators that there was another continent in the northern part of the hemisphere, and he believed it was his responsibility to reach that continent with the Lord's plan of salvation.

His diary, as you read it, reflects a devout Christian who daily sought the Lord both in Scripture and in prayer. Isn't it a shame that in our schools today none of that is reflected in our history books?

Was this God's way of reseeding Christianity—by sending Christopher Columbus? Was this God's method of bringing the Word to the New World? I believe it was. We are the most Christian nation in the world and God has used us as no other nation.

Join me in paying tribute to this brave Christian.

Larry Burkett

Daily Scripture Reading: Matthew 12:22-50;
Mark 3:20-35; Luke 8:1-21

*"Call to me and I will answer you and tell you
great and unsearchable things you do not know"*
(Jeremiah 33:3 NIV).

DIVINE INSPIRATION

Our world contains some 300,000 species of plants and 900,000 species of insects. And in the observable universe, there are an estimated 170 billion galaxies. Our God is awesome, and He provides for us in unseen ways through creativity and ideas.

Imagination and creativity are avenues through which God shares His thoughts with us. He wants us to turn to Him and ask for new ideas, insights, and inspiration.

When we receive these thoughts, it is important to acknowledge that they come from Him. We should never take credit for divine inspiration. Instead, we should follow the example of Daniel, who gave credit to God after he was divinely inspired not only to interpret King Nebuchadnezzar's dream but also to first tell him what he had dreamed (Daniel 2:27-28).

You must seek the Lord and know His Word in order to determine if your thoughts are consistent with His. Be very, very humble and walk in reverence before God. Be careful not to open yourself up to vain, conceited thoughts and claim they are from Him.

Divine inspiration should be combined with work, diligence, and planning. Don't ask God for the correct numbers to win the lottery or seek to manipulate Him in some other way to become rich quickly. God commended Solomon for not asking for foolish things (1 Kings 3:11-14).

Chuck Bentley

Daily Scripture Reading:
Matthew 13:1-53; Mark 4:1-34

"Who regards you as superior? And what do you have
that you did not receive? But if you did receive it,
why do you boast as if you had not received it?"
(1 Corinthians 4:7).

WHAT FAULTS?

In order to cure a disease, we must first be able to recognize its symptoms, which are visible, outside indicators. Although we may not always recognize these symptoms in ourselves, others will. So it becomes vital for us to stay open to criticism, particularly from those who are spiritually discerning.

The people most consistent in discerning our faults are usually our spouses. God has placed them in our lives as a balance, and they will help to offset our extremes if we will listen.

This works both ways, because we also are balance for them. I'll have to say that more often than not it is the husband who refuses to take counsel from his wife. Why? Pride.

Once we are trapped by pride, we can be of no service to God. We must accept criticism, humble ourselves, call on His mercy and forgiveness.

Make me aware, Father, of any pride in my life, and help me to overcome it.

Larry Burkett

Daily Scripture Reading: Matthew 8:18, 23-24; 9:18-34;
Mark 4:35-5:43; Luke 8:22-56

*"Just as you abound in everything, in faith and utterance
and knowledge and in all earnestness and in love. . . , see
that you abound in this gracious work also"*
(2 Corinthians 8:7).

CHRISTIAN BUSINESS

The goal of Christian businesspeople should be to use their organizations as vehicles to share Christ with other people.

Businesspeople should be Christ's representatives to employees, to creditors, and to customers.

Also the minimum expected from a Christian business must be a quality product or service at a fair price. Sadly, not all Christian organizations measure up to this standard. It's a small wonder that so many unbelievers have a bad perspective of Christianity.

If Christian businesses don't have excellence, they will not be able to witness to the customers.

Though there's nothing specifically mentioned in God's Word about it, I'm sure Paul made the best tents and Jesus, the carpenter's son, made excellent furniture. We can do no less.

"Do you see a man skilled in his work? He will stand before kings; he will not stand before obscure men" (Proverbs 22:29).

Larry Burkett

Daily Scripture Reading: Matthew 13:54-58, 9:35-11:1, 14:1-12;
Mark 6:1-30; Luke 9:1-10

"A scoffer does not love one who reproves him, he will not go to the wise"
(Proverbs 15:12).

YOUR SINS WILL FIND YOU OUT

There is nothing more devastating to a believer than looking spiritual while living in defeat. The immediate consequence is the loss of esteem in the eyes of family and close friends.

One couple shared how God had used their daughter to shake them out of their complacency about deception and hypocrisy. It seems they were selling their home, which had a significant problem with flooding in a basement playroom. During the dry winter season, they replaced the carpets and put the house on the market.

They were showing it to a very interested buyer, and when they went to the playroom the potential buyer mentioned that the carpet looked new.

"Sure," the small daughter replied, "the old carpet got wet every time it rained."

This came as a shock, since the couple had skillfully avoided any mention of a water problem. The buyer left, but not without a thorough discussion of ethics and Christianity.

You see, the couple selling the home was a well-known pastor and his wife. Later he told me, "We allowed our personal needs to choke out our spiritual values. God simply used the honesty of a young child to expose us."

The truth revealed will make you truly free; concealing facts will make you a captive of your own hypocrisy.

"Do not let kindness and truth leave you . . . write them on the tablet of your heart. So you will find favor and good repute in the sight of God and man" (Proverbs 3:3).

Larry Burkett

Daily Scripture Reading: Matthew 14:13-36; Mark 6:31-56;
Luke 9:11-17; John 6:1-21

*"[God] alone is my refuge, my place of safety;
he is my God, and I am trusting him"*
(Psalm 91:2 TLB).

SHOULD I HAVE FEAR?

Fear has a very useful function. If you didn't have fear, you'd be roadkill.

I have a friend who has no fear of physical peril, and it's a real detriment to him. In his lifetime, he's probably had 200 broken bones and is a terror to be around.

He goes hang gliding in the Alps, jumps off buildings, scuba dives in underwater caves, jumps motorcycles for fun—crazy things.

We are supposed to fear some things. However, there are some people who live in dread and fear, and that's wrong too. They let fear control their lives.

There should be a healthy balance for fear in your life. You should have a cautious regard for your own safety but not enough to let it control your life.

The writer of Hebrews says, *"Since we, God's children, are human beings. . . he became flesh and blood too. . . . Only in that way could he deliver those who through fear of death have been living all their lives as slaves to constant dread"* (Hebrews 2:14-15 TLB).

Larry Burkett

Daily Scripture Reading: Matthew 15:1-20;
Mark 7:1-23; John 6:22-7:1

"The fear of the Lord is the beginning of wisdom"
(Psalm 111:10).

FEAR OF THE LORD

We know that *"perfect love casts out fear"* (1 John 4:18), so you would think that there would be no place for persistent fear. We are assured time and again in God's Word that we don't need to fear the future; He will take care of us.

But what about another kind of fear—fear of God? Do I fear God? Oh yes, but it's the kind of fear that is the beginning of wisdom. You can replace the word "fear" with "reverence" or "awe." We should be in awe of God: His power, His love, His grace, His compassion. How could we not be in awe of Him?

As believers, we should have that kind of fear, which is actually reverence for God.

Then there's the fear of God's judgment. *"Justice for man comes from the Lord"* (Proverbs 29:26). *"We shall all stand before the judgment seat of God"* (Romans 14:10).

I believe I would sum it all up by quoting yet another verse: *"The fear of the Lord prolongs life, but the years of the wicked will be shortened"* (Proverbs 10:27).

God said it. I believe it!

Larry Burkett

Daily Scripture Reading: Matthew 15:21-16:20;
Mark 7:24-8:30; Luke 9:18-21

"The heart of the discerning acquires knowledge;
the ears of the wise seek it out"
(Proverbs 18:15 NIV).

SEVEN PRINCIPLES OF INVESTING

When it comes to investing, there are pitfalls and blessings, rewards and penalties, events that are unexpected and some that are unpredictable.

Surviving the world of investing requires wisdom, and the best source of wisdom is God. Seven principles will help you make the most of your investing experience.

1. All debt should be short-term, it should not be your normal way of operating, and it should be taken on without surety (only borrow up to the value of the collateral asset). Use cash whenever possible.

2. Diversify your investments, and place your money in things with a proven record of long-term growth. Never completely turn your money over to someone else, avoid fads, and invest in something you know.

3. Avoid a get-rich-quick mentality. Have the wisdom to show restraint, and pursue your goals slowly.

4. Invest intelligently, because anything else is like gambling. Read a book and study the field you are interested in learning about.

5. Seek godly counsel. Make sure your heart and the heart of your counselors are matched. Be sure that your counselors are looking out for your best interests.

6. Check your motive for investing, which should be to help your family and God's Kingdom. Determine how much is enough and give the rest to the Lord.

7. Count the cost. Understand that the money you invest is at risk and that you could suffer losses. If you're not comfortable with risk, you're a saver, not an investor.

Chuck Bentley

Daily Scripture Reading: Matthew 16:21-17:27;
Mark 8:31-9:32; Luke 9:22-45

"A friend loves at all times, and a brother is born for adversity"
(Proverbs 17:17).

LOYALTY

Although I've taught and written a lot about integrity being important, there is another characteristic that is vital in living: loyalty. Loyalty seems to be a lost art in our society. When people are in the midst of adversity, all too often others tend to abandon them.

Webster says that to be loyal means to be "unswerving in allegiance" and to be "faithful to a person, cause, ideal, custom, institution, or product."

Christians have a reputation for being a group that "kills their wounded." When people are down, we tend to judge them instead of help them.

Even if people have brought the trouble on themselves, God's Word teaches that we are to act in love. It says that if we see someone in need and have the ability to help and don't, how can we say that the love of God abides in us?

In the Old Testament Absalom asked Hushai: *"Is this your loyalty to your friend? Why did you not go with your friend?"* (2 Samuel 16:17).

Certainly integrity should be a minimum requirement in Christians, but the second most valuable quality is loyalty.

To whom can you show your loyalty today?

Don't forget, Jesus said, *"A new commandment I give to you, that you love one another, even as I have loved you, that you have love for one another"* (John 13:34).

Larry Burkett

Daily Scripture Reading: Matthew 8:19-22; 18
Mark 9:33-50; Luke 9:46-62; John 7:2-10

"God is faithful, through whom you were called into
fellowship with His Son, Jesus Christ our Lord"
(1 Corinthians 1:9).

GOD IS FAITHFUL

Through my suffering I have learned one thing for sure: God is a faithful God. He also is a forgiving God who will forgive anything and everything on the basis of the sacrifice of His Son, the Lord Jesus.

In contrast, He forgives nothing, no matter how small the offense, on the basis of how good we are or how acceptable we are or whether we have more positives than negatives in our lives.

God is merciful. He cares about your suffering, whether it is mental, physical, emotional, or spiritual.

My favorite Bible character, in regard to suffering, is King David, who suffered a lot in his life. He suffered at the hands of a maniacal King Saul and ran for his life with Saul in hot pursuit. Yet God protected David because He still had plans for his life.

Yes, David did die—as all flesh must. Bear in mind, though, that no one can remove us one second before God decides it's our time.

God has plans that are at work in your life. He hasn't completed His work in you, so be sure you are putting Him first in your life and seeking His will for you.

Father, I read in Lamentations 3:22-23 that Your lovingkindness never ceases and Your compassion never fails but is new every morning. Thank You, Father.

Larry Burkett

Daily Scripture Reading:
John 7:11-8:59

*"You ask and do not receive, because you ask with
wrong motives, so that you may spend it on your pleasures"*
(James 4:3).

HOW TO BE A SUCCESS

The world's view of success does not agree with God's view. What are you willing to sacrifice to achieve success according to God's way?

In many national magazines, there are ads promising to reveal the secrets of being a "success" today. Naturally, the ads are obscure enough that they don't reveal these "secrets" unless you respond. But the implication is clear enough: Success today is related to money, power, and position.

It's really not much different today than it has been. We first look at the material accumulation to determine if someone is successful. The admiration of society is carried one step further because even those who earn their wealth by deceit, extortion, or pornography are elevated to a platform of success today.

Most of those we call successful people today are frustrated and miserable, with terrible family lives; and, quite often they terminate their lives because they have nothing left to live for. The worst thing that can happen to those without Christ is to accomplish their goals, because then there is the potential that they may turn out to be worthless.

A successful person is one who accomplishes goals and is able to enjoy the benefits that result.

Larry Burkett

Daily Scripture Reading:
Luke 10:1-11:36

"Lord, my heart is not proud. . .nor do I involve myself
in great matters, or in things too difficult for me"
(Psalm 131:1).

BUSINESS BONDAGE

Business bondage is anything that disrupts your priority system as a Christian. If you are a stay-at-home wife and your husband is in business, you are a part of that business with him. God created you as a working unit, so you need to understand God's principles and then help your husband.

A Christian's priority system should begin with an active, viable personal relationship with Jesus Christ. That means reading and getting truth and direction from God's Word on a regular basis. It also means communicating with and praying to God.

Any Christian who is so involved with business that he or she has no time to study God's Word, to pray, or to get involved with other people and their needs is in bondage.

Also, a Christian who is unable to communicate and meet the needs of his or her spouse is in business bondage.

Third, a Christian must be able to meet the needs of his or her children. We are responsible for the training of our children, and if we fail in raising our children God is not pleased.

Being in balance with the world's system is risky, because the world has never been in balance with God's system.

If you or your spouse are required to work 10, 12, or 14 hours a day to do a good job, to make more money, or just to get ahead, watch out. That's bondage.

If you are in bondage, because of business or for any other reason, ask God to help you bring balance into your life today.

Larry Burkett

Daily Scripture Reading:
Luke 11:37-13:21

"The waywardness of the naive shall kill them,
and the complacency of fools shall destroy them"
(Proverbs 1:32).

LEARNING SELF-DISCIPLINE

Being legalistic and rigid is not a cure for the lack of self-discipline. Both conditions are extremes and are beyond scriptural boundaries.

Self-sacrifice does not ensure spirituality and often is the indicator of self-centeredness. For instance, if the time you spend watching television is robbing you of time in God's Word, set a realistic time limit. Determine to watch television only between certain hours and no more.

In financial decisions, self-discipline should be the norm, but they must be balanced by reason. Overreacting will result in frustration and failure. It also will create conflict in the home. Instead, create the goals of a budget and a balanced bank account.

Whether your lack of self-discipline is in spending, entertainment, gossiping, eating, or some other area, correcting the problem can free your mind of doubts, frustrations, and bondage.

Only by knowing and applying self-discipline can you have self-respect and develop a godly self-image.

Larry Burkett

Daily Scripture Reading:
John 9-10

"The rich rule over the poor, and the borrower is servant to the lender"
(Proverbs 22:7 NIV).

PRINCIPLES OF BORROWING

In recent decades, debt has become a way of life for many people. Personal, corporate, and government debt have skyrocketed, putting families, companies, and citizens at risk.

God's Word doesn't specifically say, "Do not borrow." However, it does contain warnings about borrowing. Following are some principles that you, as a borrower, should know.

1. Debt is not normal. The U.S. economy has become virtually dependent on a constant expansion of credit. But God's people should manage their finances differently. Instead of being servants of lenders, we need to be servants of God.

2. Avoid long-term debt. In Israel, the rule was: *"At the end of every seven years you must cancel debts"* (Deuteronomy 15:1 NIV). Today, the typical mortgage is for 30 years. Make every effort to pay off your mortgage early.

3. Avoid surety. Proverbs 6 warns against accepting an obligation to pay for someone's loan if you lack a guaranteed way to make the payments. The only way to avoid surety is by backing up what you borrow with collateral, or property, that covers the debt if needed.

4. Pay what you owe. Paying back a debt may be painful, but it will add great blessing to your life when you maintain your credibility by paying everyone that you owe.

Chuck Bentley

Daily Scripture Reading:
Luke 13:22-15:32

"A joyful heart is good medicine, but a broken spirit dries the bones"
(Proverbs 17:22).

A JOYFUL HEART

The name "Yahweh" is actually an American attempt to say a word that can't be pronounced. The word is "yhwh," with no vowels. So the closest we can come to pronouncing it is to say Yahweh.

Interestingly enough, when you say that over and over, it sounds like laughter. Laughter is universal, and it is the name of God. God is the God of Abraham, Isaac (which means laughter) and Jacob—the God of laughter!

There are many purposes for laughter, but the primary purpose would be to heal our souls, our spirits, and even to heal us physically. Science is now learning that when we laugh, we release endorphins, which help heal our bodies and stimulate our immune systems.

It's important for each of us to have a good sense of humor and be able to even laugh at ourselves sometimes. It makes it easier to go through difficult times.

I believe God gave us laughter to gladden our souls. If we are going to be "light" to the unsaved, we must act like we are happy with what we have.

"He will yet fill your mouth with laughter, and your lips with shouting" (Job 8:21).

Larry Burkett

Daily Scripture Reading:
Luke 16:1-17:10; John 11:1-54

300

"Hear, my son, and accept my sayings,
and the years of your life will be many"
(Proverbs 4:10).

LONG LIFE

God gave us a promise: If we would put into practice the principles He teaches, we would have a long life.

I believe that the illnesses we have are a result of violating many of the dietary rules. And many of the problems we encounter are the result of not living by His Word.

I would say, without hesitation, biblical ethics and long life go together. For instance, when you give your word, you keep it. When you marry, you commit yourself to your spouse for a lifetime. When you have a job to do, you do your absolute best.

God's Word says, *"As for the days of our life, they contain seventy years, or if due to strength, eighty years"* (Psalm 90:10).

Larry Burkett

Daily Scripture Reading: Matthew 19:1-15;
Mark 10:1-16; Luke 17:11-18:17

*"Godliness actually is a means of great gain, when
accompanied by contentment. . . . If we have food
and covering, with these we shall be content"*
(1 Timothy 6:6-8).

CONTENTMENT

Contentment does not mean complacency. Complacency means that I have a problem that I could change, but I don't put forth the effort.

Contentment means that I know that I'm in the center of God's will. I change the things I can. The things I can't change I am willing to accept and be content with because I know the One who is in control.

The secret of a happy life is to learn how to deal with both the good times and the bad and, like the apostle Paul, to know how to be content with either.

If anything is standing between you and contentment, pray about that right now and turn it over to the Lord.

Larry Burkett

Daily Scripture Reading: Matthew 19:16-20:28;
Mark 10:17-45; Luke 18:18-34

"Blessed are the poor in spirit, for theirs is the kingdom of heaven"
(Matthew 5:3).

POOR IN SPIRIT

When I think about the poor in spirit I think of the contrast between the humble and the haughty.

Jesus was not talking about the physically poor but those who were humble. Since He said, "Blessed are the poor in spirit," then He probably would have said, "Cursed are the haughty in spirit."

In fact, He did say that. He told us in His Word that to the extent you exalt yourself in this lifetime you will be humbled for all of eternity.

If we humble ourselves in true service to God, it will include being a servant in the true sense of the word, not just to Him but to those around us.

I think the perfect example of being poor in spirit (humble) is when Jesus washed the disciples' feet.

Our humility can be shown in taking a less prominent position at church but giving it all we've got. It means being willing to sit back and let someone else take the credit for what we've done without being resentful.

I appreciate the verse in Proverbs that says, *"Before honor comes humility"* (Proverbs 15:33).

Larry Burkett

Daily Scripture Reading: Matthew 20:29-34, 26:6-13; Mark 10:46-52, 14:3-9; Luke 18:35-19:28; John 11:55-12:11

"The word of the Lord came to Jonah. . . saying, 'Arise, go to Nineveh the great city, and cry against it, for their wickedness has come up before Me' "
(Jonah 1:1-2).

WRONG DECISION

We are servants of the Most High God and He has the right to tell us what to do. When He told Jonah to go to Nineveh, He was saying, "Do what I tell you to."

When one of my sons didn't like something I told him to do, he said, "Dad, this isn't a very democratic way to run this family." Then I reminded him that in our home he didn't live in a democracy; he lived in a benevolent dictatorship.

I think God was teaching Jonah another lesson besides obedience: that God loves all of His creation, the good and the bad.

Jonah suspected when God sent him to Nineveh that He was going to forgive the Ninevites, and Jonah didn't want to go. Instead, he chose another direction and suffered for it.

So, God taught Jonah two lessons: "Do what you are told." And "I get to decide who is forgiven and who isn't."

"When God saw their deeds, that they turned from their wicked way, then God relented concerning the calamity which He had declared He would bring upon them. And He did not do it" (Jonah 3:10).

Larry Burkett

Daily Scripture Reading: Matthew 21:1-22; Mark 11:1-26;
Luke 19:29-48; John 12:12-50

"Be sure you know the condition of your flocks,
give careful attention to your herds"
(Proverbs 27:23 NIV).

BUDGETING MYTHS AND TRUTHS

It's easy to say "I can't" when you're faced with a difficult task, but when it comes to handling money, what's comfortable and routine isn't always best. Take budgeting, for example. You may say, "I tried it once before, and it didn't work." That may be true, but you don't perfect new skills on the first try. Instead, you learn from previous mistakes and experience.

Here are six other myths concerning budgeting.

1. "Because I live on a variable income, I can't budget." Plan your budget based on your average monthly income.

2. "It's impossible to budget for contingencies and unplanned expenses." Contingencies are one of the most important items to include in your budget. Build an emergency savings account to expect the unexpected.

3. "I can't have a budget because I'm not mathematically inclined." There are many easy forms and software that do the math for you. You simply have to plug in the numbers.

4. "We don't have enough income to budget." The smaller your income, the more you need a budget. Anyone can live beneath their means regardless of what they earn.

5. "We earn too much income to worry about a budget." Unfortunately, for many, as incomes rise, expenses rise at the same or greater rate. A budget can help you be a wise manager of your surplus.

6. "I don't have time to keep track of a budget." It takes far more time to handle a financial mess than it does to keep your finances in order. A budget will help you know where your money is going, and it takes less time than determining where your money went.

Chuck Bentley

Daily Scripture Reading: Matthew 21:23-22:14;
Mark 11:27-12:12; Luke 20:1-19

"What sort of people ought you to be in holy conduct and godliness"
(2 Peter 3:11).

TOO BUSY TO SERVE

Nothing interferes with our ability to serve God more than our need to earn a living. The simple truth is, most Americans are too busy to serve God.

We have grown complacent and comfortable in God's material blessings and have forgotten the first commandment. In the meantime, immorality and cults have grown to alarming proportions, because their advocates are more zealous in their dedication.

Since God asks for obedience, rather than demanding it, many Christians simply ignore the very reason for their existence: to glorify God.

Without exception, God has a unique and meaningful plan for every believer, and it does not depend on age, income, or ability.

God calls each of us to fulfill His plan and we have to decide either to be used by Him or to be bypassed. What a loss if we allow temporary comforts and laziness to rob us of true riches, both now and for all eternity.

Ask God to reveal to you if you have been "too busy to serve."

Larry Burkett

Daily Scripture Reading: Matthew 22:15-46;
Mark 12:13-37; Luke 20:20-44

"Just tell me what to do and I will do it, Lord.
As long as I live, I'll wholeheartedly obey"
(Psalm 119:33 TLB).

DEEPER RELATIONSHIP

From the first day that I accepted Christ as my Savior, I made this commitment to the Lord: "God, You know that I'm an ignorant person; I don't know a lot about You, so I only ask that whatever You want me to do You will make it very clear. As of this day, I pledge that I will never again be willfully disobedient."

The way to know more about God is by reading and studying His Word. You can't possibly know about Him unless you know what His Word says.

The way you get to know God personally is by spending time in prayer (talking to God). As I've said before, I've never heard His voice audibly, but I have sensed His presence many times, and I have sensed His direction.

God never gives direction in contrast to what He has already said in His Word. That is His will for us: His Word.

Just accepting Christ doesn't develop a personal relationship with the Lord. That would be like getting married and the two of you moving to opposite sides of the U.S. and not seeing one another for the next 50 years. You'd still be married, but you wouldn't have much of a relationship.

To deepen your relationship with God, get immersed in His Word (God speaking to you) and spend time in prayer (you speaking to God). It must be done one-on-one if you want it to be a personal relationship.

Larry Burkett

Daily Scripture Reading: Matthew 23;
Mark 12:38-44; Luke 20:45-21:4

"Moreover it is required in stewards that one be found faithful"
(1 Corinthians 4:2 NKJV).

MANAGE WELL

With December just around the corner, there's a resolution for the coming year that I hope you'll consider.

It's summed up in two words: manage well. Here are some tips to help you be successful.

First, ask God for self-control, which is produced as a result of abiding in the Spirit.

Second, resolve to become very disciplined. Consider establishing automated transfers each pay period for a goal that is important to your financial health. Use the money only for what you resolved to do.

Third, ask your spouse or a close friend to share your resolve to manage well, and encourage each other on a frequent basis. When someone joins you to accomplish a similar goal, it can add joy to the journey.

Fourth, take no shortcuts. We'd all like to believe that there's a simple, easy formula that will bring positive results with very little effort. But every great accomplishment requires great commitment.

All of these steps involve discipline, but as Solomon noted, *"People who accept discipline are on the pathway to life"* (Proverbs 10:17 NLT). And, with some early success, you might continue this resolution for the rest of your life.

Chuck Bentley

Daily Scripture Reading: Matthew 24:1-31;
Mark 13:1-27; Luke 21:5-27

"The prayer of the upright is His delight"
(Proverbs 15:8).

POWERFUL PRAYER

When Jesus' disciples attempted to cast out a demon, they couldn't. Then Jesus came along and cast it out, and the disciples asked, "Lord, why were we unable to do this?"

Jesus replied, "Only by prayer and fasting can you do this." Our Lord knew prayer and fasting were necessary in His own life in order to do His father's bidding on the earth (see Luke 6:12).

Prayer must be an integral part of a Christian's life; it is an intergalactic, ballistic missile that can span oceans, deserts, mountains, and galaxies.

Faster than the speed of light, prayer travels at the speed of God.

You don't even have to know what to say. As the apostle Paul wrote, *"We do not know how to pray as we should, but the Spirit Himself intercedes for us with groanings too deep for words"* (Romans 8:26).

Abraham Lincoln expressed his thoughts on prayer: "I have been driven many times to my knees by the overwhelming conviction that I had nowhere to go but prayer. My own wisdom and that of all about me seemed insufficient for the day."

How powerful is your prayer life?

Larry Burkett

Daily Scripture Reading: Matthew 24:32-26:5, 14-16;
Mark 13:28-14:2, 10-11; Luke 21:28-22:6

"O Thou who dost hear prayer, to Thee all men come"
(Psalm 65:2).

QUIET TIMES

Sometimes my life is so hectic that it is difficult for me to schedule quiet times, but I believe it is absolutely imperative for a continued spiritual walk with the Lord that we have these quiet times.

It was necessary for Jesus to withdraw from the crowds and go out alone to pray. So, how much more important must it be for us, Jesus' followers, to do the same?

If you are reading this devotion book regularly, you probably already have a quiet time, and that's great.

Generally, my quiet time is when I first awake in the morning. I try to wake up at least an hour before I have to start getting ready to go to the office.

It's during that time that I go through my prayer list and ask God to bless the people who are doing His work and heal those who are sick. On behalf of my family and friends who are unsaved, I ask Him to intercede supernaturally.

It's during those quiet times that I get my inspiration from God and certainly it is when I get the majority of my answers.

As many people do, I also pray as I drive my car. Sometimes I pray as I am walking (for exercise).

Without those quiet times, I believe that my relationship with God would deteriorate, so I make time for the quiet communion with God.

"The Lord your God is in your midst. . . . He will be quiet in His love, He will rejoice over you with shouts of joy" (Zephaniah 3:17).

Larry Burkett

Daily Scripture Reading: Matthew 26:17-29;
Mark 14:12-25; Luke 22:7-38; John 13

*"If you are even angry with someone,
you are subject to judgment!"*
(Matthew 5:22 NLT).

WHAT TO DO WITH ANGER

There are different kinds of anger. The apostle Paul tells us that anger will bring the wrath of God and we should *"put. . . aside anger, wrath, malice, slander, and abusive speech from your mouth"* (Colossians 3:8). He was referring to personal relationships.

In Ephesians Paul said, *"Be angry, and yet do not sin; do not let the sun go down on your anger, and do not give the devil an opportunity"* (Ephesians 4:26-27). I believe he was saying that we should be careful not to give Satan room to work while we are angry.

However, I believe that not all anger is bad. When we see what's happening to our country because of the filth in movies and television and through politicians who care more about their own personal security than they do this county, that makes me angry (maybe I should just call it righteous indignation!).

When I'm angry I do three things: I let some time pass, which allows me to think rationally; I confess my anger to God and ask Him to forgive me; and I ask God to help me be totally honest, kind, and polite, which has to happen supernaturally.

If you are harboring anger, you need to pray and ask God to forgive you and help you to forgive. Remember, part of the Lord's prayer says, *"Forgive us our debts, as we also have forgiven our debtors"* (Matthew 6:12).

Larry Burkett

Daily Scripture Reading:
John 14-16

*"Many, O LORD my God, are the wonders you have done.
The things you planned for us no one can recount to you; were I
to speak and tell of them, they would be too many to declare"*
(Psalm 40:5 NIV).

PURSUING GOD'S PURPOSE
FOR YOUR LIFE

In Acts 13:36, Paul noted that David *"served God's purpose in his own generation"* (NIV). In order to align yourself with God's purpose for your life, ask yourself some simple questions and be honest in your answers.

Where has God designed you to have an influence? Pay careful attention to where you sense you are naturally bent or equipped to make a difference. Find your giftedness.

What matters most to you? Search your heart, read God's Word, pray, and spend time in the area of service that you most care about. If you still lack clarity, ask a few trusted friends for their input.

What do you want your life to count for? View your life purpose from an eternal perspective. Then, ask God to make your life count, not only in familiar things but also in new ways that you never could have imagined.

Make discovering and pursuing your purpose a priority.

Larry Burkett created an enduring resource called *Career Direct®* that will help you discover your gifts, skills and interests. I highly recommend it.

Chuck Bentley

Daily Scripture Reading: Matthew 26:30-46;
Mark 14:26-42; Luke 22:39-46; John 17:1-18:1

"Charm is deceitful and beauty is vain,
but [the one] who fears the Lord. . .shall be praised"
(Proverbs 31:30).

CELEBRITIES

We have a tendency to make celebrities of people and treat them as if they were superior. I have a real problem with "celebrities." Some people have even tried to make a celebrity of me because I have written books or have radio programs. No way!

First, there's no special reward in Heaven for teaching or writing any more than for the person who cleans the church or keeps the nursery.

Some Christian "celebrities" have allowed themselves to have their egos enlarged, which eventually will destroy their usefulness to God. Why? Because the Lord told us that if we exalt ourselves, He will humble us.

In the secular world we idolize professional athletes and actors. Amazingly, we allow them to speak on topics they have no knowledge of. Many times their value systems are so distorted they give the wrong signals to our young people.

The best thing we can do for celebrities is pray for them—that God would put them under conviction to accept salvation. Also, we should not promote celebrities in front of our young people. Instead, build up the pastor—one who is true to the Word. Or find heroes in the past who had good values in their lives: George Washington, Abraham Lincoln, and the like.

Remember, we are all equal in God's sight. All He desires is for our hearts to be completely His (see 2 Chronicles 16:9).

Larry Burkett

Daily Scripture Reading: Matthew 26:47-75; Mark 14:43-72;
Luke 22:47-65; John 18:2-27

"I will bless the Lord at all times;
His praise shall continually be in my mouth"
(Psalm 34:1).

PRAISING GOD

To me, praising God is an integral part of the Christian walk, because it is acknowledging God's ownership over my life.

I believe that one fundamental principle established all through God's Word is that as we praise Him, we acknowledge Him as the omnipotent, omniscient, and omnipresent Creator.

When I think about praising God, my mind always goes back to the psalms of David; he continually praised God in song, in word, and in spirit. And, of David, God said he was a man after His own heart. David's praise was an expression of his love for the Creator.

In David's day, when a subject entered a king's presence, that person bowed—an acknowledgment of authority. When we get on our knees before God we are doing the same thing: acknowledging His total dominion over our lives.

It's easy to praise God when things are going well, isn't it? But, we must continue to praise Him in all circumstances, realizing that He expects our "sacrifice of thanksgiving."

"Let them also offer sacrifices of thanksgiving, and tell of His works with joyful singing" (Psalm 107:22).

Larry Burkett

Daily Scripture Reading: Matthew 27:1-26;
Mark 15:1-15; Luke 22:66-23:25

"I have set before you today life and prosperity, and death and adversity"
(Deuteronomy 30:15).

ABORTION'S SPIRITUAL IMPACT

Obviously abortion is an abomination before the Lord. In my mind, there's no difference between aborting babies and forcing children to walk through fire that consumes them. The only difference is that one is alive in the womb; the other is alive outside the womb.

When the sanctity of life is ignored and the most helpless are killed, it reduces society to the level of animals.

To allow people to believe that the unborn is not really a human being is a lie. God said that He formed us—our innermost, hidden parts—even while we were in the womb.

Until we are willing to stand up as a people and eliminate abortion, I believe the spiritual character of our nation will continue to degrade.

Some Christians are secret abortionists. Although they profess that they are pro-life, in their hearts they believe that abortion does benefit society by getting rid of the poor, the nonproductive, and the handicapped, because it reduces the burden on all of society. To harbor these thoughts is to be an abortionist, because God's Word says that as you think in your heart, that's who you are.

All fetuses should have a chance at life. The psalmist said, *"Children are a gift of the Lord; the fruit of the womb is a reward"* (Psalm 127:3).

Larry Burkett

Daily Scripture Reading: Matthew 27:27-56; Mark 15:16-41;
Luke 23:26-49; John 19:1-30

"Righteousness exalts a nation, but sin is a disgrace to any people"
(Proverbs 14:34).

NATIONAL MORALITY

The only way we, as God's people, are ever going to restore morality to government is by demanding morality of our elected leaders.

That means we have to promote people to office who have good moral values and who have Christian ethics in their lives.

I've heard the definition of character is what somebody does when nobody else is watching. And that's precisely who we need to elect to public office: people who will do the right things when we aren't watching them.

We can reestablish morality in government by requiring certain values of our politicians and then holding them to those standards.

Until we are willing to stand up and vote against immorality and support those who share God's value systems, we are never going to change the direction of our country.

Morality is in the hands of the people, and we are the people!

"Blessed is the nation whose God is the Lord, the people whom He has chosen for His own inheritance" (Psalm 33:12).

Larry Burkett

Daily Scripture Reading: Matthew 27:57-28:8; Mark 15:42-16:8; Luke 23:50-24:12; John 19:31-20:10

"Pride goes before destruction, a haughty spirit before a fall"
(Proverbs 16:18 NIV).

SUCCESS AND PRIDE

Beware of pride.

I like to say that it is the easiest trait to spot in others but the most difficult to see in ourselves. The Lord described this paradox by saying, *"First, take the plank out of your own eye, and then you will see clearly to remove the speck from your brother's eye"* (Matthew 7:5 NIV). Did you notice how He described the bigger of the two problems?

One of the sure ways to know if you are blinded by pride is when you notice a critical spirit developing. If you seem to be constantly aware of other's faults, it is likely that you lack awareness of your own shortcomings.

When we are aware of God's mercy extended to us, a new attitude of grace will develop toward others. *"Do nothing out of selfish ambition or vain conceit, but in humility consider others better than yourselves"* (Philippians 2:3 NIV).

Since God resists the proud, but gives grace to the humble, it is our own pride that can disqualify us from receiving mercy and grace. What a terrible loss.

Beware of pride, especially when you think you are most successful.

Chuck Bentley

Daily Scripture Reading: Matthew 28:9-20; Mark 16:9-20;
Luke 24:13-53; John 20:11-21:25

"You are Peter [the rock], and upon this rock I will build My church"
(Matthew 16:18).

CHANGING MY NAME

Jesus called Peter "The Rock" because he was solid. Yes, he fell short many times (including denying Christ three times), but God saw beyond that, knew his heart, and recognized his value.

What would my name be if Jesus was going to change it? Well, sometimes I feel like it might be "Stupid," but I guess we all have times like that.

If I had a choice of what He would call me, it would be "Larry, the Faithful." Even though I sometimes fail to measure up to God's best, I try never to do anything that is disobedient to God's Word.

We read about David in the Old Testament and the terrible things he did, including adultery and murder. And yet, God looked back on David and said that David was a man after His own heart.

God is able to look past our actions and see our hearts. I trust that is what He is doing with me, because I do want to serve Him faithfully.

"It is required of stewards that one be found trustworthy [faithful]" (1 Corinthians 4:2).
What name do you think Jesus would give to you?

Larry Burkett

Daily Scripture Reading:
Acts 1-2

*"Delight yourself in the Lord; and He will give you the
desires of your heart. Commit your way to the Lord,
trust also in Him, and He will do it. And He will bring forth
your righteousness as the light, and your judgment as the noonday"*
(Psalm 37:4-6).

COMMITMENT

God calls each of us to a radical lifestyle: total commitment to Him. You can discern a great deal about spiritual commitment by what Christians treasure. God's Word says that our treasures will be wherever our hearts are.

All that truly matters is what we can do for the kingdom of God. Certainly, the things we accumulate are not important. They are simply tools for us to use in accomplishing God's work.

Sometimes commitment to God's way breaks down when a sacrifice is required. We must make a choice about commitment, and there are only two options: God or the world.

Which takes first place in your commitment?

Larry Burkett

Daily Scripture Reading:
Acts 3-5

"The fruit of the Spirit is love, joy, peace, patience, kindness, goodness, faithfulness, gentleness, self-control; against such things there is no law"
(Galatians 5:22-23).

PICKIN' FRUIT

The apostle Paul listed the fruit of the Spirit in Galatians, but I think the fruit that is most significant is the one he wrote about in 1 Corinthians 13: love.

We have all kinds of gifts—prophecy, evangelism, giving, speaking in tongues—but if they aren't based on love, they are ineffective. All those things are temporal and will pass away.

But love lasts forever, and one thing I pray for is that God would give me the ability to love more fully and much more deeply.

Some of my bad habits still haunt me from my secular life (remember I wasn't saved until I was 32 years old): irritation with people, driving too fast, and too much pride.

The only way to overcome ungodly characteristics is through love. Perfect love casts out not only fear but also anger, resentment, and pride.

All the fruit of the Spirit should be evident in our lives if we are going to be effective witnesses for the Lord. If you have love, all the other fruit will fall into place.

"Now faith, hope, love, abide these three; but the greatest of these is love" (1 Corinthians 13:13).

Larry Burkett

Daily Scripture Reading:
Acts 6:1-8:1

320

"Let the word of Christ richly dwell within you,
with all wisdom teaching and admonishing one another"
(Colossians 3:16).

FAVORITE BOOK

My favorite book of the Bible is Proverbs. This is probably because I'm a very pragmatic, practical, and objective person, and the proverbs are perfectly suited for me.

One good thing, the proverbs cover a whole variety of topics, most of which are totally functional. In other words, you can read them and apply them.

They have been especially helpful in my line of teaching about borrowing, lending, saving, investing, whom to trust and not to trust, the importance of seeking counsel, where to seek counsel, how to judge good counsel—just practical things.

Just because Proverbs is my favorite book (and the most applicable) doesn't mean that I don't love all of the other books.

The Bible is full of history and drama, miracles and promises, teachings and instructions. It is our handbook for living, and we should cherish it above all other possessions.

You'll enjoy your Bible more if you will get a modern translation, a good Bible dictionary, and a concordance. Then you can study it and learn what God has put in His Word.

"Man lives by everything that proceeds out of the mouth of the Lord" (Deuteronomy 8:3).

Larry Burkett

Daily Scripture Reading:
Acts 8:2-9:43

*"Whatever your hand finds to do, do it with all your might,
for in the grave, where you are going, there is neither
working nor planning nor knowledge nor wisdom"*
(Ecclesiastes 9:10 NIV).

BEING EXCEPTIONAL AT WORK

The quality of your work is the tangible expression of the invisible reality that the power of God is at work in your heart.

When it comes to work, God wants you to put your whole effort to the task. So, be the exceptional worker God made you to be by following these steps.

1. Have a "Yes" attitude. A cheerful attitude in your work can reduce the friction in your office, with your customers, and at home.

2. Willingly take on the difficult aspects of your job along with the desirable. Your willingness to accept responsibility for the difficult tasks—those that involve problems and challenges—will set you apart and allow you to make the most difference. Through these assignments, you will experience your human limitations and the need to rely on God's strength. You will discover that He is able to do more than you could ever ask or imagine.

3. Don't determine your best effort according to standards of perfection. Only God is perfect, but that doesn't mean you should settle for mediocrity. Instead, press on to achieve excellence. Vince Lombardi said, "Perfection is not attainable, but if we chase perfection we can catch excellence."

Chuck Bentley

Daily Scripture Reading:
Acts 10-11

"All who desire to live godly in Christ Jesus will be persecuted"
(2 Timothy 3:12).

UNDER PERSECUTION

It is my firm belief that if this country continues to evolve in the way it is going, on an anti-spiritual basis, eventually we will face physical persecution.

We already are facing a kind of a mental or emotional persecution; Christianity has been ridiculed and blamed for all the ills of the world, or at least of this country. Certainly that is true politically.

If this country continues to stay on the secular slide it is now on, we will be physically persecuted for our faith.

There's no reason to believe that God will supernaturally intercede on behalf of Americans any more than He will on behalf of someone who is saved in Saudi Arabia or in China. They are just as precious to God as we are.

The only reason we haven't suffered that kind of persecution is that our foundation was so thoroughly based in Christian principle that we are still living off the legacy of our forefathers. We can be thankful that we don't have to face persecution for our beliefs.

We need to bear in mind the principle that Jesus Christ taught us: *"If they persecuted Me, they will also persecute you"* (John 15:20).

Have you ever thought of what you would do if you were threatened with torture or death if you did not renounce Jesus Christ? God's Word says that *"If we endure, we shall also reign with Him"* (2 Timothy 2:12).

Larry Burkett

Daily Scripture Reading:
Acts 12-13

"Whenever you fast, do not put on a gloomy face as the hypocrites do, for they neglect their appearance so that they will be noticed by men when they are fasting"
(Matthew 6:16).

FASTING

It is my personal conviction that any long-term relationship with the Lord is going to be accompanied by fasting and prayer.

The significance of fasting is two-fold: spiritual and physical.

Physically, there are great benefits from fasting. It's a cleansing process for the body itself, because the body has the chance to rid itself of the toxins that are taken in on a daily basis through food.

Spiritually, fasting is the denial of something we need and literally surrendering that to God as a testimony that we love and trust Him. If our Lord considered fasting an essential part of His spiritual life, we certainly should.

I believe that fasting is a necessary element of any spiritual relationship with God and also a valuable part of good health.

"Having prayed with fasting, they commended them to the Lord in whom they had believed" (Acts 14:23).

Larry Burkett

Daily Scripture Reading:
Acts 14-15

"Enter His gates with thanksgiving, and His courts with praise. Give thanks to Him; bless His name. For the Lord is good"
(Psalm 100:4-5).

PREPARING FOR THANKSGIVING

As you think about Thanksgiving, what are you most thankful for? I think I'm most grateful for the freedom of worship. I've traveled all around the country, speaking to nearly every denomination, and I've been interested to see the various ways to worship the Lord. You can choose for yourself.

I choose to be a fundamental Christian: I believe that God's Word is infallible, inspired, and inerrant. But in this country we aren't forced to believe any certain way.

I own over a dozen Bibles of one kind or another and hundreds of Christian books. In many other countries if you even own one Bible it is grounds for imprisonment. If you have other Christian literature, that's considered to be subversive and you can lose your life.

I've heard of people in other countries, where Bibles are prohibited, who have no more than a page or two from a Bible, which they had to either memorize and destroy or take a chance on hiding it. Don't we take a lot for granted in this country?

With our religious freedom comes responsibility. We are responsible to show our gratitude by telling others about the Lord and helping them to know that their blessings come as a result of a loving God.

Think of what you are most thankful for so you'll be ready to celebrate Thanksgiving Day properly.

Larry Burkett

Daily Scripture Reading:
Galatians 1-3

"You shall freely open your hand to your brother,
to your needy and poor in your land"
(Deuteronomy 15:11).

THE CARING BUSINESS

Many years ago, when Davy Crockett was a congressman, a bill was brought before the Congress to help a widow of an American war hero because she was totally indigent.

Davy Crockett stood in that meeting and said, "I will, under no circumstances, vote money from the taxpayers of America to help this lady. It is not the role of the government to care for the needs of people. And when the people of this country begin to treat this government like it is their friend, we shall lose our freedoms."

He went on to say, "Though I will vote no money from the government treasury to help her, I will personally share from my bounty in her time of need, if others in this honored body will do the same."

What is the principle here? The government should not care for the needs of people; the people were always meant to do so.

This is the same principle we read in God's Word that says, "Share with others in your time of plenty so that when you have needs others will share from their plenty" (paraphrase of 2 Corinthians 8:14).

If the body of Christ doesn't voluntarily begin to accept the needs of other people and share with them, God may involuntarily involve us by letting us experience the same needs.

We have allowed the government to get in the caring business and people depend far more on the government to care for their needs than they do on the body of Christ.

God wants to direct our attention back to the source of all material things: Himself. The only way people in need are ever going to sense that God is their source is by God's people becoming their source.

Is there someone you can help today?

"They have drawn near and have come. Each one helps his neighbor, and says to his brother, 'Be strong!'" (Isaiah 41:5-6).

Larry Burkett

Daily Scripture Reading:
Galatians 4-6

326

"Consider it all joy, my brethren, when you encounter various trials, knowing that the testing of your faith produces endurance"
(James 1:2-3).

PROBLEMS

I have a good friend, an evangelist, who says, "There are only two kinds of Christians in this world: those who have problems and those who lie about it."

In 1 and 2 Corinthians, the apostle Paul laid to rest once and for all the idea that Christians don't have problems. Some of his best writing was done while sitting in a Roman jail with two guards—one chained to each arm. To Paul it was a golden opportunity to witness to the captive audience.

Some like to think that problems are a result of sin. (Remember the story of Job and his "friends"?) We might experience problems as a result of sin, but all problems are not the result of sin. Think for a moment. Christ had problems in His life and He was without sin. He told his disciples, "If they have persecuted me, how much more will they persecute those who come after me?"

The moment you decide to turn everything over to God you probably will have more problems than you ever thought existed. Why? Because Satan is not going to give up easily.

God promises that if you will yield your rights to Him He will do whatever is best in your life to give you maximum fulfillment and spiritual maturity.

You can have joy in the midst of problems if you believe that God hears you. He knows your requests, He knows your needs, and He is listening to you.

"Cease striving and know that I am God" (Psalm 46:10).

Larry Burkett

Daily Scripture Reading:
James

"The LORD is my rock, my fortress and my deliverer;
my God is my rock, in whom I take refuge. He is my shield
and the horn of my salvation, my stronghold"
(Psalm 18:2 NIV).

FINDING SECURITY

When bad economic news is being reported daily, you may be tempted to feel insecure about your future, even if things are going well in your life.

However, economic downturns should not be a cause for panic. As Christians, we should not allow current events of any kind to lead us into fear-based decisions. Instead, we should avoid fear and panic, reduce our vulnerability created by debt, and remain dependent on Christ, who is the never-changing constant in an ever-changing economy. He loves us, and He will be there even when the money is not.

Regardless of what happens, remember that money does not give you identity or fulfillment; it only serves to empower or prohibit the fulfillment of the life purpose that God has ordained for you.

By trusting God and His ways, you will be anchored in the only true security and avoid the economic storms that batter those who've placed their faith in the lifeless hands of money. Hebrews 13:5 says, *"Keep your lives free from the love of money and be content with what you have, because God has said 'Never will I leave you; never will I forsake you' "* (NIV). This promise from our faithful God is the only true security any of us really has.

Chuck Bentley

Daily Scripture Reading:
Acts 16:1-18:11

"Commit your works to the Lord, and your plans will be established"
(Proverbs 16:3).

PLANNING GOD'S WAY

Often Christians question whether they should do any planning. The question I'm often asked is, "Shouldn't a Christian depend totally on God?" Yes, but that doesn't mean that we are to sit back and do nothing. Our faith requires action.

Planning is essential in any life but especially in the lives of Christians. God is an orderly provider and He expects us to have an attitude of doing our best in our everyday decisions.

Don't try to develop plans with no flexibility. Remember that God's wisdom may be exercised by redirecting our paths.

Patience and caution are necessary in any venture—particularly if it is a financial decision.

The Christian home should be characterized by orderliness and excellence. Neither is possible without good planning, and there are some steps to take.

Family discussions allow each member of the family to have an active part.

Written goals provide visible objectives toward which to work.

Any plans that are made should be compatible with God's will. You should be able to find Scripture to back anything you plan to do.

Don't make your decisions based on what anyone else is doing.

If you need counsel, be willing to ask for it. Many Christians are willing to help others but are never willing to ask for help themselves. That's just ego. All of us need counsel and advice.

Pray together about every decision. Prayer brings God directly into our lives and strengthens our faith so we can trust Him in even greater things.

Larry Burkett

Daily Scripture Reading:
1 Thessalonians

"Whatever we ask we receive from Him, because we keep His commandments and do the things that are pleasing in His sight"
(1 John 3:22).

KEEPING COMMANDMENTS

Few of us willfully violate the Ten Commandments. The spiritual and emotional consequences are devastating.

Most committed Christians exercise a godly motivated self-discipline to avoid overt disobedience. Externally, most Christians appear basically moral. Internally, however, many earnest believers struggle with doubts, temptations, and failure. They have fallen for one of Satan's most subtle ploys: Don't let religion interfere with pleasures.

Violating many of God's commandments involves attitudes more than actions: lustful thoughts, selfishness, anger, pride. These attitudes arise over a period of time and are difficult to avoid. Most of us develop them without realizing how or when they started.

God's minimum acceptable attitudes are to love God totally and to love others as ourselves. Christ said that loving God foremost is a prerequisite to receiving God's best (reread today's Scripture verse).

We are fully responsible and accountable for our actions, regardless of what anyone else does. Often we desire to obey and trust God but are unwilling to stand without compromise in all situations.

As Nehemiah did when he refused to compromise God's way, even to save his own life, we must precondition all responses to temptations and problems on the basis of what God says. God promises He will prosper and protect us, so He may receive the glory.

"Call upon Me in the day of trouble; I shall rescue you, and you will honor Me"
(Psalm 50:15).

Larry Burkett

Daily Scripture Reading:
Acts 18:12-19:22; 2 Thessalonians

"If you have bitter jealousy and selfish ambition in your heart, do not be arrogant and so lie against the truth. This wisdom is not that which comes down from above, but is earthly, natural, demonic"
(James 3:14-15).

A THANKFUL ATTITUDE

It is remarkable that in America we could ever think that God has failed us materially. It is only possible by comparison, which is one of Satan's primary tools.

The primary defense against this attitude is praise to God. Satan uses lavishness and waste to create discontent and selfish ambition. Why else would we drive ourselves to acquire more than we need or can logically use and, in the process, destroy our health, families, and usefulness to God?

Thankfulness is a state of mind, not an accumulation of assets. Until we can truly thank God for what we have and be willing to accept that as God's provision for our lives, contentment never will be possible.

Have everyone in your family make a list of all he or she has to be thankful for and then share your lists with one another. It may open your eyes to how much you've been blessed by God.

In your prayer of thanksgiving, ask God to help you continue to have a thankful attitude.

Larry Burkett

Daily Scripture Reading:
1 Corinthians 1-4

*"Every good thing given and every perfect gift is
from above, coming down from the Father of lights,
with whom there is no variation, or shifting shadow"*
(James 1:17).

GIVING THANKS

What are you most thankful for? A visit from a loved one? Turkey and pumpkin pie? The sound of children laughing? Or your favorite team winning by a field goal?

Think about the first Thanksgiving—the day the forefathers set aside to give thanks. The early pilgrims gave thanks to the omnipotent Creator who provided their food. They were primarily concerned about having enough food to make it through the winters, because many of the early colonists died of starvation.

These people had no difficulty in believing in a Creator. They were simple people who lived off the land. They noticed that when acorns fell on the ground they grew into oak trees, and when pine cones fell pine trees grew. Not once did they see a pine tree come from an acorn, so they knew God had an orderly plan for everything.

They lived on the cutting edge of life and that's where they had their needs met by God.

In the excitement of Thanksgiving Day, it's easy to forget those who are less fortunate. We should always reach out to someone who is alone or hungry.

Above all, don't let your giving of thanks become a ritual. With your family and friends, either sing or recite the words to the Doxology (Praise God from whom all blessings flow...).

Larry Burkett

Daily Scripture Reading:
1 Corinthians 5-8

*"Anger is cruel and fury overwhelming,
but who can stand before jealousy?"*
(Proverbs 27:4 NIV).

JEALOUSY

If Saul, Israel's first king, had allowed David to serve under him, he would have had a faithful and daring warrior at his command. According to 1 Samuel 18 (NIV), *"Whatever Saul sent him to do, David did it so successfully that Saul gave him a high rank in the army"* (Verse 5).

But Saul became extremely jealous of David when he heard the women of Israel singing, *"Saul has slain his thousands, and David his tens of thousands"* (verse 7). From that point on, he *"kept a jealous eye on David"* (verse 9) and later tried to kill him.

Jealousy is a dangerous sin. It leads people to hurt others in ways they might never have imagined. It ends friendships and can even turn one spouse against another. Jealousy caused Cain to murder Abel, it caused Joseph's brothers to sell him into slavery, and it caused Joab to murder Abner.

Two of the chief causes of jealousy are money and possessions. *"And I saw that all labor and all achievement spring from man's envy of his neighbor. This too is meaningless, a chasing after the wind"* (Ecclesiastes 4:4 NIV).

Today, people jokingly refer to this as "Keeping up with the Joneses." But there's nothing funny about exhausting yourself in an effort to match someone else's success. *"Resentment kills a fool, and envy slays the simple"* (Job 5:2 NIV).

God has a better plan: be a good steward of what He's entrusted to you and fulfill His purpose for your life.

Chuck Bentley

Daily Scripture Reading:
1 Corinthians 9-11

*"I was a father to the needy, and I
investigated the case which I did not know"*
(Job 29:16).

WHOM TO HELP?

When you have a surplus, how do you decide whom to help? Judy and I have faced that question, and we have a kind of pecking order that we go through.

First of all, we support our local church. The Bible says that we should support those who teach the Word.

Second, we support the organizations from which we benefit—the ones that minister to us. Our ministry is Christian Financial Concepts, which Judy and I started in 1976. I don't get an income from the ministry, but I do support it, because we benefit from it.

Then we support things like our Christian radio stations and other ministries that bless us.

Next, we try to meet the special needs of individuals. The first requirement is that we must know them personally, unless it's missionaries whose needs have been presented to us (of course we wouldn't know them).

If we hear of an individual in need and don't know him or her, we give through a trustworthy organization.

Even if you give to someone and find out later that the money was misspent, you will still be blessed for your heart attitude.

Giving to others should be made a matter of prayer and good stewardship.

"The wisdom from above is first pure, then peaceable, gentle, reasonable, full of mercy and good fruits, unwavering, without hypocrisy" (James 3:17).

Larry Burkett

Daily Scripture Reading:
1 Corinthians 12-14

*"The wife of a man from the company of the prophets cried out to Elisha,
'Your servant my husband is dead, and you know that he revered the
LORD. But now his creditor is coming to take my two boys as his slaves'"*
(2 Kings 4:1 NIV).

LESSONS FROM THE WIDOW

Perhaps no story illustrates the hardships of indebtedness better than the story of the widow in 2 Kings 4. I call it "A Mother's Nightmare" or "The Worst Case Scenario for Bad Financial Consequences." A helpless widow is vulnerable to lose her children for a loan that her husband created that she cannot pay.

There are certainly many financial lessons we learn from her:

1. God provided for her after she did her part and asked for help;

2. Her neighbors and children contributed to God's plan for her deliverance;

3. God multiplied her oil through a miracle;

4. She had to go to work to sell the oil;

5. She paid her debts first;

6. She had a surplus to live on after she freed her children from enslavement by the creditors.

But I hope you don't miss the bigger picture here. This terrible financial dilemma happened to the widow of a godly man.

Although the Lord mercifully met the needs of this widow, it is a story that should cause every godly man to avoid debt and prepare his estate in such a way that his own family will not suffer financial stress while also grieving their loss.

Chuck Bentley

Daily Scripture Reading:
1 Corinthians 15-16

"Instruct those who are rich in this present world not to be conceited or to fix their hope on the uncertainty of riches, but on God, who richly supplies us with all things to enjoy"
(1 Timothy 6:17).

CHRISTMAS GIFT GIVING

We have become terribly imbalanced. We give a myriad of useless gifts at Christmas because it's expected of us, and we feel guilty if we don't. The commercialized world now makes a $100 toy seem perfectly normal.

It's easy to observe the stress that our imbalanced society places on family members. Christian parents who can't provide the latest indulgences to their children are often depressed and distraught. Obviously, no one person purposely makes them feel unworthy or insignificant, but the overwhelming emphasis we place on giving at Christmas certainly does.

So great is this social pressure that the closer we get toward Christmas Day, the more depressed and unworthy those who can't indulge feel. Unfortunately, the pressures don't end after Christmas is past either.

We must develop a plan for our families without the pressure from the commercial world. To do so, we must first believe that God's plan is different from the world's and is more, not less, fulfilling. More emphasis must be placed on the values taught in God's Word.

The key is balance, which comes from following God's wisdom.

"The Lord gives wisdom; from His mouth come knowledge and understanding. He stores up wisdom for the upright. . . and He preserves the way of His godly ones" (Proverbs 2:6, 8).

Larry Burkett

Daily Scripture Reading:
Acts 19:23-20:1; 2 Corinthians 1-4

"We establish the Law"
(Romans 3:31).

"THE ESTABLISHMENT"

The apostle Paul gave a dissertation to some Jewish converts, telling them that the Law, established in the Old Testament, was not abolished as a result of salvation.

One common idea of that generation was that once someone was saved that person was no longer bound by the Law and could do anything he or she wanted to do.

Some even believed that if God's blessing was received as a result of forgiving sin, then the more they sinned the more blessings they received—a heresy commonly accepted at that time.

So, Paul made it very clear that they were not released from the Law; being a Christian does not nullify the Law. As Christians, we either confirm or complete the Law.

We know that the ritualistic practices of blood sacrifices were no longer necessary, because Jesus Christ, the Lamb of God, was sacrificed once and forever for all sins.

But God didn't change His mind about sin. The Ten Commandments remain just as applicable as they were in the time of Moses. The good news is that now we have the means to be forgiven if we stumble and violate God's laws.

It is only through the sacrifice of the Lord Jesus Christ and the fact that we stand before God cleansed by His blood that we are not judged by the Law.

Larry Burkett

Daily Scripture Reading:
2 Corinthians 5-9

"A generous man will prosper; he who refreshes others will himself be refreshed"
(Proverbs 11:25 NIV).

DIFFERENT GIFTS

Have you finished your Christmas shopping? If not, you may be dreading the crowds and the pressure of buying more than you can afford.

As you plan your gift giving for this Christmas, I would like to suggest some alternatives to the traditional shopping treks throughout the malls.

Consider the person you want to give to and think about what they will appreciate that does not have to be purchased. Your gift should be a generous expression of your love that actually cannot be acquired through a purchase.

A handmade gift is often the ideal choice. Take the time to make something for the person you want to honor. One year, our foreign exchange student surprised us with a beautiful picture that she painted for us. We were surprised and blessed by this, knowing the countless hours she spent to express her generous love for us.

Heirlooms can be a meaningful expression of love for family. Passing along a prized antique or collection to your children can mean more to them than anything you could purchase. My grandfather once gave me a knife from a collection that he made with his own hands. It remains one of my fondest memories of him and our relationship.

One year, I wanted to be generous with a special group of friends, but I could not afford to buy gifts for each one. At our Christmas gathering, I gave each one a card with a handwritten Bible verse that reminded me of that person after praying for each one. To this day, that group thanks me for the special meaning that verse holds for them.

Chuck Bentley

Daily Scripture Reading:
2 Corinthians 10-13

*"Who are you, O man, who answers back to God? The thing molded will
not say to the molder, 'Why did you make me like this,' will it?"*
(Romans 9:20).

THE RICHES SYNDROME

Many Christians have concluded that since poverty isn't normal, riches must be. Therefore, they have assumed that God must make them wealthy to protect His image.

Then most of them set about in a totally secular way to accumulate what is supposed to be a Christian testimony. If God doesn't provide according to their preconceived plan, they rationalize that the end justifies the means and "help Him out."

So what if they don't have a personal prayer or study life? After all, just think what a witness God will get from their "success"! And even though their children don't get much parental direction, they do get the best possible "advantages."

Others try to manipulate God to work for them. They give, but usually to get. They continually demand "more" and "the best," while fervently trying to convince others that it is normal. Rarely, if ever, do they stop to consider God's plan, for fear it won't coincide with their concept of prosperity.

There is a great danger in seeing God only through worldly eyes, because then all riches and all blessings are measured in terms of what God can do for us, rather than what we can do for God.

To be a spiritual success, a Christian must be willing to relinquish all rights and accept God's plan. Of necessity, God will place believers at every tier (or income level) in society to minister to those around them.

Larry Burkett

Daily Scripture Reading:
Romans 1-3

*"They cried out to the Lord in their trouble;
He saved them out of their distresses"*
(Psalm 107:19).

LESSONS LEARNED

We can learn from all the experiences we have in life, especially the difficult times.

When I reflect on the years since I was diagnosed with cancer and underwent two major surgeries, I believe that God is teaching me how to trust Him day by day.

If somebody had asked me a few years ago if I were trusting the Lord daily, I would have said sincerely, "Yes, I am." But now I realize that I didn't understand what it meant to truly trust the Lord day by day—to wake up every day and accept that day as a true gift from God and praise Him for it and not anticipate anything long-term.

That doesn't mean that I don't do any planning. I do plan—for myself, my family, and the ministry—but I don't anticipate or take for granted a long life. I believe that has helped me learn to trust God more day by day.

"Behold, God is my salvation, I will trust and not be afraid; for the Lord God is my strength and song, and He has become my salvation" (Isaiah 12:2).

No matter what the circumstances, our sense of joy, satisfaction, and fulfillment in life will increase if we completely trust in the Lord.

Think of some difficulty you've experienced and how it has benefited your spiritual life; then praise God for it.

Larry Burkett

Daily Scripture Reading:
Romans 4-6

*"Prove yourselves doers of the word, and
not merely hearers who delude themselves"*
(James 1:22).

CHRISTIAN COMMITMENT

If most Christians in America were as dedicated to Christian activities (Bible study, prayer, evangelism) as they are to sports, we would truly have a spiritual revival today. Christians often are confronted with a conflict between God's way and the world's attractions.

One pastor of a large dynamic church confided that he had come under severe criticism for allowing the Sunday morning services to go beyond noon when the local professional football team had home games.

Obviously, it is not sports, recreation, or other activities that are the problems; it is a lack of vital, dynamic commitment to God's way.

The non-Christian world will try to test our commitment to see if it's real. If it's not, they will reject our message as just another philosophy. Quite often, the testing ground will be on the job or in our own neighborhoods.

Many Christians have lost their witness because they weren't "doers of the Word."

Larry Burkett

Daily Scripture Reading:
Romans 7-8

"If a brother or sister is without clothing and in need of daily food, and one of you says to them, 'Go in peace, be warmed and be filled,' and yet you do not give them what is necessary for their body, what use is that?"
(James 2:15-16).

UNMET CHRISTIAN NEEDS

Unfortunately, unmet needs in the church is the norm in today's Christianity. But it is the responsibility of each Christian to supply the needs of others who cannot do so for themselves.

Harry Truman made a famous statement about the presidency: "The buck stops here." And the same is true for each Christian.

If we see a brother or sister in need and we close our hearts to that need, what kind of love is that?

Of course, God will not lay every need on every Christian's heart, but He does lay on our hearts specific needs that we are to meet.

Stephan Grellet said, "I expect to pass through this world but once; any good thing therefore that I can do, or any kindness that I can show to any fellow creature, let me do it now; let me not defer or neglect it, for I shall not pass this way again."

Ralph Waldo Emerson said, "It is one of the most beautiful compensations of this life that no man can sincerely try to help another without helping himself."

And the psalmist said, *"To those who fear Him, there is no want. . . . They who seek the Lord shall not be in want of any good thing"* (Psalm 34:9-10).

Larry Burkett

Daily Scripture Reading:
Romans 9-11

"Fight the good fight, keeping faith and a good conscience, which some have rejected and suffered shipwreck in regard to their faith"
(1 Timothy 1:18-19).

YOUR CONSCIENCE, YOUR GUIDE

We received a letter at the ministry from a woman who asked how we felt about a Christian using the telephone but not paying for the calls.

She said that when her husband travels he calls back home, person to person, and asks for himself, so she will know that he's okay. They use codes so that if she says one thing he will know to call back, but if the family's okay she uses another code.

She thought this was all right since, after all, she was paying a phone bill every month. But after listening to our radio broadcast she began to wonder if it was cheating.

The general principle you have to use is to let God guide your conscience. If you think something is wrong, it probably is.

The son of a friend of mine went off to college and he and some friends devised a system of sticking battery wires down into the telephone to make the operator think they were dropping coins in. Unfortunately, the phone company found out and his father ended up paying a $1,000 fine. In addition, the son got one year of probation.

Sin is sin. Integrity is worth a lot more than what little can be saved by cheating someone. Always follow your conscience (your inner voice).

"If I regard wickedness in my heart, the Lord will not hear" (Psalm 66:18).

Larry Burkett

Daily Scripture Reading:
Romans 12-15

"Submit yourselves, then, to God. Resist the devil, and he will flee from you. Come near to God and he will come near to you. Wash your hands, you sinners, and purify your hearts, you double-minded"
(James 4:7-8 NIV).

REPENTANCE

In 1999, I experienced a genuine repentance from my double-minded ways. While reading God's Word, I suddenly saw myself as looking in a mirror. The reflection back was that of an Idolater. I worshipped God with my mouth but served money with all of my energy. My dreams, goals, and ambitions all involved the pursuit and capture of more money. In reality, money was my invisible master.

I remember a deep sense of sorrow that swept over my soul. How could I have been so easily deceived? How could I have treated the Lord with such shallow lip service? How could I have allowed money to take the throne of my heart? All of these questions rushed into my mind as I contemplated the reality of my sin.

Coveting, greed, and idolatry are often thought of as "invisible sins" in that we try very hard to hide them. Catholic priests have told me that these are the least confessed sins they hear in their confessional booth. I understand why. Most often, we think they really don't matter. We rationalize that if we say we love God that should be enough, even though our actions defy the words.

1999 was a turning point in my life that led me to become a single-minded man, loving and serving only One Master. I turned from my idol, submitted myself to God Almighty, and He came near to me.

Chuck Bentley

Daily Scripture Reading: Romans 16;
Acts 20:2-21:16

"He fell to the ground, and heard a voice saying to him, 'Saul, Saul, why are you persecuting Me?'"
(Acts 9:4).

HEARING GOD'S VOICE

In my travels as a lecturer, I've known many people who told me that God speaks audibly to them. I wish that were true in my life. I have never heard God speak to me audibly; but I know I will when I stand before Him one day.

In order to hear God speak in your spirit, you have to be in tune to God. It's kind of like turning on a radio to get your favorite program on FM 95. You aren't going to hear that program if your radio is tuned to AM 750.

Of course, being tuned to God's voice is not that simple, but I think it's a good analogy. Until your mind, your spirit, and your heart are tuned to God, you won't hear Him speak to you. (Sin will block your "reception.")

I believe I've heard God speak in my spirit and, almost without exception, He has spoken to me through His Word—through Scripture. He may speak to a particular situation or problem I'm facing, but I always hear Him speak inaudibly and with spiritual clarity.

If we want to be in tune with God and hear what He has to say to us, we have to be "tuned in" to His voice and receptive to His Word.

"He who is of God hears the words of God" (John 8:47).

Larry Burkett

Daily Scripture Reading:
Acts 21:17-23:35

345

"If you remain silent at this time, relief and deliverance will arise for the Jews from another place and you and your father's house will perish"
(Esther 4:14).

OBEYING GOD'S VOICE

Yesterday I was relating how I hear God speak to me in my spirit. I want to carry that thought further by giving you an example.

When I had been a Christian about two and a half years, I felt God calling me to do something different from what I was doing as a company vice president.

Often my pastor would take me on Wednesday visitation when he was going to visit hard cases, because he could use me as his example—"if God can save this guy He can save anybody."

This particular evening we had gone to three homes and nobody was home. So we were back at the church sitting in his car, half talking, half praying, and I mentioned that I believed God wanted me to do something different.

He asked what it was, but I had to admit that I didn't really know. At the time, I had been studying the area of biblical finances and had become the resident financial counselor for our church.

We prayed about it and during the prayer I heard God speak to me in that gentle, soft voice, and it was from His Word in Esther (our verse for today). Mordecai went on to say to Esther what I believe God was telling me, "Who knows but what you have been raised to this position for just such a time as this, but if you don't go another will be chosen."

I resigned my job, joined the Campus Crusade for Christ staff as a financial counselor, and began the greatest adventure of my life—serving God's people in the area of finances.

Be careful to listen when God speaks to you.

Larry Burkett

Daily Scripture Reading:
Acts 24-26

"Quietly trust yourself to Christ your Lord and if anybody asks why you believe as you do, be ready to tell him and do it in a gentle and respectful way"
(1 Peter 3:15 TLB).

KNOWING SCRIPTURE

If we are going to share Christ with others, and that is a requirement for all Christians, we need to know what to say to them and what Bible verses will confirm what we say. Since most of us don't usually carry a list of verses or a Bible with us, we must carry those verses in our memories.

In teaching, I often quote Scriptures dealing with finances. Friends ask me how I am able to remember so many verses. Through no credit of mine, I was given the ability to recall Scripture verses that deal with whatever question I am asked. This has to be a God-given ability, because I don't have to work at it. But, I have to stay in the Word and read the verses I need to recall. You can't remember what you have never read.

Often, when I go to bed, I spend the time until I fall asleep going back over Scripture verses so I'll remember them.

I encourage you to learn as much of God's Word as you can so you can keep it with you. Then, when given the opportunity, you will be able to share it with others. God's Word says that whatever is in your heart is going to come out of your mouth. And John 7:38 says, *"From his innermost being shall flow rivers of living water."*

Get a piece of paper and list all of the verses you can quote from memory. Which is your favorite? Now list the ones you want to learn and spend time each day working on that list.

Larry Burkett

Daily Scripture Reading:
Acts 27-28

"Train up a child in the way he should go,
even when he is old he will not depart from it"
(Proverbs 22:6).

GODLY INHERITANCE

The most important inheritance we can offer our children is a Christian influence that leads to salvation. We think of an inheritance coming after someone's death, but godly inheritance—training in Christian living—cannot be left until then.

Neither should we neglect training our spouses and our children in the use of handling the inheritance. I challenge every Christian to develop a godly approach to inheritance, beginning right now. Establish a few fundamental absolutes about your inheritance.

Knowing how to manage money is basic in preparing for the future. Teaching your children to give to God's work out of their earnings is the most essential step in molding them into good money managers and is the best inheritance you can give them.

God promises wisdom to those who trust Him.

"The beginning of wisdom is: acquire wisdom; and with all your acquiring, get understanding. Prize her [wisdom], *and she will exalt you; she will honor you if you embrace her"* (Proverbs 4:7-8).

Larry Burkett

Daily Scripture Reading:
Ephesians 1-3

"He must increase, but I must decrease"
(John 3:30 KJV).

THE PARADOX OF GREATNESS

John the Baptist knew that his purpose in life was to call people to repentance in preparation for the coming of Jesus, the Messiah.

As a result, when a group of priests and Levites asked him who he was, he replied, *"I am not the Christ"* (John 1:20 NIV).

In describing Jesus, he said, *"He is the one who comes after me, the thongs of whose sandals I am not worthy to untie"* (John 1:27 NIV).

And, when Jesus came to him to be baptized, John's response was, *"I need to be baptized by you, and do you come to me?"* (Matthew 3:14 NIV).

Like John, we must decrease, and Jesus must increase.

That's not a popular concept in our self-centered world, but it's only through this process that we come to the fullness of what we were created to be.

Each of us is a unique creation, with a certain personality, talents, gifts, and so forth. Our uniqueness is tied to the purpose God appointed for us on this earth.

Unless we put God first, become more like Christ, and live out His purpose for our lives, we'll miss the unique purpose that God wants to accomplish through us.

John the Baptist exemplified the principle that "He must increase, but I must decrease." And, regarding John, our Lord said, *"I tell you the truth: Among those born of women there has not risen anyone greater than John the Baptist"* (Matthew 11:11 NIV).

Greatness in God's eyes comes from decreasing, not increasing.

Chuck Bentley

Daily Scripture Reading:
Ephesians 4-6

*"There will always be poor people in the land. Therefore
I command you to be openhanded toward your brothers
and toward the poor and needy in your land"*
(Deuteronomy 15:11 NIV).

IS WELFARE SCRIPTURAL?

The issue of welfare is very clear biblically: We are to help those in need. There may be disagreements about how much help is necessary and who should receive it, but there should be no disagreement about the necessity to feed, clothe, and shelter the poor.

Welfare for the poor is biblical and necessary. The fact that the government has assumed that function of caring for the poor does not negate our responsibility.

No one can realistically deny that the church is no longer the prime source for meeting the needs of the poor; the government is.

Nor can there be any doubt that from this base of government welfare the "great society" has grown. From this society developed many families in permanent poverty. Because of this, many Christians have developed resentment and indifference to those who really are poor.

God's Word says there will always be needs in the world around us. The purpose is twofold: to test our commitment to obedience and to create an attitude of interdependence.

We are given clear and absolute direction about welfare in God's Word. Fortunately, the standards for welfare also are given.

Indiscriminate welfare traps the recipients by making them dependent. Biblical welfare meets needs and always looks toward restoring individuals to positions of productivity.

How do you feel about the poor? What are you doing about it?

Larry Burkett

Daily Scripture Reading:
Colossians

*"Having been freed from sin, you became slaves of
righteousness. . . . Now having been freed from sin and enslaved
to God, you derive your benefit. . .the outcome, eternal life"*
(Romans 6:18, 22).

FREEDOM THROUGH RESTRICTION

As the directors of a child care center watched the children playing outside, they
noticed them staying quite close to the building, even though the yard itself was quite
large. It was evident that the busy intersection and passing cars had frightened the
children into huddling together in one spot.

One of the directors suggested putting up a fence, and the day after it was erected the
children were seen playing happily all over the yard. The fence represented security and,
consequently, freedom. Knowing their limits expanded the children's sense of freedom and
their capacity to enjoy it.

If God's love did not provide fences in our lives, the result would be chaos,
disorder, and unhappiness. God's restraints produce freedom, which brings satisfaction
and fulfillment.

What fences do you think God has provided for you in order to avoid unhappiness?

Job, during his predicament said, *"He has walled up my way so that I cannot pass; and
He has put darkness on my paths"* (Job 91:8). But we read later in Job: *"And the Lord restored
the fortunes of Job when he prayed for his friends"* (Job 42:10).

So, no matter what your situation is now, no matter how many "fences" you think
there are in your way, trust the Lord to remove them at the right time.

Larry Burkett

Daily Scripture Reading:
Philippians

*"In the beginning God created the heavens and the earth. . . . Thus
the heavens and the earth were completed, and all their hosts"*
(Genesis 1:1, 2:1).

GOD'S CREATION

Don't you wonder why the world is living so far away from God and spiritual values,
when technology has brought us access to so much information?

You would think that the advanced technology would draw people closer to God.
However, learning more about God's creation and how complex it is has done just the
opposite: It has really pushed people away from God, and some even believe that science
has refuted God.

When we split the atom and created the atomic bomb, basically, we didn't create
anything that hadn't been there since the beginning of time. The ability of that atom to
be separated and to release energy has been there since the world began.

What we've realized now is that since the beginning of the world, God's creation
has been doing exactly what we "discovered" in 1944. We haven't invented anything. All
we've done is discover another one of God's marvelous creations.

In great part, technology in our generation has been the single greatest tool used by
Satan to deceive people into believing there is no God.

Science is not incompatible with creation. In fact it confirms it. It is our refusal to
accept God's authority that causes us to rebel.

However, His Word says, *"In the beginning was the Word. . . and the Word was God. He
was in the beginning"* (John 1:1). That's what is vital to our lives.

Larry Burkett

Daily Scripture Reading:
Philemon; 1 Timothy 1-3

"May the Lord cause you to increase and abound in love for one another, and for all men. . . so that He may establish your hearts unblamable in holiness before our God and Father"
(1 Thessalonians 3:12-13).

TIME TRAVEL

Have you ever thought about what it would have been like to have lived in another time period? If you could be at any event in history, which one would you choose?

Perhaps most Christians would choose to have lived during the time Christ was on the earth. I don't think I would, and I'll tell you why. I'm not absolutely sure which side I would have been on. Would I have believed what Jesus was teaching, or would I have been one of those who opposed Him? Would I have been a zealot, screaming unbelief at Him, like everyone else? I'm not sure. I'd like to think I would have accepted His teaching, but I'm not sure.

I know that if I had lived during Christ's life and had accepted His teaching, the crowds would have done to me what they did to Paul, because I would have refused to compromise.

If the Lord would just allow me to do it, I'd go back to 1775, when the first of the real Freedom Movements began to take hold in America. The value systems and attitudes were being shaped by the Founding Fathers.

To me, outside of the birth, death, and resurrection of Christ, that is the most exciting time in all history. There are others, to be sure.

However, we were created for this particular time and environment, and it is great, because we can be a driving force for Christianity to the entire world.

"God is with the righteous generation" (Psalm 14:5).

Larry Burkett

Daily Scripture Reading:
1 Timothy 4-6; Titus

"Go to the ant, you sluggard; consider its ways and be wise!
It has no commander, no overseer or ruler, yet it stores
its provisions in summer and gathers its food at harvest"
(Proverbs 6:6-8 NIV).

MONEY BUT NO MARGIN

In the United States we are experiencing a growing problem of people who have money, but no margin. They are living without any flexibility whether it was from debt, unexpected medical expenses, maxing out on two incomes, over consumption, or poor planning.

As one pastor who has a fast-growing church in a major city once told me, he preaches every Sunday to the "affluent poor." They have outward appearances that reflect lots of money and possessions, but beneath the surface, most are stretched to their limits and beyond because they are maxed out on their lifestyles.

In times of a growing economy and rising incomes, most people can stay a step ahead of the wolves. But when the economy slows or inflation hits and financial margin is needed, the lifestyle that seemed so wonderful becomes a form of captivity. The real crisis in our nation is not because of inflation or a slow economy, it is because a high percentage of our population is unprepared for inflation or a slower economy...they have no margin.

Maybe you are one of those who is feeling margin-less. Do you feel like you have money but no margin? Does affluent poor describe you?

Maybe today is the day to truly consider the ant, and grow wise.

Chuck Bentley

Daily Scripture Reading:
2 Timothy

*"Be hospitable to one another. . . . As each one has
received a special gift, employ it in serving one another
as good stewards of the manifold grace of God"*
(1 Peter 4:9-10).

WILL IT BE MERRY?

Christmas is very close and I hope you are going to have a happy one—not because of the gifts you are going to get, but because you are celebrating the true meaning of Christmas. The saying has become almost trite; nevertheless, it is something to think about: "Jesus is the Reason for the season."

Christmas should be a joyful time, but for many people it becomes a depressing time—either because they can't afford to compete in the gift-giving activities or because they are away from their loved ones and feeling lonely.

Think of people you know who don't have much hope of having a happy Christmas—financially, physically, or emotionally. Call someone today, and tell that person that you love him or her and that God does too. See if there is anything that person needs.

The holidays can be a very lonely time for some people. If you can invite others into your home, that's great. But if not, at least call and give of yourself. The busier you are doing for others, the happier your Christmas will be.

"Commit your works to the Lord" (Proverbs 16:3).

Larry Burkett

Daily Scripture Reading:
1 Peter

355

> *"Do you not know that you are a temple of God,*
> *and that the Spirit of God dwells in you?"*
> (1 Corinthians 3:16).

MY TEMPLE

Scripture is clear that, as a believer, when we put our faith in Jesus Christ the Holy Spirit comes to reside in us.

Therefore, whatever I do and wherever I go, the Holy Spirit is with me in my words and in my actions. That's a pretty sobering thought that should cause all Christians to stop and give thought to what we say and do. We are actual temples in which the Holy Spirit lives.

I have often regretted something I've just said or done or thought because I just included the Holy Spirit in my pettiness (or anger or resentment or irritation).

In the Old Testament He chose to make His presence known in the temple (the building). Now, living under the New Covenant, the Spirit lives within each born-again person.

When Scripture speaks of grieving the Holy Spirit, I think it means that the Spirit is emotionally, spiritually, and physically entwined in each and every believer. So we must bring our thoughts, actions, and deeds under God's control.

"To each one is given the manifestation of the Spirit for the common good" (
1 Corinthians 12:7).

Larry Burkett

Daily Scripture Reading:
2 Peter, Jude

"A wife of noble character is her husband's crown,
but a disgraceful wife is like decay in his bones"
(Proverbs 12:4 NIV).

A PRICELESS CROWN

In the Northern Hemisphere, the winter solstice occurs on either December 21 or 22. The winter solstice marks the shortest day and the longest night of the year.

Do you want to know why I remember this? It is also the day of my wedding anniversary. I did not intentionally choose this day, but it marks a turning point in the change of seasons and a remarkable change in my life as well.

On December 21, 1978, Ann and I exchanged our vows before God to become man and wife. From the beginning, I loved and cherished her. However, through the years, I have grown to also truly admire her for her noble character.

There is not a single person who has had greater influence on my relationship with Jesus Christ than my beloved wife. As Solomon noted here, a wife of strong character is as precious as the crown of a king.

This asset is deemed as priceless in Proverbs 31:10-11: *"A wife of noble character who can find? She is worth far more than rubies. Her husband has full confidence in her and lacks nothing of value"* (NIV).

Men, let us thank God for these "priceless crowns" who adorn our heads.

Chuck Bentley

Daily Scripture Reading:
Hebrews 1:1-5:10

"In Hades he lifted up his eyes, being in torment. . . . He cried out and said, 'Father Abraham, have mercy on me, and send Lazarus, that he may dip the tip of his finger in water and cool off my tongue; for I am in agony in this flame' "
(Luke 16:23-24).

WHAT IS HELL LIKE?

I read a story once about a very evil man who had died. He woke in a place that was totally dark—nothing around him. He had always joked that since all his friends would be in Hell that was where he wanted to go.

He thought, I'm alone. What happened? Well, this can't be forever; nothing is forever. God will come and get me.

Time passed and he finally realized that no one was coming. Then he began to feel the heat of the flames around him. He looked down to see if he was burning, but there was no physical body; yet he could feel the flames and the pain was real.

He cried out for mercy, but there was no one to hear him. He realized he had died and gone to hell and would be there for eternity, which is forever and ever and ever. He would always be in that lake of fire. No one was coming for him. He was completely alone in his suffering.

I believe that's an accurate description of what hell probably will be like. From what we read in Scripture (see today's verse) it sounds frighteningly real.

Praise God that we don't have to fear that fate—not if we have accepted the Lord Jesus Christ as Savior and Lord of our lives.

We do have to be concerned about those who have not made that decision and do all we can to see that their eternity will be joyful.

"God did not spare angels when they sinned, but cast them into hell and committed them to pits of darkness, reserved for judgment" (2 Peter 2:4).

Larry Burkett

Daily Scripture Reading:
Hebrews 5:11-9:28

"Behold, I create new heavens and a new earth; and the former things shall not be remembered or come to mind"
(Isaiah 65:17).

WHAT WILL HEAVEN BE LIKE?

Shortly after Senator Harold Hughes became a Christian someone asked him, "Senator Hughes, what do you think is the advantage of being a Christian?" They thought he would say, "Well, God will make me the next president of the United States." But he didn't say that.

Senator Hughes replied, "The advantage of being a Christian is that this life is all of Hell I shall ever experience. The disadvantage of being an unbeliever is that this life is all the Heaven some people will ever know."

I guess everybody has their own idea of what Heaven will be like. We are told in Revelation that God is going to bring New Jerusalem down out of Heaven—a city made of jasper, gold, onyx, and other precious stones, and the streets will be transparent gold. The city will be a 1500-mile cube.

God said there will be a new Heaven and a new Earth, and that's where His people will be. I'm looking forward to it, aren't you?

I don't care if I'm a street sweeper in Heaven. After all, the streets are made of gold!

The best part of Heaven is that we will be in the presence of God. And, there will be no more pain, fear, suffering, sickness, or sorrow, as well as no cancer, diabetes, heart trouble, overweight, gray hair, or wrinkles, so why wouldn't we look forward to getting to Heaven?

What are you looking forward to?

Larry Burkett

Daily Scripture Reading:
Hebrews 10-11

*"For all that is in the world, the lust of the flesh and
the lust of the eyes and the boastful pride of life,
is not from the Father, but is from the world"*
(1 John 2:16).

KEEPING CHRIST IN CHRISTMAS

It irritates me to see Christ being taken out of Christmas. That's not limited to only non-Christians—even Christians have adjusted to the commercialism of the holiday season. Obviously, not all of it is bad; in fact, the holiday season provides opportunities for families to reunite and also provides a pleasant break from our routines.

I personally look forward to these days as an opportunity to visit with friends who are much too busy other times of the year to just stop and relax.

Gift-giving is a relatively new idea. Until a couple of centuries ago, Christmas was reserved as a religious holiday on a noncommercial basis. However, gift-giving became a generally accepted practice and was used primarily to show appreciation to loved ones.

As with most things that start out right, somewhere along the way the direction shifted. How did it happen? It seems apparent that Christians aren't as wise in the things of the Lord as non-Christians are.

The secular world is always looking for ways to shift attention from God to material things, and we've been naive enough to go along with it.

It's time for Christians to stop compromising with the enemy and put Christ back in the celebration of His birth.

"He who practices the truth comes to the light, that his deeds may be manifested as having been wrought in God" (John 3:21).

Have a wonderful day as you celebrate our Savior's birthday!

Larry Burkett

Daily Scripture Reading: Hebrews 12-13;
2 John; 3 John

"The plans of the heart belong to man. . . . Commit your works to the Lord, and your plans will be established"
(Proverbs 16:1, 3).

AFTER CHRISTMAS

Well, Christmas is past. Praise the Lord! Right? That's what you may be thinking, especially if you went into debt. Now that Christmas is over, what are your goals for the coming year?

Let me make a suggestions for next year's Christmas that you can start right now. In fact, the first goal is to budget your Christmas gifts right now, while the memory of what you have done this year is fresh in your mind. Jot down some distinct spending goals and stick to them.

Next, set aside some money in your budget every month for Christmas shopping. If you are going to spend $600, save $50 every month; if it will be more like $1,200, save $100 every month. Then don't spend any more than you have saved.

Three, think about self-made gifts. You and your family could make gifts to exchange with one another, which will be some of your finest treasures.

Four, shop bargain sales throughout the year and don't wait until November or December, when you'll pay the higher prices.

Five, get your family members together and discuss drawing names. If you swap gifts with one or two people, that simplifies gift-giving.

Begin now to set some realistic goals for next Christmas. Make it a joyful Christmas—one that can be spent in the worship of our Lord, with less focus on material things.

Larry Burkett

Daily Scripture Reading:
1 John

*"Now to him who is able to do immeasurably more
than all we ask or imagine, according to his power that
is at work within us, to him be glory in the church and in
Christ Jesus throughout all generations, for ever and ever! Amen"*
(Ephesians 3:20-21 NIV).

PEACE AND PASSIVITY

When you're facing a crisis, it's important to be peaceful rather than passive.

Being passive means you allow yourself to suffer through something that you might be able to change by making a little effort. You may even wallow in self-pity and believe you're suffering because of past sins and that God no longer cares.

Peace is entirely different. It means you're doing all you can to change your circumstances, but you're not worrying. You know that even if recovering from your crisis is difficult and requires a long time, then perhaps God wants you to learn something from the process.

Don't worry, because when you do, you take on a responsibility that belongs to God. *"Cast all your anxiety on him because he cares for you"* (1 Peter 5:7 NIV). When you worry, you're essentially saying to God, "You're not in control." Instead, be at peace, knowing He remains sovereign.

Jesus said, *"Peace I leave with you, My peace I give to you; not as the world gives do I give to you. Let not your heart be troubled, neither let it be afraid"* (John 14:27 NKJV).

In times of crisis, do all you can to change the situation and trust God to do the rest. His greatest saints had to learn to handle heartaches and disappointments. Reading about their defeats will bring you insight, and reading about their victories will give you hope.

Chuck Bentley

Daily Scripture Reading:
Revelation 1-3

*"Esther was taken to the palace of the king. . . . The king
loved Esther more than any of the other girls. . . . He set the
royal crown on her head and declared her queen"*
(Esther 2:16-17 TLB).

CHOSEN TO INTERCEDE

If we are to be fulfilled Christians, we have to make the commitment to do what
God has told us to do—no matter the outcome.

One of my favorite books in the Bible is Esther. Esther was a graphic example of
obedience, timidity, and humility.

Esther's uncle, Mordecai, heard that the king (Esther's husband) had granted a
request to issue an edict that all the Jews in the land could be killed and their property
confiscated. When Mordecai heard this, he fasted and prayed; then he wrote to Esther
and asked her to go to the king and intercede on behalf of her people.

Esther responded by saying that she couldn't go in to the king unless he summoned
her—under penalty of death.

Mordecai wrote back to tell Esther that she could do nothing else (because Esther
was also a Jew, although her husband, the king, didn't know it). He cautioned Esther that
if she didn't go and intercede for her people, God would choose someone else.

Esther agreed and said, *"Fast for me. . . . I will go in to see the king; and if I perish, I
perish"* (Esther 4:16 TLB).

Esther made sure her husband, the king, and her people were saved, but the real
point is that she was willing to face an uncertain fate to be obedient. All too often in our
generation we choose the safe way and miss the blessing.

What would you do if being obedient risked your life?

Larry Burkett

Daily Scripture Reading:
Revelation 4-9

"There is he that maketh himself rich, yet hath nothing;
there is he that maketh himself poor, yet hath great riches"
(Proverbs 13:7).

DECEITFULNESS OF RICHES

Old man Cates was a very rich man—one of the richest in the islands. He had a sizable plantation and prospered financially from its produce; but he had few friends. He was very tight with his money, and the wages he paid his hired labor were low. Over the years he spent little and amassed quite a savings. And through those years he didn't have time for God; he was too busy building "bigger barns."

After many years, old man Cates became extremely ill. Because he suffered from pain that hindered his sleep, he often rocked during the evenings. His condition grew worse until it was evident that he wouldn't live.

One evening, hearing his screams, his wife ran to him and heard him cry out, "Oh, my God! Jesus of Nazareth has passed me by!" With that on his lips, he died.

Time ran out for the man who had no time for God. The expression of terrible fright remained on his face and the sounds of his agonizing cries about the intense heat of the fire into which he was passing haunted his wife.

Just like the rich man of Luke 16, old man Cates would have traded his wealth for Lazarus' poverty, if he had only realized the deceitfulness of his riches.

We need to remind ourselves that we cannot trust in riches. Only our trust in Christ will secure our future—now and in the hereafter.

Larry Burkett

Daily Scripture Reading:
Revelation 10-14

364

"Why do you worry so for tomorrow? Are not the cares of today sufficient for this day unto itself?"
(Luke 12:22).

JUST A LITTLE MORE

We have the greatest abundance of material things in the entire world. It's not the lack of things that concerns us; it is the worry about the lack of things.

I recall a story I heard about a fellow in India who was starving. He couldn't feed his family so he began to pray, "Oh God, I ask You to give us what we need this day. Give us just one fish, Lord, and we'll be satisfied." That day he went to a rice paddy with a bent hook, dropped it into a rice paddy, and pulled out a fish. A miracle.

After the fish was gone he began to pray that God would give him a fish every day and then he would not have a need again. Every day he pulled out a fish. A miracle.

It began to rain and his roof leaked. He asked God to provide him with materials to fix the roof. A truck came by one day and some tin fell off. It kept the rain out of his house and he was thankful.

Then he prayed, "Lord, I thank You for the fish and for the tin for my roof. Now, God, if I just had a three-bedroom, two-bath house, with two cars, a color television, and a good education for my children, then God I wouldn't ask You for anything else."

Of course, the story is fictitious, but does it remind you in any way of yourself? Are you ever satisfied with what you have or do you always want more? Just a little more?

"His eyes were not satisfied with riches. . . . This too is vanity and it is a grievous task" (Ecclesiastes 4:8).

Larry Burkett

Daily Scripture Reading:
Revelation 15-18

*"For the eyes of the LORD range throughout the earth to
strengthen those whose hearts are fully committed to Him"*
(2 Chronicles 16:9 NIV).

FULLY COMMITTED

In less than a day the year will be over and the New Year will begin. In our home, we have a practice of establishing resolutions and helping each other to stick with it.

I would like to recommend two resolutions for your consideration.

First, fully commit your entire heart to God. Commit to Him your goals, dreams, ambitions, money, time, talents, health, relationships, and whatever else may be between you and God. Hold nothing back.

Second, commit to read through the entire Bible with the goal to get to know the Author. There are few resolutions you could ever derive more benefit from than that one simple, daily practice.

Make your single purpose in life to glorify God.

Each new day represents an opportunity to crown Him with the position of supremacy in your life that He deserves.

May this be the year that you become completely faithful in complete commitment to our Faithful God.

Chuck Bentley

Daily Scripture Reading:
Revelation 19-22

MONEY AND POSSESSION

Scriptures

GOD'S PART

Genesis 14:19	Acts 17:26	Joshua 24:13
Genesis 14:22	2 Chronicles 25:7-9	Nehemiah 9:15
Exodus 9:29	Isaiah 10:5-6	Nehemiah 9:36
Exodus 19:5	1 Chronicles 29:14	Jeremiah 7:5-7
Deuteronomy 10:14	Romans 11:36	Genesis 24:35
1 Chronicles 29:11,14-16	Genesis 22:14	Genesis 26:12-14
Job 41:11	Psalm 136:25	Deuteronomy 30:5
Psalm 24:1	Psalm 145:15-16	1 Samuel 18:14-15
Psalm 50:12	Deuteronomy 2:7	2 Samuel 6:12
Psalm 82:8	Deuteronomy 8:15-16	2 Chronicles 1:11-12
Psalm 89:11	Nehemiah 9:15	2 Chronicles 25:6-9
Psalm 95:4-5	Nehemiah 9:21	Job 1:9-10
Psalm 104:24	Leviticus 25:20-22	Job 42:10,12
1 Corinthians 10:26	Matthew 14:15-21	Psalm 105:37
Matthew 25:14-28	Matthew 15:32-38	Isaiah 45:3
Hebrews 1:3	Matthew 16:8-10	Jeremiah 27:5-7
Colossians 1:17	Mark 6:35-44	Ezekiel 16:13,14,17-19
Leviticus 25:23	Mark 8:1-9	Ezekiel 29:18-19
Ezekiel 16:17	Mark 8:18-20	Hosea 2:8
Haggai 2:8	Luke 9:12-17	Genesis 14:22-23
Psalm 50:10-11	John 6:5-13	Deuteronomy 8:15-18
1 Chronicles 29:11-12	John 21:2-11	Psalm 66:10-12
Psalm 135:6	Psalm 33:18-19	Psalm 127:2
Proverbs 16:33	Psalm 34:9-10	Proverbs 10:22
Proverbs 20:24	Psalm 81:13,16	2 Samuel 12:7-8
Daniel 2:20-21	Proverbs 10:3	Matthew 25:14-15
Job 42:11	Philippians 4:19	Genesis 32:9
Isaiah 45:6-7	Matthew 6:33	Genesis 32:12
Lamentations 3:37-38	Luke 12:30-31	Genesis 39:2-3
Amos 3:6	1 Chronicles 29:14	Genesis 39:21-23
Romans 8:28	Romans 11:36	Psalm 115:14
Genesis 45:5-9	1 Timothy 6:17	Psalm 118:25
Ecclesiastes 9:11	1 Chronicles 29:12,14-16	3 John 2
Proverbs 21:1	Ecclesiastes 5:19	Job 1:21-22
Genesis 39:21	Ecclesiastes 6:1-2	Job 2:9-10
Ezra 6:22	Jeremiah 27:5	1 Samuel 2:7
Nehemiah 2:8, 18	Genesis 35:12	Ecclesiastes 7:14
Exodus 3:21-22	Exodus 6:8	Judges 2:13-16
Exodus 12:35-36	Leviticus 25:38	Jeremiah 29:14
Exodus 14:4	Deuteronomy 6:10-12	Jeremiah 32:44
Deuteronomy 2:30	Deuteronomy 8:7-10	Jeremiah 33:7, 11, 26
Exodus 34:23-24	Deuteronomy 26:1-3	Jeremiah 48:47

Jeremiah 49:6
Joel 3:1-2
Zephaniah 2:7
Zephaniah 3:20
Zechariah 8:10-12

Proverbs 15:25
Ezekiel 26:12, 14
Zechariah 9:3-4
Zechariah 14:1-2
Genesis 31:6-7, 9

Genesis 31:14-16
Job 1:9-10
Genesis 31:42

OUR PART

Genesis 1:28
Psalm 8:6
Psalm 115:16
Hebrews 2:6-8
Matthew 25:14
Genesis 24:2
Genesis 39:4-6
Genesis 39:7-9
1 Corinthians 9:17
Luke 14:33
Matthew 19:27-29
Mark 10:28-30
Luke 18:28-30
Mark 1:20
Luke 5:11
Luke 5:27-28
Matthew 13:44-46
1 Corinthians 4:2, KJV
Proverbs 28:20
Matthew 24:44-46
Matthew 25:21
Matthew 25:20-23
Luke 12:42-44
Luke 19:12-26
Matthew 24:48-51
Luke 12:45-47
Luke 19:12-26
Luke 16:1-8
Deuteronomy 7:12-13

Deuteronomy 15:4-6
Deuteronomy 28:1-14
Deuteronomy 29:9
Deuteronomy 30:9-10
Deuteronomy 30:15-16
Joshua 1:8
1 Kings 2:3
1 Chronicles 22:12-13
1 Chronicles 28:8
Psalm 37:4
Psalm 128:1-2
2 Kings 18:6-7
2 Chronicles 14:7
2 Chronicles 26:5
2 Chronicles 31:20-21
Isaiah 30:22-23
Deuteronomy 28:15-18, 33
Deuteronomy 28:45-48, 63
Deuteronomy 30:15-18
Ezra 7:26
Judges 2:13-14
2 Chronicles 21:12-
14,16,17
2 Chronicles 24:20
Nehemiah 9:33-36
Jeremiah 10:21
Ezekiel 16:17-19, 39
Haggai 1:4-11
Haggai 2:15-17

Psalm 112:1,3
Proverbs 22:4
Proverbs 28:25
Proverbs 11:28
Jeremiah 17:5-6
Jeremiah 48:7
Jeremiah 49:4-5
Matthew 25:14, 19
Luke 16:2
2 Corinthians 5:9-10
Revelation 20:11-12

DEBT

Romans 13:8
Proverbs 22:7
1 Corinthians 7:23
1 Samuel 22:1-2
2 Kings 4:1
Nehemiah 5:1-5
Psalm 109:11
Isaiah 50:1
Jeremiah 15:10
Deuteronomy 28:15, 43-45

Deuteronomy 15:4-6
Deuteronomy 28:1-2, 12
Proverbs 3:27-28
Psalm 37:21
2 Kings 4:1-7
Deuteronomy 15:1-11
Deuteronomy 31:10-11
Nehemiah 10:31
Philemon 18-19
Matthew 18:21-35

Luke 7:40-43
Colossians 2:14
Proverbs 17:18
Proverbs 20:16
Proverbs 27:13
Proverbs 11:15
Proverbs 22:26-27
Proverbs 6:1-5

COUNSEL

Proverbs 1:5
Proverbs 1:25
Proverbs 1:30
Proverbs 12:15
Proverbs 13:10
Proverbs 19:20
Proverbs 20:18
Proverbs 27:9
Ecclesiastes 4:13
Luke 13:31
Proverbs 11:14
Proverbs 15:22
Proverbs 24:5-6
Leviticus 26:8
Ecclesiastes 4:9-12
Exodus 18:14-24
1 Kings 1:11-12
Job 29:21-23
2 Chronicles 25:14-16
Job 12:13
Psalm 16:7
Psalm 25:12
Psalm 32:8
Psalm 33:10-11
Psalm 73:24
Proverbs 19:21

Isaiah 9:6
Isaiah 11:2
Isaiah 28:29
Jeremiah 32:18-19
1 Chronicles 10:13-14
Joshua 9:14-15
Psalm 106:13-15
Psalm 107:10-12
2 Samuel 15:31, 33-34
2 Samuel 16:20, 23
2 Samuel 17:6-23
Psalm 119:24
Proverbs 1:8-9
Proverbs 6:20-22
Proverbs 23:22
1 Kings 2:1-4
2 Chronicles 9:23
Proverbs 13:20
1 Corinthians 12:8
1 Kings 12:6-8
2 Chronicles 10:6-8
Job 21:14-16
Psalm 1:1
Proverbs 12:5
Ezra 4:4-5
Nahum 1:11

Deuteronomy 32:28
Isaiah 41:28-29
1 Kings 12:8-10, 13-14
2 Chronicles 10:8-10, 13-14
Proverbs 11:14
Proverbs 15:22
Proverbs 24:6
Psalm 32:8
Psalm 73:24
Proverbs 6:20-22
Proverbs 13:10
Proverbs 19:20
Proverbs 12:20
1 Chronicles 10:13,14
2 Chronicles 22:3-5
2 Chronicles 25:16
Proverbs 1:24-32
Proverbs 13:10
Proverbs 15:22
Proverbs 11:14
Joshua 9:14-15
Psalm 106:13-15
Psalm 107:10-12

HONESTY

Genesis 8:21
Jeremiah 17:9
Matthew 15:19
Mark 7:21-22
Judges 17:6
Genesis 31:7
Joshua 7:11, 20-21
1 Samuel 8:3
1 Kings 21:19
Psalm 58:3
Isaiah 1:23
Isaiah 56:11
Jeremiah 6:13
Jeremiah 7:9, 11
Ezekiel 22:27, 29
Hosea 4:1-2
Hosea 5:10
Hosea 7:1
Hosea 12:7
Micah 6:10-12
John 12:4-6
John 18:40
Acts 5:1-10
Titus 1:12
Revelation 9:20-21
Luke 16:1-8
Jeremiah 7:9-11
Matthew 21:12-13
Matthew 23:25
Mark 11:15-17
Luke 11:39
Luke 19:45-46
Titus 1:10-11
John 1:14
John 14:6
John 16:13
1 John 5:7
John 8:44
Exodus 20:15
Leviticus 19:11-13
Leviticus 19:35-36

Leviticus 25:14-17
Deuteronomy 5:19
Deuteronomy 19:14
Deuteronomy 25:13-16
Psalm 34:13
Psalm 51:6
Psalm 62:10
Proverbs 3:3
Proverbs 4:24
Proverbs 6:12
Proverbs 6:16, 19
Proverbs 11:1
Proverbs 12:22
Proverbs 13:5
Proverbs 14:5
Proverbs 14:25
Proverbs 17:7
Proverbs 16:11
Proverbs 20:10
Proverbs 20:23
Proverbs 22:22-23
Proverbs 22:28
Proverbs 23:10
Proverbs 23:23
Proverbs 28:24
Lamentations 3:35-36
Zechariah 8:16-17
Luke 3:12-14
Romans 2:21-22
1 Corinthians 6:7-10
Ephesians 4:25
Ephesians 6:14
Colossians 3:9
1 Thessalonians 5:22
1 Timothy 1:9-10
Titus 2:9-10
1 Peter 1:15-16
1 Peter 4:15
Exodus 18:21-22
Proverbs 20:28
Proverbs 28:16

Ezekiel 45:9-10
1 Timothy 3:8
Titus 1:7
1 Peter 5:1-2
Malachi 1:13-14
Malachi 3:8-9
Proverbs 19:1
Proverbs 19:22
Proverbs 28:12
Numbers 16:15
1 Samuel 12:3-5
Job 31:5, 8
Daniel 6:4
Daniel 6:22
Zephaniah 3:13
Genesis 42:11, 18-20
Genesis 42:31-34
Proverbs 13:5
Proverbs 14:2
Proverbs 26:28
Romans 13:9-10
Philippians 2:15
Proverbs 4:24-26
Luke 16:10
Psalm 119:36
Proverbs 30:7-8
Galatians 5:16-17
Matthew 7:12
Philippians 2:4
Proverbs 16:6
Psalm 26:4
Psalm 40:4
Psalm 101:6-7
Proverbs 1:10-16
Proverbs 29:24
|1 Corinthians 5:9-11
1 Corinthians 15:33
Ephesians 4:28
Genesis 30:31-33
Leviticus 5:5-6
Leviticus 6:1-5, 7

1 John 1:9
Proverbs 28:13
James 5:16
Exodus 22:1-4
Exodus 22:7-9
Exodus 22:14
Leviticus 6:1-5
Numbers 5:5-8
2 Samuel 12:5-6
Proverbs 6:30-31
Ezekiel 33:14-16
Luke 19:8
Psalm 15:1-4
Psalm 24:3-4
Psalm 145:18
Proverbs 3:3-4
Proverbs 3:32
Proverbs 12:22
Jeremiah 22:15-17
Proverbs 2:7
Proverbs 10:9
Isaiah 33:15-16
Proverbs 20:7
Proverbs 10:2
Deuteronomy 25:13-15
Psalm 34:12-13
Proverbs 12:19
Ezekiel 33:14-16
Proverbs 3:3-4
Proverbs 15:6
Proverbs 28:16
Deuteronomy 25:13-16
Psalm 5:6
Proverbs 3:32
Proverbs 6:16, 19
Proverbs 12:22
Proverbs 19:9
Isaiah 57:17
Isaiah 59:2-4
Deuteronomy 27:17
Psalm 63:11
Proverbs 12:15
Proverbs 19:5

Proverbs 20:17
Isaiah 57:17
Jeremiah 5:27-29
Jeremiah 9:3-9
Ezekiel 22:13-15
Ezekiel 22:27-31
Hosea 5:10
Amos 8:4-10
Micah 6:10-16
Matthew 21:12-13
Luke 19:45-46
Joshua 7:11, 15, 25
Psalm 5:6
Psalm 52:3-5
Proverbs 1:19
Proverbs 6:12, 15
Proverbs 12:19
Proverbs 21:6
Proverbs 22:8
Proverbs 22:22-23
Jeremiah 22:17-19
Ezekiel 18:10-13, 18
Acts 5:1-10
Proverbs 15:27
Jeremiah 8:10
Micah 2:1-3
Genesis 31:7, 9
Proverbs 10:2
Proverbs 13:11
Jeremiah 6:12-13
Jeremiah 17:11
Micah 4:13
Proverbs 22:8
Proverbs 29:12
Revelation 21:8
Revelation 21:27
Revelation 22:15
Deuteronomy 27:17
Proverbs 20:17
Nahum 3:1
Job 24:1-2, 12
Proverbs 17:8
Proverbs 21:14

Psalm 26:9-10
Proverbs 17:23
1 Samuel 8:3
Isaiah 1:23
Micah 7:3
Matthew 28:11-15
Acts 24:25-26
Exodus 23:8
Deuteronomy 16:19
Ecclesiastes 7:7
Deuteronomy 10:17
2 Chronicles 19:7
Proverbs 29:4
1 Samuel 12:3-5
Job 6:22
Deuteronomy 27:25
Isaiah 5:23
Ezekiel 22:12-15
Amos 5:11-12
Micah 3:11-12
Psalm 15:1, 5
Proverbs 15:27
Isaiah 33:15-16

GIVING

James 2:14-17

1 John 3:17

2 Corinthians 8:8

Luke 10:33-35

Matthew 19:21-22

Mark 10:21-22

Luke 18:22-23

John 3:16

1 John 4:16

James 1:17

1 Corinthians 13:3

2 Corinthians 9:7

Exodus 25:2

Exodus 30:12-14

Exodus 35:5

Exodus 35:21-29

Leviticus 7:14

Numbers 18:8-24

2 Chronicles 32:23

1 Chronicles 18:11

2 Samuel 8:11

Psalm 50:14

Psalm 66:13

Psalm 68:29

Psalm 76:11

Ezekiel 20:40

Micah 4:13

1 Chronicles 29:14-16

Matthew 2:1

Isaiah 43:23-24

1 Chronicles 29:5-9

1 Chronicles 29:14-17

2 Corinthians 8:1-5

Matthew 23:23

Luke 11:42

Luke 18:10-14

Genesis 4:4

Hebrews 11:4

Philippians 4:18

Genesis 4:3-5

Amos 4:4-6

Amos 5:22, 24

Amos 5:25-27

Malachi 2:13-14

Acts 5:1-10

Proverbs 7:14

Acts 20:35

Matthew 6:21

Luke 12:34

Matthew 6:20

Matthew 19:21

Luke 12:33

Luke 18:22

Philippians 4:17

1Timothy 6:17-19

Deuteronomy 14:28-29

2 Chronicles 31:10

Proverbs 3:9-10

Proverbs 11:24-25

Ecclesiastes 11:1

Luke 6:38

2 Corinthians 9:6-11

Philippians 4:19

Malachi 3:10

Ezekiel 44:30

Luke 7:2-5

Acts 9:36-37, 40

Acts 10:1-4, 31

Genesis 14:20

Genesis 28:20-22

Leviticus 27:30-32

Malachi 3:8-9

Deuteronomy 14:22-26

Numbers 18:21-24

Deuteronomy 14:28-29

Deuteronomy 26:12

2 Chronicles 31:4-12

Nehemiah 10:37-38

Nehemiah 13:10-11

Numbers 18:26

Hebrews 7:1-2, 4-9

2 Chronicles 31:11-12

Nehemiah 10:38

Nehemiah 12:44

Nehemiah 13:12

Deuteronomy 16:10, 16

1 Corinthians 16:2

Ezra 2:69

Acts 11:29

2 Corinthians 8:12

Mark 12:41-44

Luke 21:1-4

2 Corinthians 8:1-4

2 Samuel 24:21-24

1 Chronicles 21:22-24

Malachi 1:6-14

Exodus 23:10-11

Exodus 34:19

Exodus 34:26

Leviticus 2:12

Numbers 28:26

Deuteronomy 26:1-2

Proverbs 3:9

Exodus 22:29

Deuteronomy 23:21

Ecclesiastes 5:4

2 Corinthians 9:7

1 Corinthians 16:2

Exodus 34:20

Deuteronomy 16:17

Ezekiel 45:16

Acts 11:29

1 Corinthians 16:2

1 Corinthians 16:2

Matthew 6:1-4

Exodus 25:2

Exodus 35:5

Exodus 35:21-29

2 Kings 12:4

1 Chronicles 26:20

1 Chronicles 26:26

2 Chronicles 31:14-15

Nehemiah 12:44

Nehemiah 13:13
2 Corinthians 8:18-21
Acts 11:30
1 Corinthians 16:3-4
2 Kings 12:15
2 Kings 22:7
1 Timothy 5:8
Matthew 15:4-6
Mark 7:9-13
1 Timothy 5:4
1 Timothy 5:16
Genesis 45:11
Genesis 47:12
Leviticus 2:3
Leviticus 7:14
Leviticus 7:32-34
Leviticus 10:12-14
Numbers 5:8-10
Numbers 18:8-19
Numbers 31:28-30
Deuteronomy 18:3-4
Deuteronomy 25:4
Nehemiah 10:35-36
Nehemiah 12:47
Ezekiel 44:29-30
Matthew 10:9-10
Mark 6:8
Luke 9:1-3
Luke 10:1, 4-7
Galatians 6:6
1 Timothy 5:17-18
Titus 3:13
3 John 1:5-8
Luke 8:3
1 Corinthians 9:6-15
1 Corinthians 9:17-18
2 Corinthians 11:7-9
2 Corinthians 12:14-18
1 Thessalonians 2:5, 9
2 Thessalonians 3:8-9
1 Peter 5:1-2
2 Corinthians 2:17
Titus 1:10-11

2 Peter 2:1, 3
Luke 22:35-36
Exodus 25:3-8
Exodus 36:3-7
1 Chronicles 29:2-8
1 Kings 5:17
2 Kings 12:4-11
2 Kings 22:4-6
2 Chronicles 24:4-13
2 Chronicles 34:8-11
Ezra 2:68-69
Ezra 6:4
Ezra 6:8
Nehemiah 10:30, 39
Matthew 5:42
Luke 6:30
Galatians 6:10
Romans 12:10, 13
Proverbs 25:21-22
Romans 12:20
Proverbs 28:17
Deuteronomy 15:11
Proverbs 14:31
Proverbs 19:17
Isaiah 58:6-10
Ezekiel 16:49
Exodus 23:10-11
Leviticus 19:9-10
Leviticus 23:22
Deuteronomy 24:19-21
Deuteronomy 15:7-10
Ester 9:22
Leviticus 25:10
Job 29:12-16
Job 31:16-23
Psalm 72:4, 12-13
Proverbs 31:10, 20
Luke 3:10-11
Matthew 25:31-45
John 13:27-29
Ephesians 4:28
Acts 2:44-45
Acts 11:28-30

Acts 20:35
Romans 15:26-27
Galatians 2:10
Jeremiah 22:16
Ezekiel 18:7, 9, 16-17
Psalm 112:2, 9
Proverbs 28:27
Psalm 41:1-3
Psalm 41:1-2
Psalm 112:9
Deuteronomy 15:10
Deuteronomy 24:19
Psalm 72:4, 12-15
Psalm 112:3, 9
Proverbs 19:17
Proverbs 28:8
Daniel 4:27
Titus 3:13-14
Proverbs 22:9
Proverbs 14:21
Proverbs 21:13
Proverbs 22:16
Proverbs 28:27
Job 30:25
Job 29:16
Job 22:5, 7, 9
Matthew 26:6-13
Mark 14:3-7
John 12:3-8
Acts 6:1-3
James 1:27
Acts 4:32-33
Leviticus 5:7, 11
Leviticus 12:6, 8
Leviticus 14:21-22
Leviticus 14:30-32
Leviticus 27:8
Luke 2:22-24
Exodus 30:12-15
Luke 19:8-9
Genesis 24:22, 53
Genesis 43:11-12, 15
2 Chronicles 9:8-9

2 Chronicles 9:12
2 Chronicles 31:23
2 Chronicles 32:23
2 Chronicles 35:7-9
Ezra 1:4, 6
Nehemiah 7:70-72
Esther 2:18
Psalm 72:10
Jeremiah 40:5
Genesis 32:13, 20
Genesis 33:8-11
Proverbs 21:14
Genesis 34:11-12
2 Chronicles 9:23-24
1 Kings 10:10
Revelation 11:10

Exodus 23:19
Exodus 34:26
Deuteronomy 12:6
Deuteronomy 12:11
Deuteronomy 12:17-18
Acts 3:2-6
Proverbs 19:6
2 Corinthians 9:5
2 Corinthians 9:12
Matthew 5:23-24
Nahum 1:15
Hebrews 13:16
Matthew 8:4
Mark 1:44
Luke 5:14
Acts 24:17

Mark 12:33
Hosea 6:6
1 Samuel 15:22
Isaiah 1:11
Proverbs 21:3
Ezekiel 46:11-15
Ezekiel 46:12
1 Kings 8:62-64
Ezra 1:2, 4, 6
Ezra 7:15-18, 20-22
Romans 12:6-8
Exodus 16:18
2 Corinthians 8:13-15

WORK

Genesis 2:2-3
John 5:17
Exodus 20:9
Exodus 23:12
Exodus 34:21
Deuteronomy 5:13
Ephesians 4:28
2 Thessalonians 3:8-12
Psalm 104:23
Genesis 2:15
Genesis 3:17-19, 23
Genesis 5:29
Genesis 2:15
Genesis 4:2
Genesis 9:20
Genesis 46:32
Genesis 47:3
Amos 7:14
Genesis 39:4
Genesis 41:41

Genesis 45:26
Nehemiah 4:14
Psalm 105:21
Daniel 2:48
Daniel 6:1-2
Daniel 8:27
Acts 8:27
Matthew 4:18
Mark 1:16
Mark 1:20
Matthew 13:55
Mark 6:3
Acts 18:2-3
Mark 2:14
Luke 5:27
Luke 19:2
Acts 16:14
1 Corinthians 10:31
Ephesians 6:5-9
Colossians 3:17

Colossians 3:23-24
Ecclesiastes 1:3
Ecclesiastes 2:4-5, 10-11
Ecclesiastes 2:18-24
Ecclesiastes 3:9-10, 13
Ecclesiastes 4:4-6
Ecclesiastes 5:18-19
Ecclesiastes 6:7
1 Samuel 2:28
Psalm 90:17
John 4:34
John 6:27
Acts 13:36
1 Corinthians 3:13-15
Ephesians 2:10
John 17:4
John 21:3-11
Psalm 127:1
Proverbs 16:3
Romans 2:6, 8

2 Corinthians 5:9-10
James 3:14-16
Jeremiah 45:5
Joshua 1:6-7
1 Chronicles 22:10, 13, 16
1 Chronicles 28:20
2 Chronicles 15:7
Haggai 2:4
Ezra 4:4-5
Nehemiah 4:15-22
Nehemiah 6:3, 9
Proverbs 12:27
Ecclesiastes 9:10
Ecclesiastes 11:6
Genesis 31:38-40
Nehemiah 2:18
Acts 20:34
1 Corinthians 4:11-12
2 Corinthians 11:27
Colossians 1:29
1 Thessalonians 2:9
2 Thessalonians 3:8
Proverbs 16:26
2 Timothy 2:6
Proverbs 12:11
Proverbs 27:18
Proverbs 28:19
Proverbs 10:4-5
Proverbs 13:11
Proverbs 14:23
Proverbs 21:5
Proverbs 13:4
Proverbs 12:24
Ecclesiastes 5:12
Psalm 128:1-2
Psalm 127:2
Proverbs 23:4
Proverbs 6:6-8
Proverbs 10:26
Proverbs 12:27
Proverbs 15:19
Proverbs 18:9
Proverbs 19:24

Proverbs 22:13
Proverbs 26:13-16
Proverbs 19:15
Proverbs 20:4
Proverbs 6:9-11
Proverbs 10:4
Proverbs 14:23
Proverbs 20:13
Proverbs 23:21
Proverbs 24:30-34
Ecclesiastes 10:18
Proverbs 21:25
Proverbs 13:4
Proverbs 12:24
Genesis 2:2-3
Exodus 20:11
Exodus 31:17
Hebrews 4:4, 10
Exodus 12:16
Exodus 20:9-10
Exodus 23:12
Exodus 34:21
Leviticus 23:3
Deuteronomy 5:13-14
Nehemiah 10:31
Jeremiah 17:21-22, 24
Exodus 31:15
Numbers 15:32-35
Nehemiah 13:15-18
Jeremiah 7:27
Exodus 23:10-11
Leviticus 25:1-5
Nehemiah 10:31
Leviticus 26:34
Leviticus 26:43
Leviticus 25:11
Numbers 28:18
Numbers 28:25
Deuteronomy 16:8
Leviticus 16:29
Leviticus 23:27-31
Leviticus 23:7-8
Leviticus 23:34-36

Numbers 29:12, 35
Leviticus 23:21
Leviticus 23:24-25
Numbers 28:26
Numbers 29:1
Numbers 29:7
Exodus 28:3
Exodus 31:1-3
Exodus 31:6
Exodus 35:30-35
Exodus 36:1-2
1 Chronicles 22:12
2 Chronicles 1:11-12
2 Chronicles 9:23
Ecclesiastes 2:26
Daniel 1:17
Daniel 2:21, 23
Genesis 39:2-3
Ruth 2:12
1 Chronicles 22:11
Nehemiah 2:18, 20
Nehemiah 4:15, 19-20
Nehemiah 6:15-16
John 3:27
1 Chronicles 29:12
2 Chronicles 9:8
Psalm 75:6-7
Daniel 2:37-38
Daniel 5:21
Haggai 1:14
Jeremiah 22:13
Malachi 3:5
Genesis 29:15
Genesis 30:28
James 5:1, 3-4
Matthew 20:1-16
Leviticus 19:13
Deuteronomy 24:14-15
Colossians 4:1
Ephesians 6:7-9
Job 31:13-15
Isaiah 58:3
Proverbs 29:12

Exodus 21:2	2 Chronicles 34:12	Proverbs 22:29
Deuteronomy 15:12-14	Proverbs 25:13	James 4:13-15
Genesis 30:27	Ephesians 6:5-8	1 Thessalonians 4:11-12
Genesis 39:5	Colossians 3:22-24	Acts 19:24-28
Nehemiah 5:14-18	Titus 2:9-10	Psalm 107:11-12
Exodus 1:13-14	1 Peter 2:18-19	1 Kings 5:6
Proverbs 26:10	1 Timothy 6:1	2 Chronicles 2:9-10
Daniel 6:4	Titus 2:9	1 Kings 9:10-12
1 Timothy 6:2	Proverbs 30:10	Number 8:24-26
Proverbs 17:2	Luke 3:14	Proverbs 31:10-28
Proverbs 27:18	Genesis 39:7-9	Titus 2:4-5
Daniel 6:28	2 Corinthians 6:14-17	Proverbs 12:11
2 Kings 12:15	Proverbs 24:27	Proverbs 28:19
2 Kings 22:7	Proverbs 14:4	

SAVING AND INVESTING

Matthew 6:19-21	Ezekiel 44:28-30	1 Timothy 6:10
Matthew 6:24-33	Genesis 15:2-4	1 Timothy 6:11
Matthew 19:16-21	Genesis 24:35-36	Matthew 4:8-10
Mark 6:8	Genesis 25:5	Luke 4:5-8
Luke 5:11	Genesis 31:14-16	Proverbs 21:20
Luke 12:22-34	Genesis 48:21-22	Proverbs 21:20, LB
Luke 18:18-30	Joshua 24:32	Proverbs 30:24-25
Luke 12:13-21	Ruth 4:5-10	Genesis 41:34-36
Matthew 25:14-28	2 Chronicles 21:3	Isaiah 48:17
Luke 19:12-24	Ecclesiastes 5:13-14	Ecclesiastes 11:2
1 Timothy 5:8	Ecclesiastes 7:11	Proverbs 24:27
Proverbs 13:22	1 Chronicles 28:8	Matthew 8:14
Proverbs 19:14	Ezra 9:12	Mark 1:29
Isaiah 38:1	Psalm 25:12-13	Luke 4:38
2 Corinthians 12:14	Proverbs 17:2	Matthew 8:20
Leviticus 25:46	Luke 15:11-31	Acts 28:30
Numbers 27:8-11	Luke 12:13-15	Ecclesiastes 5:13-14
Numbers 36:2-9	Proverbs 20:21	Ecclesiastes 5:13-16, LB
Deuteronomy 18:8	Galatians 4:1-2	Proverbs 21:5
Deuteronomy 21:15-17	Ecclesiastes 2:18-21	Proverbs 21:5, LB
Ezekiel 46:16-18	Ecclesiastes 4:8	Proverbs 21:5
Numbers 18:20-24	1 Timothy 6:9	Proverbs 28:20

Proverbs 28:22	Isaiah 5:8	Ezekiel 22:12-13
Ecclesiastes 3:1	Leviticus 25:14-17	Habakkuk 2:6-7
Proverbs 27:23-27	Proverbs 20:14	Deuteronomy 23:20
Luke 14:28-29	Proverbs 31:10, 16, 24	Exodus 22:26-27
Proverbs 20:18	Deuteronomy 15:7-9	Deuteronomy 24:6, 10-13
Proverbs 21:5	Psalm 112:5	Deuteronomy 24:17
Proverbs 24:3-4, LB	Matthew 5:42	Job 22:5-6
1 Corinthians 14:40	Exodus 22:25	Ezekiel 18:7, 9, 16-17
1 Corinthians 14:33	Leviticus 25:35-37	Ezekiel 33:15
Jeremiah 9:23-24	Deuteronomy 23:19	Ezekiel 18:10, 12-13
1 Timothy 6:17	Nehemiah 5:3-12	Amos 2:6, 8
James 1:9-11	Deuteronomy 23:20	Job 24:3, 9
Jeremiah 48:7	Psalm 15:1, 5	Luke 6:34-35
Jeremiah 49:4-5	Ezekiel 18:7-17	
1 Timothy 6:17	Proverbs 28:8	
1 Timothy 6:18	Ezekiel 18:10, 13	

CHILDREN

Deuteronomy 4:9	Deuteronomy 11:18-19
Deuteronomy 6:6-7	Proverbs 22:6

BUDGETING

Proverbs 27:23-27	1 Corinthians 14:33	Proverbs 24:3-4, TLB
Luke 14:28-29	Proverbs 20:18	
1 Corinthians 14:40	Proverbs 21:5	

CONTENTMENT

Philippians 4:11-13	Hebrews 13:5-6	Psalm 73:25
Matthew 6:25-34	1 Timothy 6:8	1 Timothy 6:6
Luke 12:22-31	Luke 3:14	Proverbs 6:35

COVETING

Exodus 20:17
Deuteronomy 5:21
Deuteronomy 7:25
Joshua 6:18
Micah 2:1-3

Joshua 7:11-25
1 Corinthians 10:6
1 Corinthians 6:9-10
Ephesians 5:3, 5
1 Corinthians 5:9-11

Acts 20:33
Exodus 34:23-24
Romans 7:7-8

EVIL USES OF MONEY

Matthew 26:14-15
Matthew 27:3-10
Mark 14:10-11
Luke 22:3-5
Acts 1:18

Genesis 37:28
Numbers 22:7
Numbers 22:18
Numbers 24:13
Esther 3:9-11

Esther 4:7
Judges 16:4-5
Judges 16:18
Judges 9:4

GREED

Ephesians 5:3, 5
Colossians 3:5
Luke 12:15
Proverbs 23:1-3
Psalm 73:25
1 Thessalonians 2:5
1 Corinthians 10:6
Numbers 11:4-5

1 Samuel 14:32
Isaiah 56:11
Romans 1:28-29
Psalm 10:3-4
Proverbs 11:6
2 Peter 2:1-3
2 Peter 2:14-15
Proverbs 30:15

Ezekiel 33:31
Numbers 11:34
2 Kings 5:20-27
Jeremiah 6:12-13
Jeremiah 8:10

IDOLATRY

Exodus 20:23
Psalm 135:15
Hosea 1:8, 13

Colossians 3:5
Ezekiel 23:29-30
Micah 1:7

Isaiah 30:22-23
Judges 17:2-4

PARTIALITY

Deuteronomy 10:17	James 2:8-9	Deuteronomy 16:18-19
2 Chronicles 19:7	James 2:1-9	2 Chronicles 19:6-7
Job 34:19	Exodus 23:3	Malachi 2:9
Ephesians 6:9	Leviticus 19:15	Romans 12:16
Proverbs 28:21	Deuteronomy 1:17	Philippians 2:3

TAXES/TRIBUTE

Romans 13:5-7	Ezra 6:8	2 Chronicles 17:12
Matthew 22:17-21	1 Samuel 17:25	2 Chronicles 27:5
Mark 12:14-17	Ezra 7:24	2 Chronicles 36:3
Luke 20:22-25	Matthew 17:24-27	Ezra 4:20
2 Kings 3:4	1 Kings 4:21	Ezra 4:13
2 Kings 15:20	2 Kings 17:1-3	
2 Kings 23:33, 35	2 Chronicles 17:5	

POOR

Exodus 22:21-24	Amos 8:4-6	Exodus 23:6
Job 34:28	Zechariah 7:9-12	Deuteronomy 24:17
Proverbs 28:3	Malachi 3:5	Daniel 4:25-27
Isaiah 32:6-7	Psalm 94:2, 6, 7	Jeremiah 5:27-29
Proverbs 28:15	Jeremiah 2:34	Ezekiel 16:49
Proverbs 30:14	Mark 12:38-40	Isaiah 1:23
Job 20:10, 15, 18-20, 26, 28	Luke 20:46-47	Proverbs 14:31
Psalm 37:14-15	Ecclesiastes 5:8	Proverbs 17:5
Psalm 109:11, 16	Proverbs 31:8-9	Deuteronomy 10:18
Proverbs 22:16	Isaiah 1:17	Job 5:15
Proverbs 22:22-23	Jeremiah 21:12	Psalm 9:18
Isaiah 3:14-15	Proverbs 29:7	Psalm 10:14
Isaiah 10:1-2	Job 30:25	Psalm 12:5
Jeremiah 22:1-5	Psalm 41:1-3	Psalm 34:6
Ezekiel 22:7, 29	Proverbs 19:17	Psalm 35:10
Amos 2:6-7	Proverbs 29:14	Psalm 40:17
Amos 4:1-2	Jeremiah 7:5-9	Psalm 68:6
Amos 5:9-12	Luke 14:12-23	Psalm 68:10

Psalm 69:33	Ecclesiastes 6:8	Psalm 86:1
Psalm 102:17	Proverbs 14:20	Lamentations 1:11
Psalm 107:4	Proverbs 19:4	Luke 2:22-24
Psalm 109:31	Proverbs 19:7	1 Corinthians 4:11-12
Psalm 113:7	Proverbs 13:23	2 Corinthians 6:4-5, 10
Psalm 132:15	Proverbs 18:23	2 Corinthians 11:27
Psalm 140:12	Proverbs 22:7	Philippians 4:11-14
Psalm 146:7	Ecclesiastes 9:14-16	1 Corinthians 11:18-22
Psalm 146:9	Proverbs 10:15	Leviticus 25:11-13
Psalm 147:6	Proverbs 30:7-9	Leviticus 25:39-54
Proverbs 15:25	Luke 6:20, 24	Jeremiah 34:13-17
Isaiah 11:4	James 2:5	Proverbs 13:18
Isaiah 14:30	Isaiah 61:1	Proverbs 20:13
Isaiah 25:4	Matthew 11:2-5	Proverbs 21:17
Isaiah 41:17	Luke 4:18	Proverbs 23:20-21
Jeremiah 20:13	Luke 7:22	Deuteronomy 15:4-5
Psalm 72:4, 10, 12-15	Proverbs 13:8	2 Kings 24:14
Psalm 74:21	Luke 16:19-25	2 Kings 25:12
Psalm 82:3-4	James 1:9-10	Jeremiah 39:10
Psalm 109:21-22	Isaiah 29:19	Jeremiah 40:7
Job 24:2-12, 14	Proverbs 28:11	Jeremiah 52:15
Revelation 2:9	Proverbs 19:1	OTHER AREAS
Revelation 3:17-18	Proverbs 19:22	ADDRESSING POOR:
1 Corinthians 1:26-27	Proverbs 28:6	Lending, Partiality, Work
Proverbs 22:2	1 Samuel 18:23	
Proverbs 29:13	Psalm 70:5	

RICHES

Revelation 2:9	1 Timothy 6:7	1 Peter 1:18
Job 5:5	Psalm 39:6	Philippians 3:7-8
Job 15:29	Psalm 49:5-8	1 Timothy 6:17
Job 20:10, 15, 18-20, 26, 28	Proverbs 11:4	Ecclesiastes 2:4-11
Job 21:13, 16	Matthew 16:26	Job 28:15-19
Job 22:23-25	Mark 8:36-37	Psalm 37:16
Job 27:13, 16-17	Luke 9:25	Psalm 119:14
Job 36:11	Proverbs 14:20	Psalm 119:72
Job 36:19	Proverbs 19:4	Psalm 119:127
Ecclesiastes 7:11-12	Proverbs 23:4-5	Proverbs 3:13-16
Psalm 49:16-20	Hebrews 11:24-26	Proverbs 8:10-11
Ecclesiastes 5:13-15	1 Peter 1:7	Proverbs 8:18-21

Proverbs 15:16
Proverbs 16:8
Proverbs 16:16
Proverbs 16:19
Proverbs 19:1
Proverbs 20:15
Proverbs 22:1
Proverbs 28:6
Luke 12:48
Proverbs 13:21
Proverbs 15:6
Psalm 1:1-3
Psalm 22:29
Psalm 106:5
Psalm 122:6-7
Psalm 128:5
3 John 2
Genesis 12:5
Genesis 13:2
Genesis 15:13-14
Genesis 24:1
Genesis 24:16
Genesis 24:35
Genesis 26:12-14
Genesis 30:43
Genesis 33:11
Genesis 41:42
Genesis 45:13
Genesis 46:6
Genesis 47:27
Joshua 22:8
Ruth 2:1
2 Samuel 1:24
1 Kings 10:4, 7
1 Kings 3:11-13
1 Chronicles 29:23
1 Chronicles 29:28
2 Chronicles 1:11-12
2 Chronicles 9:22
2 Chronicles 17:5
2 Chronicles 17:11-12
2 Chronicles 18:1
2 Chronicles 32:27-30

Nehemiah 9:25
Job 1:3
Daniel 3:30
Matthew 27:57
1 Corinthians 4:8, 11-12
Philippians 4:11-18
Psalm 35:27
Hebrews 11:36-40
Revelation 5:12
Proverbs 14:24
Proverbs 24:3-4
Proverbs 21:17
Proverbs 22:16
Psalm 62:10
Ezekiel 28:4-5
1 Timothy 6:17
James 1:9-11
Jeremiah 9:23-24
Proverbs 10:15
Proverbs 18:11
Psalm 30:6-7
Psalm 49:10-12
Genesis 13:5-11
Genesis 26:12-16
Genesis 36:6-7
Isaiah 5:8
1 Corinthians 11:18-22
Proverbs 11:18
Matthew 13:4-5, 7, 22
Mark 4:2-3, 7, 18-19
Luke 8:7, 14
Matthew 19:16-26
Mark 10:17-27
Luke 18:28-30
Luke 16:19-25
Proverbs 28:11
Proverbs 18:23
Proverbs 22:7
James 2:6-7
Deuteronomy 6:10-12
Deuteronomy 8:9-18
Deuteronomy 31:20
Proverbs 30:7-9

Jeremiah 22:21-22
Revelation 3:17-18
Genesis 26:12-14, 16
Genesis 31:1
Proverbs 13:8
Ecclesiastes 5:12
Luke 6:24
James 5:1-5
Psalm 10:3-5
Psalm 37:1-2, 7, 9-11
Psalm 73:1-20
Proverbs 11:16
Jeremiah 12:1-2
1 Samuel 25:2
Esther 1:4
Esther 5:11
Isaiah 2:7
Ezekiel 27:33
Daniel 11:2
Luke 19:2
Deuteronomy 23:6
Ezra 9:12
Hosea 12:8
Zechariah 11:5
Judges 17:13
Proverbs 2:4
Ecclesiastes 10:20
Proverbs 13:7
Matthew 13:44-46
Proverbs 10:20
Isaiah 15:7
Jeremiah 51:13
Ezekiel 27:3, 12-27
Hosea 10:1-2
Zephaniah 1:11, 13, 18
Zechariah 9:3-4
Deuteronomy 17:16-17
1 Kings 4:26
1 Kings 10:14-28
2 Chronicles 1:14-17
2 Chronicles 9:8-27
Psalm 45:12
Isaiah 39:2, 4-6

Isaiah 60:5-6, 9, 11
Isaiah 61:6-7
Haggai 2:7
Zechariah 1:17
Zechariah 7:7

Revelation 6:15-16
Revelation 13:16-17
Revelation 17:4
Revelation 18:3
Revelation 18:11-19

Genesis 34:10-12
Genesis 34:21, 23
1 Samuel 17:25

MISCELLANEOUS

1 Kings 10:29
Proverbs 20:14
James 4:13-15
Proverbs 5:10
Proverbs 6:35
Proverbs 29:3
Proverbs 23:6-8
Ezekiel 33:31
James 3:14-16
James 4:2-3
2 Peter 2:3
Deuteronomy 21:14
Isaiah 13:17
2 Samuel 21:4
Ruth 3:10
Proverbs 11:26
Proverbs 12:9
Proverbs 23:23
Isaiah 53:9
Matthew 13:52
Mark 5:25-26
Acts 22:28
Proverbs 17:26
Isaiah 7:23
Isaiah 23:18
Isaiah 52:13
Isaiah 53:10
Isaiah 55:1-2
Ezekiel 16:33-34
Ezekiel 48:14
Zechariah 11:12-13
Mark 4:24-25
Luke 15:8-10

Acts 2:44-45
Acts 4:32-37
Acts 19:18-19
Genesis 20:16
Genesis 34:27-29
1 Samuel 17:53
1 Kings 20:1-6, 8
2 Kings 14:12, 14
2 Chronicles 20:25
Ezra 9:7
Esther 8:11
Esther 9:5, 10
Isaiah 10:5-6
Isaiah 10:12-14
Ezekiel 26:12
Ezekiel 30:4
Hosea 13:15
Amos 3:11
Obadiah 1:13
Obadiah 1:6, 11
Micah 4:13
Nahum 2:9-10
Nahum 3:1
Habakkuk 2:6-8
Zephaniah 1:11, 13, 18
Zephaniah 2:9
2 Corinthians 8:13-15
1 Timothy 2:9
Exodus 21:18-19
Exodus 21:22
Exodus 21:28-30
Exodus 21:32-36
1 Samuel 8:10-11, 14-17

Ezekiel 45:7-8,
Jeremiah 32:6-7, 9, 14-15
Jeremiah 32:25
Ezekiel 7:11-13, 19
Ezekiel 38:10-13
Daniel 11:24
Daniel 11:38
Daniel 11:43
Zechariah 14:1-2
Zechariah 14:14
Luke 17:28
2 Timothy 3:1-2
Revelation 6:6
Revelation 6:15-16
Revelation 9:20-21
Revelation 13:16-17
Revelation 17:4
Revelation 18:3
Revelation 18:11-19
Jeremiah 7:5-9, 11
Micah 3:11
Matthew 21:12-13
Mark 11:15-17
Luke 19:45-46
John 2:14-16
2 Corinthians 12:14
1 Timothy 3:2-3
1 Timothy 3:8
1 Timothy 6:5-6
Titus 1:10-11
1 Peter 5:1-2
Ecclesiastes 5:10-11
Song of Solomon 8:7

Isaiah 24:2	Colossians 3:1-5	Isaiah 59:2, 4
Isaiah 52:3	1 Timothy 4:4	Matthew 5:25-26
Lamentations 4:1-2	Hebrews 10:34	Matthew 5:40
Matthew 22:5	Hebrews 11:24-26	Luke 6:29-30
Luke 12:13-15	1 John 2:15-17	Luke 12:58-59
Luke 16:1-14	2 Samuel 18:11-12	1 Corinthians 6:1-8
Acts 8:18-24	1 Kings 15:16-20	Acts 16:16-19
1 Corinthians 10:33	2 Kings 16:5, 8-9	Acts 19:24-27
2 Corinthians 6:4, 10	2 Chronicles 16:2-4	

For a full listing and explanation of scriptures please visit
crown.org/scripture.